John F. Edgar

PIONEER LIFE IN DAYTON [OHIO] & VICINITY, 1796-1840

BY JOHN F. EDGAR

HERITAGE BOOKS
2008

HERITAGE BOOKS
AN IMPRINT OF HERITAGE BOOKS, INC.

Books, CDs, and more—Worldwide

For our listing of thousands of titles see our website at
www.HeritageBooks.com

Published 2008 by
HERITAGE BOOKS, INC.
Publishing Division
100 Railroad Ave. #104
Westminster, Maryland 21157

Copyright © 1896 John F. Edgar

Other books by the author:
CD ROM: Pioneer Life in Dayton [Ohio] & Vicinity, 1796-1840

All rights reserved. No part of this book may be reproduced or transmitted in any form or by any means, electronic or mechanical, including photocopying, recording or by any information storage and retrieval system without written permission from the author, except for the inclusion of brief quotations in a review.

International Standard Book Numbers
Paperbound: 978-0-7884-1276-9
Clothbound: 978-0-7884-7099-8

IN GRATEFUL REMEMBRANCE

OF

THE TRIALS THROUGH WHICH THEY PASSED
THIS LITTLE BOOK IS AFFECTIONATELY DEDICATED

TO

The Makers of Dayton

PREFACE.

AT the suggestion of a friend, I have undertaken to collect reminiscences of the early history of Dayton, including the names and personal history of the pioneers of the township and county previous to 1840, when Dayton assumed the proportions of a city, receiving her charter in 1841.

So far as I can learn by careful inquiry, I am the only person living in Dayton whose father was here the first year of its settlement (1796), and having known personally some of the original settlers,— Granny Thompson, Mr. and Mrs. George Newcom, William Van Cleve, Jerome Holt, and others,— it seemed good for me, in the centennial year of the first surveying party (1895), to undertake this work, reviving memories of the heroic pioneers, the hardy men and women who braved the dangers of a new and unbroken wilderness. When possible, I have endeavored to trace the history of each family down to the present day, not making mention of any whose connection with Dayton commenced after 1840. There are many whose history I was anxious to give, but could not do so, being unable to secure the necessary data. Others whom I would have been glad to mention, had their names been suggested to me, and without whom a history of Dayton is hardly complete, have unfortunately and unintentionally been overlooked in the work of writing a history of this kind. I can only say to them that it is a matter of great regret to me that such is the case. My idea has been that the people have made the town, and their individual history is the history of the town. I have been at great pains to look up all the older citizens in Dayton that I could hear of, as well as my own acquaintances; I have written many letters to people who once lived here, but are now residing elsewhere, and have made every endeavor to reach all who were in any way connected with the development and growth of our "Gem City." Dayton is a city of homes. The people who came here have many of them married here, made their money here, spent it here, and died here. There has never been a bubble boom — inflated only to burst, leaving the town in a state of helpless depression.

For assistance I am under obligations, first, to James C. Reber for his kindly suggestion; also to John H. Patterson, Edward Brenneman, Wickliff Belville, Frank Bruen, Charles A. Stone, Mrs. Annie Lowe Rieman, Mrs. W. D. Bickham, Mrs. Anner Bacon Carroll, Mrs. Henrietta Dover Simpson, Prof. A. W. Drury, D.D., W. A. Shuey, and to many others, for valuable information and almost priceless documents freely entrusted to my care.

For historical facts and data I am indebted to Curwen's "Sketch of the History of Dayton"; "The History of Montgomery County"; John Littell's Family Records, etc., of the Passaic Valley of New Jersey; "Western Address Directory," by W. G. Layford; "Sketches of Pioneers of Southern Ohio," by Judge Barclay Harlan; "Historical Collections of Ohio," by Henry Howe; "History of Dayton, Ohio," published by the United Brethren Publishing House; Dr. Drake's "Cincinnati"; Kirchwell's "Valley of Virginia"; Chase's Statutes; "Biographical Cyclopedia and Portrait Gallery of Ohio," edited by J. Fletcher Breman; "Pennsylvania Genealogies," Egle; Stewart's "Memoirs of Virginia"; early Dayton papers, court records, records of deeds, etc.

I wish also to acknowledge my obligation to my daughter, Elizabeth B. Edgar, without whose assistance this volume could not have been published, and to Miss Minta I. Dryden, librarian of the Dayton Public Library, and the assistant librarians, for their uniform courtesy and valuable aid.

I have endeavored to be accurate as to dates, family names, etc., but, to quote from Henry Howe, "whoever expects to find this volume free from defects has but little acquaintance with the difficulties ever attendant upon procuring such materials. . . . . I must here close with the observation that I have passed the allotted age of human life, and, although in sound health, cannot expect for many more years to witness its mysterious, ever-varying changes."

JOHN F. EDGAR.

DAYTON, OHIO, June 1, 1896.

CONTENTS.

CHAPTER I.

INTRODUCTORY.

LA SALLE—Treaties with the Indians—General George Rogers Clark—Indian Hunting-ground—Gist—John Cleves Symmes's Purchase—Boundary Lines—No. 1 Miami Land Warrant—Surveyors—Major Stites—Venice—Death of John Van Cleve—Fort Recovery—Battle of "Fallen Timbers"—General Wayne's Victory—Daniel C. Cooper and John Dunlap—Spring of 1796—Israel Ludlow and Party—Naming the Town—Copy of an Old Certificate, - - - - - - - - - - - - - 13

CHAPTER II.

THE SETTLEMENT AND THE FIRST SETTLERS.

WILLIAM HAMER—Birth of Dayton Hamer—Jonathan and Edward Mercer—George Newcom and Party—Samuel Thompson—Mary Van Cleve—The Pirogue—Arrival of the Party—The First House in Dayton—Agreement Between Colonel Newcom and Robert Edgar—The Tavern—Official Positions—Thomas Davis—John Davis—First Death—William Chenoweth—John Dorough—Daniel Ferrell—James Morris—Solomon Goss—Abraham Grassmire—John Van Cleve and Family—Benjamin Van Cleve—First Recorded Wedding—Obituary of Mrs. Thompson—Mrs. McClure—William Gahagan—Daniel C. Cooper—Headgates—Digging a Race—First Mill Started—Article of Agreement—Mrs. Sophia Greene Burnett—First Colored Person—New Plat of Dayton—Transfers of Property—Governor Meigs's Order—Robert Edgar—The Quarry—Mrs. George's Death—Biographical Sketches, - - - - - - - 22

CHAPTER III.

DAYTON TOWNSHIP FORMED.

DAYTON TOWNSHIP—Boundary Line—James Brady—Tax on Single Men—Andrew Lock—Blockhouse—Officers of the Town—Location of the First Settlers—General Brown—Original Topography—Household Furniture—Nuggins—David Lowry's Trips to New Orleans—Ebenezer Wead—John Stewart Wead—John Miller—George Adams—Blockhouse—Dr.

viii   CONTENTS

John Hole—Hole's Station—Jerome Holt—Census—State of Ohio—William King—Rates of Ferriage—William Ruffin—Five Families in 1802—Philip Wagner—John Bradford—Daniel Miller—John H. Williams—James Lockhart Williams—Harbert S. Williams—James Bracy Oliver—John Neff—Henry Leatherman—Gilbert Kennedy—Isaac Spining—Commission of Governor Edward Tiffin—Charles Spining—John Whitten Van Cleve—Woodland Cemetery—Bachelor's Alley,   - - - - 48

CHAPTER IV.

MONTGOMERY SEPARATED FROM HAMILTON COUNTY.

LOCAL Officers—Order Issued by the Court—Montgomery County Formed—County-seat—First Election—Second Election—Sheriff—Contract for New Jail—Prisoners Escape—First Term of Court—New Court-house—Furniture of Court and Jury Rooms—Curwen's Description—First Appearance Docket—Letters of Administration—Third Term of Court—Grand Jury—Court Docket—Colonel Robert Patterson—Luther Bruen—David H. Bruen—Luther Barnett Bruen—Henry Brown—Female Charitable and Bible Society—Robert Patterson Brown—Henry L. Brown—Judge A. Barr Irwin—Captain Hugh Andrews—Nathan Worley—Joseph H. Crane—Joseph G. Crane—Mathias Dennison—Jefferson Patterson—David McConnaughey—John C. McConnaughey—Aaron Baker—David C. Baker—Philip Gunckel—Lewis B. Gunckel—John Martin Shuey—Martin Shuey—Adam Shuey—Rev. William J. Shuey, - 77

CHAPTER V.

THE TOWN OF DAYTON INCORPORATED.

ACT of Legislature—Town of Dayton—Meetings of Council—Charter—Flood of 1805—Licenses—Ferries—Colonel John Grimes's Tavern—Taylor Street Bridge—Alexander Grimes—Colonel David Reid—Daniel Kiser's Tavern—General Fielding Loury—John Howard—Fielding Loury, Jr.—David Squier—Timothy Squier—Matilda Owens—William Roth—Matthew Patton—Joseph Peirce—Jeremiah Hunt Peirce—Joseph Crane Peirce—Horatio Gates Phillips—Dayton Hydraulic Company—Jonathan Dickinson Phillips—John G. Lowe—George S. Houston—Charles Russell Greene—John Rench—Jonathan Harshman—Jacob S. Brenner—William George—Sarah George—First Sunday-School Superintendent—William Bomberger—William G. George—Augustus George—Abraham Darst—William Eaker—George W. Smith—George Umbaugh—Henry Butt—Peter Lehman—David Lehman—Samuel Boogher—Daniel G. Boogher—Jesse Boogher—Lewis Kemp—George W. Kemp—John Folkerth—Justice of the Peace—Russel Folkerth—John Bonner—George Fryberger—Valentine Fryberger—James Steele—First Opera-house—Robert W. Steele—A Few Important Changes—Roads Opened—*Repertory*—Paul Butler—Henry Disbrow—First Carding-machine—Weaving Establishment—James Hanna—Peter Bellaw—A Manufacturing Town—Secret Society—First County Convention—Mail Route—Postage—List of Postmasters—1809—Three Physicians—Rev. James Welsh, M.D.—List of Medicines—Dr. P. Wood—First Drug-store—Service at the Court-house—*Repertory* Discontinued—*Ohio Centinel*—

CONTENTS ix

Ohio Republican—Fourth of July Celebration—Census for 1810—Town Election—Sidewalks Made—Two Tickets—Names of Suburbs—Standard Half-bushel—State Corduroy Road—Dr. Este—Earthquake Shocks—David Lindsley—John Perrine—James Perrine—Stephen Johnston, - 106

CHAPTER VI.

THE WAR OF 1812.

ENROLLMENT—James Madison—President's Call—General Munger—Dayton the Headquarters—First Companies to Arrive—Governor Meigs's Arrival—General Hull—Camp Meigs—Hull's Surrender—Seventy Brave Men—Governor Meigs's Order—Wagon Boy of Ohio—Shirts Made by the Ladies—First Recruiting Office—Peace Declared—Population Increased—Current Prices—Charles Tull—Eddy Fairchild—Henderson & Elliott—Rolling-pins, - - - - - - - - - - - - 156

CHAPTER VII.

DAYTON TO 1840.

JOHN ENSEY—Alexander McConnell—Benjamin Kiser—Daniel Kiser—Henry Diehl—John Rouzer—John Compton—Thomas Cottom—Leven Cottom—William Tyler—James Grimes—William Huffman—William P. Huffman—Samuel Shoup—Joel Ohio Shoup—Samuel Tate—Mary A. Darst—Obadiah Burlow Conover—Temperance Question—Harvey Conover—Wilbur Conover—Obadiah M. Conover—Hiram Strong—Collins Wight—The Dayton Manufacturing Company—Directors—New Charter—The Dayton Branch of the State Bank—Directors—Dayton National Bank—Directors—Workingmen's Association—Bible Society—Second Flood—Dr. A. Coleman—Revenue of the County—New Court-house—Social Societies—First Market-house—Market-house Moved—Moses Stout—David Stout—Moses Simpson—Robert Strain—Daniel Stutsman—John Grove Stutsman—First to Do Gas-fitting—Jonathan Stutsman—Robert McReynolds—Thomas Morrison—Shinplasters—David H. Morrison—Thomas G. Carpenter—Silas Broadwell—Ephraim Broadwell—David Heck—Henry Stoddard—George B. Holt—Dr. William Blodget—Dr. Job Haines—Samuel Forrer—James H. Mitchell—John Bimm—Robert J. Skinner—*Ohio Watchman*—Bridge Across Mad River—Ferries—Bridge Company Incorporated—Toll-house—First Stage Line—First Show—First Circus—Elisha Brabham—Cut Money—Lewis Hamblin Brown—Bible Society Formed—Cooper's Mills Burned—Fire Department—First Fire-wardens—The *Gridiron*—Thespian Society, - - - 162

CHAPTER VIII.

DAYTON TO 1840—CONTINUED.

LOCATION of the Canal—First Canal-boat Built, *Alpha*—Suppers and Toasts—First Steam Packet, *Enterprise*—Aqueducts—Cost of Canal—Census in 1820-30—Two Newspapers—Jephthah Regans—Richard N. Comly—Dayton *Journal*—Major W. D. Bickham—*Log Cabin*—Flood of 1828—First

CONTENTS

Book Published—John Dodson—Augustus George—Dayton Temperance Society—Extracts from a Letter—Lovell Bebee—Emson Brown—Underground Railway—James F. Thompson—Gorton Arnold—John W. Dryden—Andrew Wiggim—James Dodds—John Engle—Rev. Thomas Winters—Rev. David Winters—Valentine Winters—Thomas Clegg—Exhibition of Gas—William Westerman—Peter Perlee Lowe—Edward W. Davies—Andrew Gump—Edward Weakley—Dayton *Evening Herald*—Henry Herrman—Charles Soule—Benjamin Wicks Mead—Peter Light—David Stone—William B. Stone—John Belville—Dr. Hibbard Jewett—John W. Harries—David Altick—Gideon Beall—Joseph Weston—Frederick Boyer—Thomas J. S. Smith—John Bidleman—Thomas Brown—James Findlay Schenck—Robert C. Schenck—Dr. John Boyd Craighead—Daniel W. Iddings—Joseph Barnett—Harrison Convention—Hezekiah Loomis—James Decatur Loomis—Peter Post Conover—Peter Odlin—Eliam E. Barney—Augustin King—Colonel Edward King—James Greer—Christopher Thompson—Frederick Gebhart—Hiram Wyatt—John Achey—David Laymon—William Hoff—Francis Ohmer—William Dickey—Horace Pease—William Clark—Beniah Tharp—Jacob Sturr—Thomas Mathison—Miss Maria Boyd—Charter Amended—Locomotive Exhibition—Morris Seely—Philip Keifer—Alexander Swaynie—The National Hotel—Calvin Francisco—Cholera—Flood of 1832—David Zeigler Cooper—Wild-cat Currency—Dayton Philharmonic Society—Joseph Wheeler—Colored People Mobbed—National Road—Dam Across Mad River—Race Dug by the Soldiers of 1812—Original Map—The Mad River & Lake Erie Railroad Company—First Locomotive, "Seneca"—Census of 1796 and 1896—Retrospect, - - - - - 197

CHAPTER IX.

CHURCHES, SCHOOLS, AND LIBRARIES.

BEAVER CREEK—Shakers—Presbyterians—First Meeting-house—Burying Ground—First Sunday School—Methodists—First Minister—Camp-meeting of 1819—First Town Clock—Baptist Church—Christ Episcopal Church—New Light Society—German Reformed Church—First United Brethren Church—United Brethren Publishing House—First English Lutheran Church—First Catholic Priest—The African Methodist Episcopal Church—First and Second Schools—Dayton Academy—Manual-labor School—Public-school Tax—The Old Eastern School—Central High School—Dayton Library Association—Dayton Lyceum—The Mechanics' Institute—The Adelphic Society—Public School Library, - 242

ILLUSTRATIONS.

JOHN F. EDGAR,	*Frontispiece*
	Opposite Page
FIRST HOUSE IN DAYTON,	24
GENERAL WAYNE'S ICE HOUSE AT GREENVILLE, OHIO,	25
COURT-HOUSE IN 1858,	80
MAIN STREET, LOOKING NORTH FROM BELOW THIRD STREET,	81
FIRST PRESBYTERIAN MEETING-HOUSE IN 1804,	144
FIRST PRESBYTERIAN CHURCH IN 1896,	145
MR. AND MRS. TIMOTHY SQUIER,	160
THE HENDERSON & ELLIOTT SHOP,	161
CANAL-BOAT,	200
OLD HAY MARKET,	201
THOMAS MORRISON'S SHINPLASTERS,	234, 235
ORIGINAL MAP, SHOWING CHANGE IN BED OF MAD RIVER, ETC.,	*Page* 238
GRACE METHODIST EPISCOPAL CHURCH,	246
FIRST COLORED METHODIST EPISCOPAL CHURCH IN 1840,	247
OLD EASTERN SCHOOL,	252
STEELE HIGH SCHOOL,	252
DAYTON PUBLIC LIBRARY AND COOPER PARK,	253
SHINPLASTER OF VINCENNES BANK OF INDIANA,	254
MAP OF DAYTON,	255

PIONEER LIFE IN DAYTON AND VICINITY.

CHAPTER I.

INTRODUCTORY.

IN 1669 La Salle, a Frenchman, discovered the Ohio River, and the French consequently claimed all the territory watered by it and its tributaries as belonging to France. The English resisted, claiming that the discovery of the Atlantic coast gave them the possession of the whole continent, and, to strengthen their claim, in 1664 made treaties with the Iroquois Indians of the Six Nations for the purchase of all their lands, for which they received legally executed deeds. Seventeen years later a treaty of peace was signed between the Iroquois and French, which enabled the latter to keep possession of the Great Lakes. In 1726 the English made another treaty, which they claimed confirmed the treaty of 1664, and eighteen years later, in 1744, made another treaty at Lancaster, Pennsylvania, by which they purchased the Ohio basin for four hundred pounds (twenty thousand dollars). This treaty was confirmed at a village called Logstown, in Pennsylvania, in 1752. At the close of the War of the Revolution, by the treaty of Versailles, which secured the independence of the United States, Great Britain relinquished her claim to the Ohio Valley.

From 1752 the Indians were complete masters of all the Northwest Territory. They made frequent raids into Kentucky and West Virginia.

In 1780 General George Rogers Clark led an expedition of Kentuckians to Ohio. One of the officers who held command under him was Captain Robert Patterson, one of the founders of Lexington, Kentucky, and of Cincinnati, Ohio,—the father of Colonel Jefferson Patterson. This expedition was successful, defeating the Shawnees at their town of old Piqua, west of Springfield, Ohio, where it is said the great chief Tecumseh was born.

In the fall of 1782 the Indians were so troublesome that General Clark raised one thousand Kentuckians, and led a second expedition into the Indian country, Colonel Patterson accompanying the expedition. They saw no Indians and were not molested until they reached the mouth of Mad River, where, on November 9 of that year (1782), they had the first skirmish on the site of Dayton, in which the Kentuckians were victorious.

In 1786, the Indians still being troublesome, Colonel Logan, of Kentucky, raised another force, Colonel Robert Patterson having command of one brigade. This expedition was also successful. Among the Indians taken captive was a lad whom Colonel Logan took to his Kentucky home, and to whom he became much attached. The boy took the name of Logan, and was for life a strong friend of the whites. After a few years he was allowed to return to his tribe, and became the friendly Shawnee chief Logan. He was mortally wounded in the War of 1812, while in command of a detachment under General Harrison against some Indian allies of the British.

On returning from the expedition in 1786, Colonel Logan encountered a party of Indians in camp at the mouth of Mad

River, Tecumseh, then about fourteen years of age, being with them. After a slight skirmish, the Indians were driven up Mad River, the whites thus gaining the second victory on the site of Dayton. The party remained here for two or three days, examining the land with a view to settlement.

In 1784 Virginia, claiming the territory northwest of the Ohio by purchase from the Indians, ceded it to the United States. Tradition says that the land bounded on the south by the Ohio, on the east and west by the two Miamis, and by Mad River on the north, was reserved by all the Indian tribes as a hunting-ground. It was the home of all kinds of game,—bear, deer, elk, panthers, wolves, wild turkeys, birds, and fish,—and it is probable that no wigwam was ever erected here. The Indian villages were numerous west of the Great Miami and east of the Little Miami. The Indians claiming this Miami Valley were called the Miami tribes. The word *Miami* means, in the Indian language, "mother." The Miamis belonged to the Algonquin tribe, and came here from Michigan. They were noted for their intelligence and force of character, and were at the head of a powerful confederacy. Their principal village was near Piqua, Ohio.

In 1751, when Gist, the agent of the Virginians who formed the Ohio Land Company, visited this valley, he wrote: "The land upon the Great Miami River is very rich, level, and well timbered, some of the finest meadows that can be. The grass here grows to a great height on the clear fields, of which there are a great number, and the bottoms are full of white clover, wild rye, and blue grass." In his account of his visit to the Indian village near Piqua, he says: "It is accounted one of the strongest Indian towns upon this part of the continent. The Twightwees [or Miamis] are a very numerous people, consisting of many different tribes under the same form of government." The remnants of the Miami tribes are now domesticated and living on farms in Miami County, near Peru, Indiana.

In the winter of 1786 Mr. Benjamin Stites, of Red Stone, Pennsylvania, on the Monongahela, having been to the mouth of Mad River, probably with General Clark, and being impressed with the fertility of the soil and beauty of location, went to New York with the intention of purchasing from Congress a tract of land on the Great Miami River. On becoming acquainted with John Cleves Symmes, then a member of Congress from New Jersey, he represented to him the character of the Miami Valley, and solicited his influence and coöperation in effecting the purchase. Mr. Symmes preferred having some personal knowledge of the country before he would engage in the enterprise, and accordingly crossed the mountains and descended the Ohio River as far as Louisville, Kentucky. In July, 1787, Congress authorized the sale of lands in the Northwest Territory in tracts of not less than one million acres, and John Cleves Symmes made application on August 29, 1787, in his own name, for the purchase of the lands (the consideration being sixty-six cents per acre) lying within the following limits:

"Beginning at the mouth of the Big Miami River, thence running up the Ohio to the mouth of the Little Miami, thence up the main stream of the Little Miami River to the place where a line to be continued due west from the western termination of the northern boundary line of the grant to Messrs. Sargent, Cutler & Company shall intersect the said Little Miami River, thence due west, continuing the said northern line, to the place where the said line shall intersect the main branch or stream of the Big Miami River, thence down the Big Miami River to the place of beginning."

Mr. Symmes must have felt confident that there would be no check in his negotiations for these lands, as on the 26th of the following November he issued a manifesto announcing his purchase and a plan for colonization. The next month the first land warrant was issued, as follows:

"No. 1, MIAMI LAND WARRANT.

"[SEAL.] This entitles Benjamin Stites, his heirs, or assigns, to locate one section, in which the fee of six hundred and forty acres shall pass, subject to the terms of settlement.
"December 17, 1787.
(Signed,) "JOHN CLEVES SYMMES.
(Countersigned,) "BENJAMIN STITES."

On the warrant is found the following note:

"SPESHEL.—At the point betwixt the mouth of the Little Miami and the Ohio, in the pint."

The Treasury commissioners, however, denied having made a contract with Judge Symmes, and were disposed to repudiate his claim. In the meantime Mr. Symmes, in July, 1788, had started west with a colony of sixty persons in fourteen four-horse wagons, arriving at Pittsburg on August 20. After a short stay there and at Marietta, they went on to Limestone, Kentucky.

Judge Symmes, being anxious to know more of the Miami country, in 1788 organized two companies of surveyors, with Captain John Dunlap and Major Benjamin Stites in command, who explored the valley from the mouth of the Great Miami to Honey Creek. Major Stites, remembering former impressions of the land around the mouth of Mad River, commenced negotiations for its purchase, and succeeded in interesting others in his purpose to locate a colony at that point. On June 13, 1789, he purchased of Mr. Symmes, for John Stites Gano, William Goforth, and himself, the whole of the seventh range of lands, for which they were to pay eighty-three cents per acre, and at once commenced plans for a town, to be called Venice. One of the stipulations was that a road should be opened to the mouth of the Tiber (Mad River). The town was to be laid off in squares, each square to contain eight half-acre lots. The streets were to cross at right angles. At the center of the town spaces were to be left at each of the four quarters for market-house and public square. One square was to be given to the first Baptist church in the town, and "each denomination of pious and religiously disposed people, who worship the God of Israel, formed in the town within two years after the founding of the settlement" was to receive one half-acre lot. Three half-acre lots were to be given for "a capitol, a court-house, and a gaol." Half-acre lots were to be sold for four dollars each. The articles of agreement for the above were signed at the blockhouse, near Columbia, commanded by Major Stites, on June 13, 1789; but owing to Indian troubles and Mr. Symmes's failure to meet his obligations to the Government, the scheme fell through.

The last surveying party previous to Wayne's treaty at Greenville, August 20, 1795, was sent to the Miami country on August 7, 1789. It consisted of Mr. Matthews, a surveyor, with four assistants and a guard of seven soldiers. While eating breakfast one morning they were fired upon by Indians in ambush, a bullet passing through the bosom of Mr. Matthews's shirt, just grazing the skin. As the men rose to their feet the forest seemed to be filled with savages; another volley was poured upon them, and six of the soldiers fell dead. Out of the party of twelve six only remained, and they returned at once to Cincinnati.

In 1790 and 1791 numerous parties of Indians were

organized for raids on the frontier settlements at Marysville, Cincinnati, etc., the mouth of Mad River being their principal and favorite rendezvous. They were constantly skulking around Cincinnati, watching for an opportunity to kill or steal. It was in one of these raids that John Van Cleve, grandfather of our deceased fellow-citizen, John W. Van Cleve, was killed at Cincinnati. In the spring of 1793 it was felt that a decided effort must be made to conquer the Indians, and General Wayne was made commander-in-chief of the Western army—about three thousand six hundred men. On Christmas day, 1793, a detachment of this army encamped on the ground made memorable by St. Clair's defeat. A reward was offered for every human skull found, and over six hundred were gathered by the soldiers. A fort was built on this ground, appropriately called Fort Recovery.

Early in 1794 General Wayne, hoping to avoid the terrors of Indian warfare, sent three men acquainted with the savages,—Freeman, Trueman, and Hardin,—to make overtures of peace to the Indians, but they were most inhumanly murdered. From this time on General Wayne was busily employed preparing for an engagement, until on August 20, 1794, he met the British, Spanish, and Indians combined, on the banks of the Maumee, in the battle of "Fallen Timbers," and succeeded in putting the entire army to rout. This was certainly a victory over the British and Spanish, who had joined with the Indians hoping to crush out General Wayne. The British, for the sake of trade, refused to give up their forts south of the Great Lakes until 1796, and continued to supply the Indians who fought against St. Clair and Wayne with provisions, muskets, cannon, and ammunition, and frequently numbers of painted Canadians accompanied the Indians to the battle-field. The evil influence of the British did not cease until after the War of 1812.

After General Wayne's victory on the Maumee and the treaty of Greenville, August 20, 1795, which had a decided influence on the settlement of Dayton, General Jonathan Dayton, of New Jersey, afterwards United States Senator from that State, General Arthur St. Clair, Governor of the Northwest Territory, General James Wilkinson, of Wayne's army, and Colonel Israel Ludlow, of Morris County, New Jersey, contracted with John Cleves Symmes for the purchase of the seventh and eighth ranges between the Miami rivers. They employed Daniel C. Cooper, a surveyor, to be their agent. On September 21, 1795, two surveying parties started from Cincinnati, one in charge of Daniel C. Cooper, and the other under John Dunlap. The first night they camped at Voorhees's Station, nine miles out of Cincinnati, and the next morning separated. Benjamin Van Cleve accompanied the Dunlap party, to "run the boundaries of the seventh and eighth ranges between the Miami rivers." After being out for five or six days, their packhorse was stolen by the Indians during the night, and they were compelled to carry all their luggage to the mouth of Mad River, which they reached on Sunday, the 27th. Mr. Cooper's party, consisting of two chain-carriers,—Jerome Holt and Robert Edgar,—one man with an ax, and a hunter, who was also cook (whose names I cannot recall), was "to locate and mark a road, partially cutting out the underbrush, from Fort Hamilton up the east bank of the Miami River to the mouth of Mad River." I have often heard my father say that the road then laid out is practically the present Cincinnati road through Miamisburg and Middletown. This party reached camp on one day, and started on their return trip the next morning. In the spring of 1796 three of the party—Cooper, Edgar, and Holt—came to Dayton and made it their permanent home. Dunlap, with his party, consisting of Benjamin Van Cleve, William Gahagan, David Lowry, Jonathan Mercer, and Jonathan Donnell, remained surveying in the neighborhood for several days, and reached Cincinnati on the 6th of October.

On November 1 Israel Ludlow accompanied a surveying party to the mouth of Mad River, and on Wednesday, November 4, 1795, laid out the town, calling it Dayton in honor of Jonathan Dayton, one of the proprietors. Curwen says the town was divided "into two hundred and eighty inlots, one hundred feet front by two hundred feet deep, and fifty ten-acre outlots, which lay south of Third Street and east of St. Clair Street." The next day those of the party who expected to settle here drew lots for location, and acted as proxy in drawing for others who expected to locate here in the spring, the proprietors giving to each *bona-fide* settler one inlot and one outlot, provided they would clear and fence the same. Judge Symmes had made this agreement, which on his part was not fulfilled. The following is a copy of one of his certificates:

"This will certify that Robert Edgar has complyed with the conditions of settlement in the town of Dayton and is entitled to receive a deed for the following lots so soon as the Honorable John C. Symmes shall obtain a patent from Congress, including the premises, viz.: Town lot numbered on the plat of said town Thirty-two, and ten-acre outlot number Five.
"For the proprietor,
"D. C. COOPER.
"DAYTON, March 17, 1798."

Unfortunately for my father, after his work of clearing the above lots, the new proprietors refused to recognize Judge Symmes's contracts.

CHAPTER II.

THE SETTLEMENT AND THE FIRST SETTLERS.

During the winter of 1795–96 forty-six men agreed to settle in Dayton in the spring of 1796. When the time came to start only nineteen responded, and they set out in three sections, two overland and one by water.

William Hamer, who owned a wagon and two horses, had charge of one section. He was born in Maryland about the year 1750, and moved west with his wife and children in 1792. He and his son Solomon, who was then sixteen years old, built a flatboat, in which the family descended the Ohio River to Cincinnati, and then used the lumber in the boat to erect a house. Here they lived until they started for Dayton in March, 1796. With him on this trip to Dayton were his wife, Mary; his children, Solomon, Thomas, Nancy, Elizabeth, Sarah, and Polly; and Jonathan and Edward Mercer. The party was somewhat delayed, and was the last of the three to reach Dayton.

Mr. Hamer, who was a local Methodist preacher, has the honor of being the first minister of the gospel to live in this place. He evidently was of the opinion that he should be known by loud speaking, as it is said he could be heard three miles at family prayers.

Mr. Hamer located on a quarter-section of land, east of the town, known recently as Tate's Point, now owned by William Focke & Sons, the butchers. It was at this home that a son was born, December 9, 1796, and in honor of his being the first white boy born in the settlement his parents named him Dayton. Of his children, Nancy married William Gahagan, who came here on the pirogue; Elizabeth married William C. Lowry; Sarah married David Lowry, in 1801, and lived on Mad River, near the mouth of Donnell's Creek. They were about the first to settle in Greene County. Polly married Joseph Culbertson, of Miami County, and Dayton Hamer married Catharine Haney, and moved to Illinois, and from there to California, where he died. William Hamer, Jr., married Hannah Culbertson, and moved to Indiana; Susan married a Mr. Krider, and Ruth a Mr. Wagoner. Ellen never married. Mrs. Elizabeth Croy, of Sidney, Ohio, and Mrs. E. E. Berkdoll and Fletcher Lowry, of Dayton, are the only living grandchildren of William Hamer. Mr. Hamer's wife, Mary, died at their home, August 9, 1825, and he died in 1827 from an accident received on his way to Cincinnati.

After reaching Dayton with Mr. Hamer's party, Jonathan and Edward Mercer, with all their worldly possessions in the panniers of one horse, went on up Mad River several miles, and located on prairie land that is now in Bath Township, Greene County. They were the first white people to settle there. It was an exposed position and they were twice driven to Dayton for safety during the first two years.

On March 21, 1796, the other two parties made their start. George Newcom was the leader of the one overland. With him were his wife, Mary Henderson Newcom, his father, an old man, George Newcom, Sr., his brother, William Newcom, Thomas Davis and family, William Chenoweth and family, William Van Cleve, James Morris, John Dorough and family, Daniel Ferrell and family, Solomon Goss and family, John Davis, and Abraham Grassmire.

Samuel Thompson, the leader of the party by water, in the pirogue, was accompanied by his wife, Catherine Benham Van Cleve, their little daughter, Sarah, but two years old, baby Matthew, three months old, and Mrs. Thompson's daughter, Mary Van Cleve, nine years old, the first white girl to step on Dayton soil; Benjamin Van Cleve; the widow McClure and her children, James, John, Kate, and Ann, and William Gahagan.

The pirogue was a long, narrow boat, pointed at each end, with boards on either side on which the men walked in poling the boat up stream. There was a deck to protect the women, children, and freight. In order to ascend the rapids a rope attached to the boat would be fastened to a tree up stream, and then all hands pulling on this rope would draw the boat slowly along, one man with his pole keeping it in the current of the stream.

The first day's journey brought the party to the mouth of the Miami, where they camped for the night. The second night they camped at Dunlap's Station (Colerain), the third night at Fort Hamilton,—and so they proceeded, camping each night, until, ten days after starting, on April 1, 1796, they arrived at their destination, and landed at St. Clair Street, the first of the three parties to reach Dayton.

When this little party arrived, of course they found no shelter. The pirogue was carefully taken apart, piece by piece, and rebuilt on dry land, forming the first house in Dayton. The accompanying illustration is taken from a drawing now in my possession, made by George L. Croom, an engraver, who lived in Dayton about 1850. This house stood as built for eighty-four years, and for many years was owned and used by John W. Harries to store charcoal, which he used in making malt. It was a fine hiding-place for slaves, in the early days, on their way to Canada.

FIRST HOUSE IN DAYTON, BUILT FROM THE LUMBER OF THE PIROGUE.

GENERAL WAYNE'S ICE HOUSE AT GREENVILLE, OHIO.

THE SETTLEMENT AND THE FIRST SETTLERS 25

The other picture, from a drawing made by the same gentleman, is of General Wayne's ice-house at Greenville.

The party led by George Newcom overland met with few difficulties as far as Fort Hamilton, the road to that place being kept in good condition by the army. From that point on, the road had been only recently surveyed by Mr. Cooper and his corps of helpers, and was in such primitive condition that it was necessary in crossing small streams to fell trees for foot-bridges. For the larger streams rafts were made to carry the people and the freight, the cattle and horses swimming across. All the property was carried in creels on packhorses, the children that were too small to walk being also carried in the creels, their heads only showing. Game being plentiful the party suffered no hardship from lack of food, but the nights were cold and the hastily constructed camps afforded but little shelter, the beds being made in the open air by spreading blankets over brush. This party was about two weeks on the road.

Colonel George Newcom, the leader of this party, was born in Ireland in 1771, and came to America with his parents in 1775. They first settled in Delaware, and afterwards removed to near Middletown, Pennsylvania. He married, in Washington County, Pennsylvania, Mary Henderson, aunt of Thomas W. Henderson, recently deceased, and of Abraham Henderson, formerly sheriff of this county. In 1794 they emigrated to Cincinnati, and on March 21, 1796, he started with his little company for Dayton.

On arriving at Dayton, Colonel Newcom at once chose lot 13, at the corner of Main and Water streets, on which to erect a tavern. He first built a round-log house on Water Street (now Monument Avenue) for his family to live in while the tavern was being built, and it afterwards served as a kitchen to the tavern. When this round-log house was completed, Colonel Newcom employed Robert Edgar (who was handy with tools, having learned the millwright trade), to build a hewed-log house, eighteen by twenty-two feet. The agreement between Newcom and Edgar was that Newcom should pay Edgar six shillings (seventy-five cents) per day for cutting and hewing the logs for the "best house in Dayton," to front on Main and Water streets, and Edgar for his board agreed to furnish Newcom the carcass of a deer once every week, retaining the skin. This was full payment for his board and lodging. In order to comply with this part of his contract without breaking a day's work, my father would rise early, hide in the bushes on this side of the river at Main Street, and watch for the deer to come down to the river on the north side for their morning drink, when, choosing the best-looking one, he never failed to drop him. He would then, with his canoe, bring his week's board across the river before breakfast. The rifle used at that time is still in my possession. Edgar worked faithfully at the house, getting out the clapboards for the roof, floors, and doors.

The building, being the east half of the Tavern as it now stands in Van Cleve Park, was two stories, had two rooms, and was the largest house in Dayton. It was enlarged to its present size in the winter of 1798–99. It was the first whitewashed house here, and a little boy who saw the work progressing went home and told his mother that Mr. Newcom was making his house white with flour. In it the first store was opened, the first court was held, and at the same time it was tavern and jail. It was the favorite resort for prospectors and settlers, being at a point where all roads met, and Colonel Newcom, a man who knew every one, occupied almost as many official positions as did the house, being host, hostler, and bar-keeper, as well as sheriff of the county. He was a soldier in Wayne's army, and served in the War of 1812. The same year he was elected State senator, in 1815 was representative in the State Legislature, and in 1821 he succeeded Benjamin Van Cleve as clerk of the court and as president of the first bank here, called the Dayton Manufacturing Company.

Colonel Newcom had three children: Elizabeth, born in 1794, died in Cincinnati; John W., born September 9, 1797, at the farm of Samuel Dick, near Hamilton, and Jane, born in Dayton on April 14, 1800, said to be the first white girl born here. John Newcom married Martha Grimes November 21, 1820, and died July 7, 1836. They had five children, of whom Martha A., wife of John E. Greer, is the only one now living. Jane married Nathaniel Wilson on May 20, 1819, and died April 5, 1874, at the residence of her daughter, Susan, now Mrs. Josiah Gebhart, having lived her entire life on one street—Main Street. She had nine children, three of whom, Clinton Wilson, a farmer, and Mrs. Mary J. Hunt and Mrs. Susan Gebhart, both of Dayton, are still living.

Colonel Newcom's wife, Mary Henderson, died April 3, 1834, and in 1836 he married Mrs. Elizabeth Bowen, who died October 29, 1850. Colonel Newcom died February 25, 1853, at the age of eighty-two years. He, like Benjamin Van Cleve, was a brave, upright, noble man.

The "Old Tavern" stood on the original site, in constant use, until 1895, when Mr. John Cotterell, who owned the property, donated the cabin to the city, and it has been removed to Van Cleve Park.

George Newcom, Sr., a very old man, died probably before 1805.

William Newcom, the youngest brother of Colonel George Newcom, was about twenty years of age when he reached Dayton. He married Charlotte Nolen, of Kentucky, and had one son, Robert, who was the father of Milo G. Newcom, now living on North Wilkinson Street, this city. William Newcom died from the effects of the hardships and exposures which he endured as a soldier in the War of 1812. After Mr. Newcom's death, his widow married John Baker, father of John L. Baker, at present a member of our Board of City Affairs.

Thomas Davis, one of the Newcom party, was a native of Wales. He was in the Revolutionary War, was taken prisoner, and exchanged at Philadelphia. Mr. Davis settled near the bluffs, two or three miles south of Dayton, where he died many years ago. He married before coming to Dayton, and had a large family. His son, Owen Davis, was one of the first settlers in Yellow Springs, and had one of the first mills in Greene County. He married Jane Henderson, sister of James Henderson, who was in partnership with James Elliott. They had four children—two daughters and two sons. The boys died when quite young. Eliza Henderson Davis married David Stevenson, and Mary Jane Davis married Ralph Langton Thompson. Owen Davis died at the home of his son-in-law, Ralph L. Thompson, in Terre Haute, Indiana, in 1874. Lewis Davis, the oldest son of Thomas Davis, lived for some years at New Paris, Preble County, Ohio.

John Davis, a brother of Thomas Davis, settled south of Dayton, on the west side of the Miami River. While chopping ice from the water-wheel at Cooper's Mill, in 1799, the wheel started suddenly, drawing him under in such a way that the life was crushed out of him. This is said to have been the first death that occurred in Dayton.

THE SETTLEMENT AND THE FIRST SETTLERS

William Chenoweth came from Kentucky. He was about thirty-five years of age, and was a blacksmith by trade, but it is not known that he worked at his trade here. The reconstruction of the county about the year 1803 placed his farm in Greene County.

John Dorough, a married man, between twenty and thirty years of age, was by trade a miller. He operated a small mill built in 1820, after the burning of the first mill, on the north bank of a race on what is now Cooper Street, at the north end of Antrim's large tobacco warehouse, East First Street. The mill was reached by a foot-bridge, made by placing two trees across the race about five feet apart and laying puncheons crosswise on them. A puncheon was made by sawing a log five or six feet long, and splitting it into as thin pieces as possible. It required considerable skill to make puncheons.

Daniel Ferrell, a man of about fifty years of age, came with his family from West Virginia. But little is known of him. He left one daughter, whose descendants moved to near Honey Creek, Miami County, Ohio.

James Morris came west from Pennsylvania, and was in General Harmer's expedition in 1790. He was a farmer. Although married twice, he left no children.

Solomon Goss probably did not settle in Dayton. It is known he was not living here in 1799, although it is not known where he did settle.

Abraham Grassmire, a young unmarried German, was a weaver by trade. He was handy with tools and made looms for the settlers, as it was customary for every family to have a loom and weave their own linen, cloth, and blankets. Mr. Grassmire moved to Honey Creek about the year 1802 or 1803.

John Van Cleve, son of Benjamin and Rachel Van Cleve,

of New Brunswick, New Jersey, was born May 16, 1749. He was a soldier in the War of the Revolution, serving in his father's company. In 1772 he married Catherine Benham, and resided for some years in Monmouth County, New Jersey. Here four of his children were born— Benjamin, Ann, William, and Margaret. Some time after the birth of Margaret the family moved to Washington County, Pennsylvania, where Mary and Amy were born. In December, 1789, John Van Cleve, with his family, started for the West and arrived at Losantiville, Ohio, January 3, 1790, the day the name of the town was changed to Cincinnati. While at work here on an outlot, on June 1, 1791, Mr. Van Cleve was ambushed and murdered by the Indians, who, after stabbing him in five places and scalping him, left his body lying in the field and made their escape in the woods. His wife afterwards married Samuel Thompson, who was in the pirogue with the first party to arrive in Dayton.

Mary Van Cleve, in June, 1804, married John McClain, a farmer from Lexington, Kentucky. They had ten children. Mr. McClain died December 12, 1826, and Mrs. McClain married Robert Swaynie. After Mr. Swaynie's death his wife went to live with her daughter, Sarah Jane McClain Swaynie, where she died.

Ann Van Cleve married Colonel Jerome Holt. Amy married Isaac Shields and died in Preble County. Margaret married George Reeder, of Cincinnati, and died in September, 1858.

William, who was not quite twenty years of age when the family came to Dayton, purchased a quarter-section of land in Van Buren Township, and married Effie Westfall. They had several children. His wife died, and he was married the second and third time. In 1812, in response

THE SETTLEMENT AND THE FIRST SETTLERS   31

to a call for men, Mr. Van Cleve raised a company of Dayton Riflemen, and in June they were ordered out to protect the frontier, with Mr. Van Cleve in command as captain. After the war, Captain Van Cleve returned to Dayton, and kept a tavern at the junction of Warren and Jefferson streets, where he died in 1826. The old two-story frame house was moved from there a few years ago to the corner of Bachelor's Alley (now Lathrop Avenue) and Fillmore Street, where it is used as a double tenement.

Benjamin Van Cleve, the oldest child, was only eighteen years old when his father was killed. He at once assumed the care and support of his mother and the other children. It was harder to obtain an education in those days than it is now, but Benjamin, being a boy of strong mind and determined will, managed to master surveying and other branches of education, thereby fitting himself for the many offices of trust which he held during his lifetime. He was an honest, upright man, and was trusted with important dispatches to Philadelphia, New York, and other points. Benjamin Van Cleve was in Dunlap's surveying party just after Wayne's treaty with the Indians at Greenville. He was from the first one of the most prominent citizens of the place, taught the first school in Dayton in the blockhouse in the winter of 1799–1800, served as clerk of the court from the organization of the county until his death, in 1821, and was the first postmaster of Dayton, continuing to occupy that office until his death. Colonel John Johnston, of Piqua, Ohio, in his obituary, said, "God never made a better man than was Benjamin Van Cleve."

On August 28, 1800, Benjamin Van Cleve married Mary Whitten, daughter of John and Phœbe Whitten, born February 17, 1782, and died December 28, 1810. This was the first recorded wedding in Dayton. Mrs. Van Cleve's marriage portion was a few household and kitchen utensils, a bed, a cow and heifer, a ewe and two lambs, a sow and pigs, a saddle, and a spinning-wheel. They had five children: John Whitten Van Cleve, who was born in Dayton June 27, 1801, and died September 6, 1858; William James Van Cleve, born October 10, 1803, and died October 30, 1808; Henrietta Maria Van Cleve, born November 16, 1805, married, first, to Samuel B. Dover, and second, to Joseph Bond, and died May 18, 1879; Mary Cornelia Van Cleve, born December 2, 1807, married James Andrews November 20, 1827, and died February 19, 1878; and Sarah Sophia, born November 24, 1809, married David C. Baker on February 11, 1830, and died October 18, 1839. On March 10, 1812, nearly two years after his first wife's death, Benjamin Van Cleve married Mary Tamplin, of Champaign County. He died November 29, 1821. His wife died December 19, 1825.

Samuel Thompson, originally from Pennsylvania, moved west to Cincinnati, where he married Mrs. Catherine Van Cleve, widow of John Van Cleve. They had two children. Sarah, the oldest, married John Ensey, and had six children, all of whom are dead except Dennis Ensey, who lives on Tecumseh Street. Matthew married Margaret Gillespie, and moved to Hagerstown, Indiana, at an early date. Samuel Thompson was drowned in Mad River about the year 1817.

The following is an obituary of Mrs. Thompson:

"DIED.

"In this place on Sunday last at the age of eighty-two years, Mrs. Catherine Thompson, formerly Mrs. Catherine Van Cleve, mother of the late Benjamin and William. She was the first female resident of this town and county, to which place she came on the 1st of April, 1796. She was also one of the earliest inhabitants of Cincinnati, having come to that place before its name was changed from Losantiville, when two small hewed houses and a few log cabins constituted the whole town. Her first husband, John Van Cleve, to whom she was married by the Rev. William Tennant, of Monmouth County, New Jersey, was killed by the Indians on the 1st day of June, 1791, within the present corporate limits of Cincinnati. Her second husband, Samuel Thompson, was drowned in Mad River near this place about twenty years since.

"She was the mother of thirteen children; her grandchildren have numbered eighty-seven, and her great-grandchildren upwards of ninety.

"She was a worthy member of the Methodist Church for the last twenty years of her life, and died in Christian resignation.

"DAYTON, August 8, 1837."

Mrs. McClure, with her three sons, James, John, and Thomas, and two daughters, Kate and Ann, came to Dayton in the pirogue. Mrs. McClure's husband had been killed at St. Clair's defeat. The family moved to Honey Creek, in Miami County. Thomas afterwards returned to Dayton. I have not been able to learn anything of their descendants.

William Gahagan came to Cincinnati with General Wayne's army in 1793, and served through 1794 and 1795. After the treaty at Greenville he made his home with William Hamer. He married Nancy Hamer, and about the year 1805 removed to Miami County, on a prairie south of Troy. After his wife's death he married Mrs. Tennery. He died at Troy about 1845. His descendants still live, I believe, in Miami County, but they have not responded to my inquiries for more particular information.

Daniel C. Cooper, the oldest son of George Cooper, a farmer, of Morris County, New Jersey, was born November 20, 1773. He was educated for a surveyor, an important profession in those days. Prospecting around Dayton as a surveyor gave Mr. Cooper great opportunities for seeing good sites and locating choice lands. In 1796 he built a cabin on the southeast corner of Water and Jefferson streets, and during the following two years entered over one thousand acres south of town, now known as the Patterson farm, onto which he moved, having built a cabin, in 1798. There was a strong spring branch running through this farm, fed by springs on the Wade farm, now partly owned by the Asylum, on which, in 1799, Mr. Cooper built a corn-cracker, sawmill, and still-house. For many years there was enough water in this branch to run the mills all the year.

The first panic that struck Dayton was when Judge Symmes failed to meet his obligations to Congress. The people were much alarmed at the prospect of losing their labor and lands. Many moved away disheartened, and many who stayed, as well as those who left, sold their claims for what they could get. Others who had thought of coming did not come, and the town was in serious danger of a collapse. The settlers at length petitioned Congress for relief, and in compliance with this petition, on March 2, 1799, a law was passed giving any person who had a written contract with Judge Symmes dated prior to April 1, 1797, the privilege of purchasing United States lands at two dollars an acre, payable in three annual installments. In consequence of this law Mr. Cooper entered over eight hundred acres within the town limits. He then began to develop the natural resources of the place, getting ready to build mills by erecting head-gates and throwing a dam across Mad River at the east end of the ground now owned by the Car Works, and digging a race beginning about where the canal now crosses First Street, running westward through Pond Street, and northward, crossing First and

Sears streets, thence north of where Whitmore's coal office now stands to the grist-mill which was erected on the ground now occupied by a red shop and the canal immediately north of Monument Avenue.

The first mill started at the head of Mill and Water streets was a "tub-mill," made of four posts, about four feet high, set in the bed of the stream four to six feet apart, on which sills were laid, and the plank, or puncheon, floor pinned down with wooden pins. In the center of this floor was a small pair of mill-stones, with the shaft through the bed stone and floor, at the lower end of which was the horizontal tub-wheel. The current of the stream was directed to the wheel by a dam running diagonally up stream. The burrs were made from granite bowlders found here, and were about two feet in diameter. Posts at the four corners upheld a clapboard roof, to keep the rain out of the hopper, and sometimes the west and north sides were boarded up. This was a corn-cracking mill.

In 1800 Mr. Cooper built a grist- and sawmill. The grist-mill foundation was in the bed of the present canal. The sawmill was just north of the grist-mill, and was run by the same water-wheel. On October 18, 1801, these mills were completed and ready for use, and the following contract was made by Mr. Cooper:

"Article of Agreement made and concluded on this 8th day of October, in the year of our Lord one thousand eight hundred and one, between Daniel C. Cooper, of the County of Hamilton and Territory Northwest of the Ohio, and Robert Edgar, of the county and Territory aforesaid,

"*Witnesseth*, that the said Cooper, for the consideration hereafter mentioned, hath demised, granted, and to farm let, and doth hereby grant and to farm let, unto the said Edgar, his grist-mill and sawmill at Dayton, to have and to hold the said premises until the first day of April next, and the said Edgar doth agree on his part to take special care of said mills, and to make use of all possible industry, and to render monthly a just and true account of the profits of each mill: to give the said Cooper two-thirds of the profits of the grist-mill and an equal share of the profits of the sawmill, and the said Edgar doth further agree to saw the said Cooper's logs in such stuff as he may want on the following terms, to wit: two-inch plank and under at sixteen pence half-penny, and all plank above two inches thick and scantling at one-quarter of a dollar per hundred, measuring scantling side and edge, and plank side only; and the said Cooper doth agree to pay the said Edgar in cash for the above sawing, or in plank, at the rate of one dollar per hundred for inch oak plank, and others in proportion to the selling price; and the said Cooper doth agree to find files, tallow, and grease for the said mills, and in consideration of which the said Edgar doth agree to finish the roof of the sawmill and inclose the grist-mill so as to make it comfortable for this season, set the bolt agowing by water, etc., etc., the said Cooper finding the materials; and for the faithful performance of the above we do bind ourselves, our heirs, our executors and administrators, firmly each unto the other in the penal sum of five hundred dollars: as witness our hands and seals the day and date above written.

"Witness,   D. C. COOPER,
    "PAUL BUTLER.   ROBERT EDGAR."

These mills were burned in 1820.

Mrs. Sophia Greene Burnett was born in Rhode Island in 1780. Her father, Charles Greene, was a member of the Ohio Company, and emigrated to Marietta in 1788. G. W. Burnett, brother to Judge Jacob Burnett, a young lawyer in Cincinnati, married Miss Greene in 1801, and shortly after, while in company with his wife and Thomas Ewing, traveling on horseback to Marietta, was taken sick and died on the roadside, in the woods. Mr. Cooper met Mrs. Burnett, who was young and handsome, sought and won her hand, and they were married in the year 1803. They had several children, all of whom died young except David Zeigler, who was born November 8, 1812. He graduated from

Princeton, and returning to Dayton married Letitia C. Smith, of Baltimore, but died shortly afterwards and left no children.

After his marriage, Daniel C. Cooper brought a colored girl here, the first colored person in Dayton, to be a servant in his family. Soon after coming she gave birth to a boy, naming him Harry Cooper. When about two and a half years old he was bound to Mr. Cooper until his twenty-first birthday, and proved to be a faithful hand, driving the oxen and working in the sawmill. While at work in the sawmill he broke his leg, so that it had to be amputated, but he was supplied with a wooden leg and could work almost as well as before. Mr. Cooper pensioned him with a dollar a day as long as he lived. He was drowned in the sawmill race, near where it crossed Third Street.

Daniel C. Cooper was the first justice of the peace in Dayton, having been appointed October 4, 1799, and served until Montgomery County was erected, May 1, 1803. Before his appointment all differences had been settled by neighbors. In 1804, 1807, and again in 1817 he was elected to the Legislature, and was sent to the State Senate in 1808, 1809, 1815, and 1816. He was a member of the Town Council and was president of the Council in 1810 and 1812.

In 1804 Mr. Cooper sold his farm to Colonel Robert Patterson, and built an elegant hewed-log house on the corner of First and Ludlow streets, lining it inside with cherry plank, where he continued to live until his death. He commenced a large brick house on the southeast corner of First and Wilkinson streets, but did not live to finish it. This house, which was bought and completed by Hon. T. J. S. Smith, was for many years the finest house in Dayton. It was finally destroyed by fire on the night of December 31, 1859, the cold being so intense that the hose froze solid, rendering the fire-engine useless.

In 1809 Mr. Cooper made a new plat of Dayton, of which the following is an explanation:

"Wilkinson Street, four poles wide, and the western boundary of the town lots.

"First Street, west of the town lots, four poles wide.

"Third Street, west of the town lots, six poles wide.

"Fourth Street, west of the town lots, four poles wide.

"Fifth Street, west of the town lots, four poles wide.

"St. Clair Street, south of the town lots, four poles wide.

"Lots 94, 95, 96, 97, 98, 99, 100, 101, 142, 143, and 144 for the use of the town for a common."

In this new plat the fifty-four outlots on the southeast corner are omitted, only two outlots, lying west of Wilkinson Street and north of Third, being on the plat.

The following is the agreement between the county commissioners and the Town Council:

"We, the subscribers, do hereby certify that the above plan is a true representation of the town lots and streets of the town of Dayton, and under the restriction of a law passed the 17th day of February, 1808, we do hereby agree that the original plan be so vacated and amended as is herein specified; and it is agreed that the proprietor shall have the privileges contained in the original record, and that all advantages not expressly given remain with the proprietor.

"Given under our hands and seals this 3d day of January, 1809.
      "JOHN FOLKERTH,
      "DANIEL HOOVER, JR.,
          "*Commissioners.*
      "JAMES WELSH,
      "HUGH MCCULLUM,
      "WM. MCCLURE,
      "BENJ. VAN CLEVE,
      "ISAAC G. BURNETT,
          "*Members of Council.*"

(Deed Book B, page 147.)

THE SETTLEMENT AND THE FIRST SETTLERS 39

Prior to 1809, when Mr. Cooper made the new plat of Dayton, few, if any, transfers of property were made by deed. The commissioners made it a rule that the name opposite the number of a lot was the name of the owner of a lot, and in order to transfer the property, all that was necessary was for the owner to say, "I transfer lot number — to ————." Of such changes of ownership no record seems to have been kept, but the list of lot owners filed when the plat of 1809 was recorded is the basis of title to the original three hundred and twenty-one lots in Dayton. All records of transfers by patent from the Government to individuals, and sales of Montgomery County property made by the individuals, are on the records of Montgomery County; so it is useless to go to Hamilton County records for information. There are no records of Montgomery County transfers there. As Judge Symmes never received a patent, he could not make transfers.

On July 18, 1812, the United States by patent transferred to D. C. Cooper four hundred and seventeen and sixty-three hundredths acres, being the residue of all south of Mad River in fractional Section 4, after deducting such lots as had already been sold and transferred.

In 1816 Mr. Cooper was sent to the State Legislature. He was also president of the Town Council.

Mr. Cooper was public-spirited and liberal, donating ground to the county for public buildings, a common to the town for a "public walk," lots to the religious organizations for meeting-house and graveyard purposes, and to trustees for the Academy, realizing that the prosperity of the town depended largely on the mental and moral development of the inhabitants. He contributed largely to the First Presbyterian Church, and when the first bell for this church arrived in Dayton, and was unloaded from the wagon at the Phillips store, on the southeast corner of Main and Second streets, Mr. Cooper loaded it on a wheelbarrow and wheeled it to the church, on the northwest corner of Second and Ludlow streets. The exertion was too much for him; he ruptured a blood-vessel, and died July 13, 1818. This bell was afterwards sold to the Shakers.

Mr. Cooper's executors, H. G. Phillips and James Steele, managed his estate so well that his investments grew to be very valuable, giving his son, David Zeigler Cooper, a good estate when he arrived of age.

Mrs. Sophia Cooper, a few years after Mr. Cooper's death, married General Fielding Loury, and died May 17, 1826, leaving one son—Fielding Loury.

Colonel Jerome Holt, one of the chain-carriers with the surveying party, was born February 21, 1763, and died near Dayton December 28, 1840. He was a brother-in-law of Benjamin Van Cleve, having married Ann Van Cleve, daughter of John and Catherine Van Cleve. They had ten children, none of whom are now living. One of his grandchildren, Mrs. F. R. Gustin, still lives in Dayton, on Albany Street.

In 1800 Mr. Holt was appointed constable of Dayton Township. I have in my possession a receipt, which reads as follows:

"December 22, 1800. Received of Robert Edgar his tax in full for the present year, it being D. Cts.
0. .60
"JER. HOLT, *Collector*."

He was elected sheriff of this county in 1809, and was colonel of the Fifth Regiment of militia from 1810 to 1812. During the latter year Governor Meigs issued the following order:

"HEADQUARTERS, DAYTON, May 26, 1812.
"Captain Van Cleve's company of Riflemen will march to the frontier of the State west of the Miami under the direction and charge of Colonel Holt. Colonel Holt will assist the frontier inhabitants in erecting blockhouses in suitable places and adopt any mode he may think best for the protection of the frontier and the continuance of the settlements."

Robert Edgar was born in Staunton, Augusta County, Virginia, February 8, 1770, and was ten years old when his father, Robert Edgar, Sr., about 1780, settled on a grant of three hundred and thirty-six acres received from the Commonwealth of Virginia, near Wheeling. While planting flax on Good Friday, 1792, as was the custom in those days, Robert Edgar, Sr., heard hooting as of owls, which he knew to be the calling and answering of Indians. After finishing his work, he felt it his duty to notify his neighbors of the fact that Indians were about, and, on returning to his home at a late hour, was waylaid by nine Indians, shot a number of times, stripped, scalped, and left where he fell. His son Robert, the oldest of the children, settled up the estate, giving the property to the widow—she being Mr. Edgar's second wife—and her children, and, together with his own brother and sister, Andrew and Nancy, came down the Ohio River to Cincinnati in a flatboat. The following is a copy of a bill in my possession:

"1795. Henry Coleman
              "To Robert and Andrew Edgar.
"May 19. To assisting with 2 boats from Short Creek
              to Cincinnati, at twenty dollars each, $40 00
"Contra Cr.
"June 4. Received for the above of Henry Coleman,
              cash, $18 00
              and 1 barrel of flour,   4 50   22 50
                                                             ───────
                                                              $17 50"

The balance is still due to Mr. Edgar, April 1, 1896.

Andrew Edgar located at Hillsboro, Highland County, Ohio, and died at that place from the bite of a rattlesnake.

Nancy married David Robinson, of near Lebanon, Ohio, afterwards moved to the West, and all trace of her descendants has been lost.

Robert came to Dayton in September, 1795, with Daniel C. Cooper, as chain-carrier, and in 1796 returned and remained as a citizen. Soon after coming here he contracted with Colonel Newcom to build the Tavern. After completing the Tavern, and clearing and fencing inlot 32 and outlot 5, in compliance with Judge Symmes's proposal to settlers, Mr. Edgar built a cabin on the prairie north of the old bed of Mad River, on the ground now owned by the Water Works and Ezra Bimm. He then went to Cincinnati, on foot, and on September 27, 1798, married Mrs. Margaret Gillespie Kirkwood, widow of David Kirkwood. She had one son, Joseph Kirkwood, who died a bachelor. Mr. and Mrs. Edgar took their wedding journey to the new home on the prairie, the bride and her child on horseback, and the groom on foot, with knapsack and rifle over his shoulder, a packhorse carrying all their worldly possessions. They were three days making the trip, which now we make in less than three hours.

While living on the prairie Mr. Edgar had frequent visits from the Indians, with whom he was always very friendly. At night they would come and sleep around his log fire. It not being considered safe to lock the doors, it was an easy matter for them to gain admittance to the house at all hours, and not infrequently they would call to Robert ("Wobet," as they said) to get up at midnight and play bullets with them. It is hardly necessary to say that he never refused. One night, on arriving home from

THE SETTLEMENT AND THE FIRST SETTLERS 43

town after dark, as Mr. Edgar went to care for the horse, Mrs. Edgar, with a child in her arms, thought to kick the log in the fire and make a blaze, and found her foot caught by the Indian she had kicked in its place. Mr. Edgar would frequently be away for several days at a time on walking trips to Cincinnati for flour, cornmeal, and groceries, which he would carry home on his back. At such times his wife would come to the Tavern for Colonel Newcom's father to stay on the prairie with her. As the horse would be swimming Mad River,—the only way of crossing it in those days,—she with her baby in her arms, old Mr. Newcom would say (he was an Irishman), "Faith and Peggy, we will, baby and all, be drowned here some day."

Mr. Edgar, who, as has been stated, was a mechanic, was constantly engaged during these years, and up to 1800, in building head-gates and forebays for Mr. Cooper, and in getting out timber for the grist-mills and sawmills, until, upon their completion, he entered into an agreement with Mr. Cooper to run the mills. At this time, in compliance with the agreement, he moved into the miller's house, a log cabin on lot number 1, corner of Monument Avenue and Mill Street. He continued to work for Mr. Cooper, running the mills and building houses, until he received a certificate from the land office at Cincinnati for what became the home farm, now known as the Edgar Plat, on south Wayne Avenue, for which he paid two dollars an acre. Here a cabin was built and the work of making a home commenced in earnest. It was on this farm that he used the first iron-moldboard plow that was ever brought to this valley, and which excited universal comment among the people here.

Mr. Edgar discovered a smooth white stone cropping

out of the ground near his farm. He at once procured an iron rod and on moonlight nights followed up the bed of stone far enough to feel sure he had found a stone quarry, and determined to buy that quarter-section. Some short time after, while at breakfast one morning, he saw a neighbor pass his door on horseback, and said to his wife, "That man is after the quarry." He at once got out his rifle and money, only enough to pay for eighty·acres, and started on foot for Cincinnati, stopping at his brother-in-law, George Gillespie's, of Warren County, where he procured the balance of the money necessary for the purchase. He reached Cincinnati, and was leaving the land office with the papers in his hand just as his neighbor on horseback rode up. The neighbor exclaimed: "Why, Bob! when I passed your house yesterday, I saw you eating your breakfast. How did you get here?" Mr. Edgar's frequent trips on foot to Cincinnati had given him such a knowledge of the country through which he had to pass that he could take advantage of all short cuts, and follow paths which a horse could not travel.

Hardly was the start made in this new home until the War of 1812 called all able-bodied men to the front, and Mr. Edgar joined a company of horsemen, equipping himself with a sword costing five dollars and twenty-five cents, the receipt for the same, as well as the sword, being now in my possession. The company was sent to protect the frontier settlements, thus leaving Mrs. Edgar at home alone, in a lonely place, to care for the farm and children. In addition to all the work which must, of necessity, be done about a farm in the wilderness, Mrs. Edgar devoted herself to baking for the army what is now called hardtack. The large brick oven would not be allowed to cool from Monday morning until Saturday night. Fortunately

THE SETTLEMENT AND THE FIRST SETTLERS 45

the farm was out of the direct line of Indian travel, so the little family was not annoyed by such uncomfortable visitors. Mr. Edgar returned safely from the campaign, and devoted himself to farming until the canal was being built, in the year 1827. Then the Legislature gave contractors the right to select any timber for bridges and locks that they might choose, and, in order to protect his own choice timber, Mr. Edgar contracted to build two bridges—one at Fifth Street and the other at Third Street.

Mr. and Mrs. Edgar were both devoted members of the First Presbyterian Church from its earliest organization, and continued their membership until death. Mr. Edgar was elected a member of the first board of trustees, and I was one of the original members of the first Sunday school in Dayton. Mr. Edgar died December 19, 1838, and his wife died November 25, 1844.

While living on the prairie two children were born— George, August 4, 1799, who died an infant, and Jane Allen, November 24, 1800. After moving to the Cooper Mills, Robert Andrew was born, and on the farm four children—Samuel Dick, William Gillespie, Mary, and John Farris Edgar, the youngest, and only one living.

Jane Allen married Augustus George December 11, 1817, and died in 1826. Mr. and Mrs. George were then living on a farm on the north side of the Miami River, part of it now owned by Jozabed L. Ensley,—Idylwild. At the time of Mrs. George's death the river was high and wide, and the current swift, but the only way to cross was by dug-out canoe. The coffin was carried on a bier along a slight elevation to a point near the entrance to Idylwild, there balanced crossways on the canoe, and rowed by careful men to the other side, the canoe returning for the family. The coffin was then taken in a wagon to the old graveyard on

Fifth Street, the friends following in wagons. She left four little children—Marcella, Margaret Jane, Mary, and Martha, Martha dying when a child. Marcella married Nathaniel Hart, of Chicago. They had three daughters, all of whom are living.

Margaret Jane George, in November, 1844, married Thomas Alexander Phillips, who settled in Dayton May 1 of that year. He was born September 29, 1810, in Cecil County, Maryland, and moved with his father to near Wilmington, Delaware, in 1814 or 1815. Mr. Phillips entered a cotton-factory on the Brandywine when quite young, and in 1835, on coming west, was made superintendent of the old cotton-mill at Covington, Kentucky, at the end of the present suspension bridge. After coming to Dayton Mr. Phillips took charge of the cotton-mill here, afterwards so well known in Dayton by the name of T. A. Phillips & Sons. Mr. Phillips was made director of the Dayton branch of the State Bank, was one of the organizers of the Cooper Hydraulic Company, and continued one of the directors until his death, and was one of the directors of the Dayton Gas Light and Coke Company for about twenty-five years. Mr. Phillips and his wife were members of the First Presbyterian Church for many years. He died of heart disease November 27, 1877. His wife died in 1882. They had four sons—George Levis, John Edgar, Charles Alexander, and William Thomas. John Edgar and William Thomas died when quite young. George Levis was born in Dayton August 22, 1845, and on May 15, 1867, married Mary Adele Bronson in Dubuque, Iowa. Mr. Phillips was for many years engaged with the Chicago Telephone Company, and moved to Chicago, where he died on January 29, 1889, leaving a wife and four daughters. One daughter, Mary Golden, died in New York just the

THE SETTLEMENT AND THE FIRST SETTLERS 47

week before her father's death. Charles Alexander married Susie O'Hara, and is living in Covington, Kentucky. He has one son, Thomas Alexander, living.

Mary George married Daniel Storms, and is living in Walla Walla County, Washington. She has no children.

Robert Andrew Edgar was born March 25, 1800. He married Catharine Iddings and had one son, George, who is now living in Kansas. Mr. Edgar died of cholera in 1833.

Samuel Dick Edgar was born March 25, 1806, married Minerva A. Jones, and died October 1, 1874, leaving three children: Mrs. Margaret Edgar Herrman, Mrs. Marianna Edgar Gebhart, and Charles, who died one year after his father, leaving a wife and three little children—Margaret, Emma, and Robert.

Mary Edgar, born April 8, 1811, married Stephen Johnston, of Piqua, Ohio. She and her husband both died of cholera the same week in July, 1849, leaving five small children—James, Margaret, Robert, William, and Eliza. Of these only two are living—Robert and Eliza, who married Philip Kingsland, of Chicago.

John Farris Edgar was born October 29, 1814. On April 23, 1843, he married Effie Allen Rogers, of Springfield, Ohio. They had five children—Robert Rogers, Jane Allen, Isabel Rogers, Elizabeth Barnett, and Frank Rogers, three of whom are still living. Mrs. Edgar died August 19, 1891.

CHAPTER III.

DAYTON TOWNSHIP FORMED.

DAYTON TOWNSHIP, Hamilton County, with other townships, was formed in Hamilton County in 1796-97. It included a part of the counties of Greene, Champaign, Clark, Logan, Shelby, Miami, and Montgomery, and was bounded as follows:

"Beginning at a point on the east bank of the Big Miami, where it was intersected by the north line of the fifth range of townships; thence up that river in all its meanderings to the Indian boundary line, at a point where said river crossed the Indian boundary line in Section 18, Township 2, in the fourteenth range of townships, between the Miamis; thence along said line to Ludlow's line, and down that line to the southeast corner of Section 5, Township 6, in the eighth range of townships, between the Miamis, where was a branch of the Little Miami River; thence down the river to the north line of the fifth range of townships; thence west with said line to the place of beginning."

On June 10, 1797, the commissioners of Hamilton County appointed James Brady assessor, Calvin Morroll collector, and Cyrus Osborn constable of this township. It was the duty of the constable to make returns of persons and property to the assessors, who made the assessments and then placed them in the hands of the county commissioners and assessors as a court of appeals to hear complaints against over-assessments. After this they were placed in the hands of the collector. The following orders show the fees allowed these officers:

"*To Stephen Wood, Treasurer of the County of Hamilton.*

"SIR: You will pay James Brady five dollars and twenty cents out of the first monies that come into your hands, the same being his perquisites in full as assessor for the Township of Dayton for the year 1797, and this shall be your warrant for so doing.

(Signed,) "WILLIAM McMILLEN,
"ROBERT BENHAM,
"Nov. 24, 1797. *Commissioners.*"

"*To Stephen Wood, Treasurer of Hamilton County.*

"SIR: You will pay Cyrus Osborn, constable of Dayton Township, one dollar and ninety cents, which by law he is entitled to for his trouble and attention in executing and returning the commissioners' warrant for ascertaining the taxable property for the present year, and also fifty cents for one quire of paper used in the aforesaid business.

"WILLIAM McMILLEN,
"ROBERT BENHAM,
"November 24, 1797. *Cincinnati Commissioners.*"

Stationery for the year 1797 cost the township fourteen dollars and thirty-four cents, and the commissioners' fees were seven dollars and fifty cents each.

In 1798 James Thompson was appointed constable, D. C. Cooper assessor, and George Newcom collector. The commissioners and appraisers fixed the following rates for taxation:

"Single men, with no property, $1; cleared land, per acre, $20; cattle, per head, $16; horses, $75; cabins, $20; houses, $600; grist- and sawmills, each, $600; boats, $600; ferries, $1,000; stud-horses, $1,000.

"There were 156 persons listed; total amount collected, $186.66½. D. C. COOPER,
"*Assessor of Dayton Township.*"

The average for each taxpayer was one dollar and nineteen and two-thirds cents, the highest being D. C. Cooper and Valentine Oyer, his miller, six dollars and twenty-five cents, and the lowest, a number being the same, thirty-seven and a half cents. Mr. Cooper's fee was seven dollars and twenty-one cents.

Andrew Lock, who entered six hundred and forty acres of land in Sections 5 and 11, north of the mouth of Mad River and east of the Miami,—what is now known as the Phillips farm,—was taxed in 1798 one dollar and thirty-seven and one-half cents. The ford over the Miami, where the bridge now is, just this side of Idylwild, was long known as Lock's Ford.

In 1799, the Indians appearing unsettled and unfriendly, a blockhouse was built at the head of Main Street, about where the Soldiers' Monument now stands. It was a large house, built of round logs, with a projecting upper story, to enable the occupants to overlook and protect the entrances. The Indians, seeing the preparations for defense, and remembering General Wayne's victory at Maumee, concluded to be peaceable; and in this instance the ounce of prevention was worth more than the pound of cure. It was never necessary, fortunately, to use this blockhouse for a fort, but it was not built for naught, as that winter it was used as a school-house. Mr. Benjamin Van Cleve says in his journal: "On the 1st of September I commenced teaching a small school. I had reserved time to gather my corn, and kept school until the last of October." After securing his corn Mr. Van Cleve went to Cincinnati to assist the clerk of the First Territorial Legislature, and on the adjournment of the Legislature returned and reopened his school for about three months.

In 1799 Samuel Thompson was appointed constable, John McGrew assessor, John Ewing collector, and D. C. Cooper justice of the peace.

DAYTON TOWNSHIP FORMED

The Big Miami River being a navigable stream, the first settlers located in its vicinity, as they supposed property would be more valuable near the landing.

At this time Samuel Thompson was living on Water Street, Mrs. McClure at the corner of Mill and Water streets, George Newcom on lot 13, Water Street, Paul Butler on Water Street, General Brown at the corner of Water and Jefferson streets, Thomas Arnett at the northwest corner of First and Ludlow streets, John Welsh at the southeast corner of Fifth and Main streets, John Williams on the southeast corner of Water and Wilkinson streets, the last four being at the extreme limits of the town. Robert Edgar was living on the prairie north of Mad River, now Bimm's ice park, D. C. Cooper on the Patterson farm, Jerome Holt north of town about four miles, and William Hamer east of town, on what is now called Tate's Point.

General Brown kept bachelor's hall in a two-story house, the first story of stone, the second of logs. He distinguished himself for bravery in the War of 1812, and was granted a vote of thanks and a gold medal by Congress for his conduct in the battles in the vicinity of Niagara Falls and the siege of Fort Erie, and was afterwards made Commander-in-Chief of the United States Army, which position he held until his death, February 24, 1828.

The original topography of the town site was rough and broken. Commencing on the east side of Mill Street the water almost constantly flowed through the low ground now occupied by the canal basin. All the land from First and Perry streets west to the river and south as far as the Fair-ground hill, was prairie. There was a prairie extending from Mad River, through which a bayou of the river ran most of the time, south to about Sixth Street, and east from St. Clair to near Madison Street. There was a gully commencing at the head of Jefferson Street, running east through lot 42, now owned by Ex-Sheriff A. C. Nixon, entering the low ground where the basin is now. At the corner of Main and Second streets there was a deep washout, and another at the corner of Main and Main Cross streets (Main and Third), which had its outlet in the prairie near Fifth Street. Then there was a quicksand swamp where Messrs. S. N. Brown & Company now have their shops.

It will probably be interesting to know what constituted the house furniture of our pioneer ancestors. First, the cooking-utensils, simple and few in number, consisted principally of an iron pot,—holding six or eight gallons, with iron lid, ears for a bail, and four iron feet,—called a "Dutch oven," used for rendering lard and tallow, boiling water, etc.; a smaller iron pot of the same shape, for boiling the meats and vegetables; a skillet, also of iron, about four inches deep, the sides square up from the bottom, iron lid, legs, and long handle, used for frying meat, baking pone, wheat-bread, etc. In order to cook in these various utensils before cranes came into use, a bed of live coals was arranged at one side of the hearth, on which they were placed, and then coals piled on top of the lid and around the sides. When cooking in this way the long-handled shovel and tongs were indispensable accessories. The fire was made first with a large log three or four feet long, ten to fifteen inches in diameter,—usually of Buckeye, as that wood does not burn out rapidly,—rolled into the fireplace, with stones in front and near each end to hold up the front wood. Johnny-cake was made by mixing cornmeal and water just stiff enough not to run. The dough was flattened out about an inch thick on a smooth board, and the board placed before the fire at an angle of forty-five degrees. Among the cooking-utensils was a long, smooth stick, one end sharpened, upon which the cook, or one of the children, would impale a strip of lean meat and hold it before the fire to toast. Nothing sweeter than this meat and the Johnny-cake was ever eaten. A wedge of wood, about six inches long, was driven between the stones of the chimney, above the arch, to which was tied a stout piece of string, and to roast, a turkey, spare-ribs, or saddle of venison would be tied to this string, the string given a tight twist, and the meat left to twirl in front of a hot fire. The twisting kept the roast constantly in motion, so that it required little attention. For tables, for the first two or three years, until the sawmills were started, rude benches, with legs fastened in holes in each corner, were used, and the tableware consisted of a few pewter plates, dishes, and spoons, and iron knives and forks. These all had to be carried from the East, as nothing of the kind was made west of the mountains. Gourds were used for carrying water until "nuggins" were made. A nuggin was made like our wooden buckets, with one stave, double length, for a handle. They did not have bails. The first few years, when salt was scarce, the meat was cut in long strips, run on rods, and hung where it would dry. This was called jerk. The supper meal usually consisted of mush and milk. After a few years the crane and andirons came into use, and aided in a measure in the difficulties of cooking for many years, as cookstoves were not brought to Dayton for a long time.

One of the old customs that have naturally long since passed away, was the coming around from town to town, and house to house, each year, of the—well, we would not call him a tinsmith, for tin was unknown; a blacksmith? I don't know. At any rate he had iron molds, and would melt the old pewter dishes and spoons and remold them, and the housewife would have an entirely new set of tableware. Then there was the shoemaker, who would bring his kit and fit out the entire family with shoes for the year; and the tailor, looking after the comforts of the men.

The first four or five years of the settlement of Dayton were not idle ones for our forefathers. Sometime between 1800 and 1803 William Robinson, who was also a minister, and his brother Henry built a flour-mill in this township on Mad River, now Harries' Station. I remember, when quite young, accompanying my father when he would go to Robinson's Mill with grist to be ground while he waited for it.

In the spring of 1800 sufficient produce had been raised to warrant the building of a flatboat by David Lowry, to transport it by way of the Miami River to the Ohio, and on down to New Orleans. The first trip was a very successful one, as Mr. Lowry sold his boat, as well as his cargo, consisting of grain, saddles of venison, deerskins, etc., to good advantage, and returned to Dayton on foot, after an absence of two months. Mr. Lowry had one son, Archibald, who lived in Springfield, Ohio, and was the father of Mrs. Eaker. From the time this first boat was built and loaded until the canal was opened, in 1829, this line of navigation was an important one. It was customary for the men making this trip to sell their boats and make their way home as best they could, often walking a great part of the way.

The first accidental death that occurred during the first four years of the settlement of Dayton was that of Thomas Davis, killed at Mr. Cooper's mill. The population during these four years was increased by a number of births, among them Dayton Hamer, George Edgar, Jane Newcom, Jane Edgar, Mary Bradford, and Jane King, who died an infant and was buried on the Presbyterian church lot. There were also some other additions to the town. Mr. McDougal brought a stock of goods from Detroit and opened a general store in the second story of Newcom's Tavern, where he did a flourishing business.

Ebenezer Wead came here from Lexington, Kentucky, in 1799. The year before he had entered fractional Section 24, in Van Buren Township, where he settled. He had two sons — John, who married Sarah Schoffe, and Robert, a tailor by trade, who worked in Dayton, going from house to house. In 1805 he bought eighty acres of land where the Insane Asylum now stands, and by hard work gradually purchased more land, until he had three hundred and twenty acres. He first married Jane Gibson, by whom he had two children, and after her death married her sister, Mary Gibson. They had six children, all of whom are dead.

John Stewart Wead inherited the farm southwest of the Asylum, on which he lived for over fifty years, and died on August 21, 1893, in his eighty-seventh year. His widow, Mrs. Sarah Wead, is still living on the farm. They were early members of the United Presbyterian church south of Beavertown, and later united with the First Presbyterian Church in Dayton.

John Miller came here in 1799. He was born in Westmoreland County, Pennsylvania, December 30, 1766, and when a young man emigrated to Kentucky, where he married. In the spring of 1799 he entered a hundred and twenty acres of land (now the Mumma place, on North Main Street), and settled there, but after some years moved to a farm about three miles north of Dayton, where he resided until his death on October 17, 1825. Mr. Miller was one of the first trustees of the First Presbyterian Church, and his name appears as elder on the first recorded list of elders of that church. After Mr. Miller's death, his family, with the exception of one daughter, Sarah, who married Obadiah Conover, moved to Indiana and Illinois.

George Adams was born in Virginia October 26, 1767, served as drummer boy in the War of the Revolution, and in 1790 came to Fort Washington with dispatches to General Harmer. General Harmer had just set out on an Indian expedition, and Adams, on horseback, provided with rifle and ammunition, parched corn, and a little flour, started to find him. He overtook the army at the old Indian town of Chillicothe on the fourth day, where he delivered the dispatches. He then joined the army, and on October 22, in hand-to-hand fights with the Indians, was wounded five times. The surgeons dressed his wounds, but said he could not live until morning, and ordered his grave dug. The next day, as he was still living, although unconscious, he was carried on a litter between two horses. When the halt for the night was made, a second grave was dug, and in this way from day to day he was carried back to Fort Washington, where he finally recovered entirely, becoming a strong and robust man. On January 26, 1792, he married Elizabeth Ellis, who was born March 31, 1773, in Virginia. Mr. Adams was constantly in the service, scouting through the Indian country, and was made captain of scouts in Wayne's army. On one of his trips a comrade pointed out his two graves, neither of them occupied. For services as drummer boy in the Revolutionary War Captain Adams received a warrant from the Government for one hundred acres of land, and for services in the Indian wars he received warrants for four hundred acres, which he located below Hole's Creek, near Alexandersville, built his cabin, and moved his family in 1797. In 1799, there being an Indian alarm, Captain Adams organized the neighbors for defense, and built the blockhouse on Zechariah Hole's land, but the little settlement was not molested. After Montgomery County was erected, Captain Adams was commissioned major of the regiments organized, and held that position at the beginning of the War of 1812. He was in constant service through that war, and was in command of Fort Greenville when peace was declared, but was not released from duty until the Indians were quieted. While located at this fort he entered land on Greenville Creek, where he built a cabin and moved his family, and later built a corn-cracker and sawmill. In 1829 and 1830 he was appointed associate judge by the Ohio Legislature, which office he held until his death, November 29, 1832. Adams Township, Darke County, was named in his honor. Mrs. Adams died February 22, 1847. They had eight children, four sons and four daughters,—George, Thomas, William, Caleb, Elizabeth, Cynthia, Martha, and Nancy.

One of the most interesting characters to settle in this vicinity in the early days was Dr. John Hole. He was born in Virginia in 1754, and on August 4, 1778, married Miss Massie Ludlow, of New Jersey. In 1796 he moved west in a covered wagon, and located in Cincinnati, but after prospecting up the Miami Valley, in 1797 he moved his family to Silver Creek, where he located one thousand four hundred and forty acres, paying for the land in military land bounty warrants, which he had earned as an officer in the Revolutionary War. He had studied medicine under Dr. Fullerton, was commissioned assistant surgeon in the Continental Army, was engaged in the battle of Bunker Hill, and was present when the army was reorganized under Washington as Commander-in-Chief. He was on the medical staff of Brigadier-General Montgomery (after whom Montgomery County was named) when he fell at Quebec. In speaking of this battle he has said, "I dressed the wounds of the soldiers beneath the walls of the fort by the flash of the cannon."

Dr. Hole was the first physician in this vicinity, and although his practice extended over miles of territory he found time to build and run two sawmills, south of Dayton. Dr. Hole and his family were Baptists, and the Doctor was the first person baptized in Silver Creek. Here he built his cabin, reared his family of six children, and died July 6, 1815. His wife died July 24, 1842. Owing to his prominence as a doctor, and also to the fact that he was one of the largest land owners in the county, the creek on which he located was soon called Hole's Creek, and retains the name to this day.

About a year after Dr. Hole entered his land, his father,—Zechariah Hole,—his wife, and three sons bought land on the east bank of the Miami River, opposite the mouth of Bear Creek. It was on this land that the blockhouse was built by Major Adams in 1799. The blockhouse and stockade, known as Hole's Station, became a favorite halting-place for newcomers, while prospecting around the valley, and was the beginning of Miamisburg, which was platted in 1818.

On July 18, 1800, Jerome Holt was appointed constable for this township, and was ordered to list the free male inhabitants of twenty-one years and over, for which he received nineteen dollars and fifty cents. The rates were: for young or single men, each, 50 cents; bond-servants, each, $2; stud-horses, the rate they stand at the season; horses, 40 cents; cattle, 10 cents; on each $100, 40 cents.

In that year the census of the Northwest Territory showed that there were forty-two thousand inhabitants in

DAYTON TOWNSHIP FORMED

that part included within the boundaries of Ohio. Application was at once made for admission as a State into the Union. On the 30th of April of the same year the enabling act of Congress, forming the State of Ohio, was approved by John Adams, then President of the United States. Under this act, on the 1st of November, 1802, the first constitutional convention assembled at Chillicothe, and on the 29th of the same month the constitution was adopted and signed and the convention adjourned. The act of Congress "to provide for the due execution of the laws of the United States within the State of Ohio" was approved by the President on February 19, 1803, by which act Ohio was admitted into the Union. Salmon P. Chase, in his statistics of Ohio, says in reference to its system of laws, "It may be doubted whether any colony at so early a period after its first establishment ever had one so good." And in reference to the settlement of Ohio, he says, "Before the end of the year 1798 the Northwestern Territory contained a population of five thousand free male inhabitants, of full age, and eight organized counties."

William King was born in York County, Pennsylvania, January 3, 1764. Nancy (Agnes) Waugh was born in Adams County, Pennsylvania, in 1762. They were married April 2, 1787, and soon after removed to Kentucky and settled near Lexington, where he worked at his trade. They had three sons: Victor, born March 11, 1790; John, born October 16, 1791; Samuel, born November 11, 1793, and a daughter, Susan, born October 15, 1796. Being conscientiously opposed to slavery, he decided to move to Ohio, and in 1799, having procured a good team, he crossed the Ohio River. Hearing of the new settlement then starting at Dayton, up the Great Miami River, he journeyed in his wagon to that place. On his arrival he found but a few log houses in the surrounding forests, and he had but one dollar left in his pocket. Leaving his family camping in the wagon at the new settlement, he concluded to cross the Miami and reconnoiter the west side. There was no settlement or house on the west side, and he had to cut his way through unbroken forests. Looking for a site to suit him, he found a beautiful knoll about two miles west, and setting down his stakes, said, "Here is where I want my farm." The next thing was to arrange for buying the land. He found he could not buy simply the tract he wanted for his home, as the Government would only sell land commencing at the river, but he also found he could buy land upon payments. So, in order to secure the spot he had selected and set his heart upon as his future home, he purchased the fractional Section 33, about five hundred and twenty acres, beginning at the Miami River, and the whole Section 32, six hundred and forty acres immediately west. As fast as payments became due, he sold a portion of land, and did this so successfully that by 1807 he had his purchase from the Government fully paid, and received his patents.

While his family camped in the wagon at Dayton, he took one man and rations for a week at a time, went out to the selected spot, hewed the timber, and built a cabin. While thus engaged an incident of pioneer life happened which it may not be amiss to mention here. They had raised the cabin, sawed out the logs for a door, and hung up their provisions inside. While they had gone off a short distance to split clapboards to cover the cabin, a bear entered it and ate up all their provisions, and they were left hungry.

Having finished the cabin, he moved his family out to it, and commenced clearing in 1799. He remained at the spot until his death in 1863. A second daughter, Jane, was born to them in 1800. About 1813 the two oldest sons, Victor and John, moved to Madison, Indiana. In 1817 his daughter Susan died. The third son, Samuel M., remained with his parents, and in 1822 was married to Mary C. Williams, daughter of John H. Williams, and oldest sister of Lockhard and Herbert S. Williams, who all owned and lived on parts of the sections named. On July 1, 1839, his wife Nancy (Agnes) died. For several years previous to her death the duties of housekeeping had been turned over to Samuel and Mary, and William King lived with them. His daughter Jane married David Osborn about 1824, and died in 1829, leaving three children—William K., David S., and Jane, now Mrs. Stevenson. David and Jane are still living.

The third son, Samuel M. King, died in October, 1849, leaving eight children living, his son Victor having died in infancy. William B. King owns and lives now on the same knoll originally selected by his grandfather, which has ever since remained in possession of the family. He married Louisa, a granddaughter of Isaac Spining, and daughter of Charles H. Spining, who came to Dayton about 1801 and settled about five miles east of Dayton on a farm that remained in that family until the death of Charles H. Spining in 1879. John W. King, the second son, owns and lives on a knoll a short distance west of the original home now owned by William B. King. Samuel D. King, the fourth son, died in the United States Army in 1864. The daughters, Nancy J. King and Mrs. Harriet A. Scott, own and live on a portion of the original tract immediately adjoining the old homestead site. Susan married James S. Alexander, and their home is at Monongahela, Pennsylvania. Eliza married Edward Breneman, and they have always lived in Dayton. Lucy W. married Rev. William Greenough, D.D., who is, and has been for more than twenty years, pastor of Cohocksink Presbyterian Church of Philadelphia, Pennsylvania. The beloved mother, Mrs. Mary C. King, died in 1886.

William King, Sr., was an elder in the First Presbyterian Church of Dayton before 1817 and continued in office until retired by the infirmities of age. Samuel M. King was an elder in the same church from 1840 until his death. All the persons mentioned in this sketch of the King family are or have been influential members of the Presbyterian Church.

Among the old papers belonging to William King are found a few items relating to early days that may be of interest. As there were no bridges over the Miami, William King in 1811 took out a license to run a ferry. It is as follows:

"THE STATE OF OHIO,
"MONTGOMERY COUNTY.

"To all who shall see these presents be it known, that license is hereby given to William King to keep a ferry below the town of Dayton for one year from the date hereof, according to the statutes made and provided.

"By the Court. In testimony whereof I have hereunto set my hand, and affixed the seal of our Court of Common Pleas at Dayton, Jan. 2, 1811.

"B. VAN CLEVE, *Clerk, M. C. P.*"

"*Rates of Ferriage.* Foot person, $6\frac{1}{4}$ cents; man and horse, $12\frac{1}{2}$ cents; loaded wagon and team, 75 cents; any other four-wheeled carriage, 50 cents; loaded cart and team, 50 cents; empty cart and team, $37\frac{1}{2}$ cents; sleigh or sled and team, $37\frac{1}{2}$ cents; horse, mule, ass, or head of neat cattle, $6\frac{1}{4}$ cents; sheep or hog, 3 cents.

"Price of license, $3.00.

"B. VAN CLEVE, *Clerk, M. C. P.*"

This ferry, *below* the town of Dayton, as stated, was located at the foot of Fourth Street. The license for

1812 is worded the same, except that "north of mouth of Wolf Creek" is added.

Some of his old tax receipts are interesting: For 1800, $1.36.9, direct tax due United States; 1802, $1.22; 1803, $1.58; 1804, $2.64; 1807, $6.53; 1808, $7.10; 1816, $19.56; 1817, $15.15; 1818, $14.30.5; 1827, $15.62.7; 1828, $20.31.6.

As he received his patents in 1807 from Thomas Jefferson, President, after that date, as the town grew, the taxes increased.

W. Craig ran a sawmill near by, as appears from a bill of fourteen dollars paid for sawing lumber.

In 1830 William King had sold all but three hundred and ninety-five acres.

In 1801 William Ruffin was appointed county commissioner, and Benjamin Van Cleve county surveyor, and also county lister. He found three hundred and eighty-two free males over twenty-one years of age east of the Big Miami, and twenty east of the Little Miami. He was paid twenty-nine dollars and fifty cents for listing. Curwen says: "In 1801 the total free male population over twenty-one years old between the two Miamis, from the present southern line of Montgomery and Greene counties, and extending probably as far north as Vienna, Springfield, New Carlisle, and the mouth of Honey Creek, was three hundred and eighty-two. Calculating on the data which the election returns now furnish, this would make the total white population of that district not far from one thousand eight hundred souls," being an average increase from 1796 of over four hundred per annum.

In 1802 there were only five families living in Dayton— George Newcom, Paul D. Butler, the Rev. James Welsh, Samuel Thompson, and George Westfall. The McClures had moved to Miami County, and other settlers had moved onto farms. However, new people commenced coming in and settling in this vicinity. Among them we find the names of Wagner, Bradford, Miller, Williams, Kennedy, Leatherman, Neff, and Spining.

Philip Wagner emigrated from Rockingham County, Virginia, to Columbia about the year 1800, and, after staying there a short time, removed to this county, settling in Harrison Township, near the Soldiers' Home, where he died. He had eight children, the youngest of whom, Philip, Jr., in 1810, bought a tract of about eight hundred acres in Mad River Township. He married Esther Bowman, and also had eight children, among them another Philip.

John Bradford was born in 1759, and on July 15, 1785, married Mary Gillespie, who was born in 1764 and died in 1812. Mr. Bradford came to Ohio in 1800, entered one hundred and sixty acres of land south of Dayton, and in 1801 moved his family to the farm. He died in 1820. They had twelve children: George G., the father of James J. and George D. Bradford; Robert, John, Jean Eleanor, James G., William, Samuel D., the father of Mrs. Alexander McConnell, and Robert Bradford; Mary, who married John Bigger, and was the mother of Joseph and Samuel Bigger; Margaret, who married Joseph Bigger, and died without heirs; David D., Martha Allen, and Allen, who married Eliza Johnson. He died in 1866. Mrs. Eliza Bradford is still living. They reared a large family, of whom Johnson P., George G., and Richard are the only ones living.

Daniel Miller came west from Pennsylvania in 1802, prospecting for land, and finding Billy Mason "squatted" on Section 30, Harrison Township, he agreed to enter the land and pay him for what he had cleared, and his cabin. Mr. Miller then went to the land office in Cincinnati and made the entry, and the next year moved his family west

DAYTON TOWNSHIP FORMED

and took possession of the Mason cabin. In 1804 or 1805 Mr. Miller built a grist- and sawmill on his land, long known as Miller's Mills. He was a German Baptist, and much respected. He built a large brick house on a rise of ground south of the Wolf Creek pike, probably at one time (many years ago) the bank of Wolf Creek, where he died. The family are all buried on this same rise, a little east of the house.

Miller's Mills were built by John H. Williams, a millwright, who emigrated to North Carolina, and from there to Kentucky, where he married Jane Crothers in 1799, and moved to Warren County, stopping at Franklin. In 1802 he located on Section 25, Madison Township, being obliged, like all other settlers, to go to the land office at Cincinnati to make his entry. Mr. Williams was a member of the First Presbyterian Church, and was a trustee of the church at an early day. His wife died in 1817, leaving him with eight children—James L., Mary, Sarah, Lucinda, Harbert S., Susan C., Anna M., and Elizabeth. Mr. Williams was after this twice married: first, to Mrs. Boal, who died in 1822, leaving a daughter, Eliza J., who married Charles Sherman, and, second, to Mrs. McConnell, by whom he had one child—Francis. Mr. Williams died in 1841.

James Lockhart Williams, the oldest son of John H. Williams, was born October 7, 1800, and on November 14, 1820, married Charity G. Crowell. He was a farmer by occupation, his farm being bounded by what are now Third Street and Germantown Street on the north and south, Broadway on the west, and the river on the east. He had seven children, of whom Jane C., the wife of Hiram Lewis, Mary C., the wife of D. C. Rench, Susan S., and Charles C., are still living. He afterwards sold his farm to his brother, Harbert Williams.

Harbert S. Williams was born in April, 1807, on the farm now owned by Wilson Sloan. Later his father, with his family, moved to the Long farm, now a part of Miami City, the house standing just west of North Summit Street. In 1830 Harbert married Mary Ann Weakley. They had four children, all of whom are dead. They lived in a frame house on the east side of Williams Street, near Third Street, while Mr. Williams was opening up the surrounding farm. In 1837 he was engaged in the grocery business with David Davis, on Market Street. He afterwards returned to his farm, and lived there several years; but the property becoming valuable, he sold it, and bought a farm on West Third Street, outside of the city limits, built the homestead, and moved there. His wife died, and in 1860 he married Agnes Whitmore. They had three children, two of whom — Mrs. John Campbell and Miss Nannie B. Williams — are still living. Mr. Williams was a successful business man, and accumulated a large property. In January, 1847, he was ordained deacon in the First Presbyterian Church, and in 1853 ordained elder in the same church. When a colony formed the Fourth Church, on Summit Street, Mr. Williams was elected and ordained an elder in that church, and held that office until his death. He contributed liberally to the support of the church.

James Bracy Oliver, born in Augusta Springs, Augusta County, Virginia, left there in 1802 on a pony, crossed the Ohio at Huntington, and reached Dayton with fifty cents in his pocket. This he gave to one of the "old residents" to keep the pony for a month. This "old resident" was building a mill, and Mr. Oliver at once commenced work on the race, and continued helping around until he was able to purchase a piece of ground near the Soldiers' Home, which he afterwards sold to the county commissioners for an infirmary, and became the first poorhouse overseer in Montgomery County.

After some time he purchased the farm, north of the Eaton pike, now owned by William King, and having, in 1809, married Mary, he built one of the largest brick houses in the county, and reared a large family. He was very fond of sport and kept a pack of hounds. He and Jeff McConnell and Adam Houk, three old cronies, were so often out fox- and deer-hunting that they became well known over the country, and many anecdotes are told about them. Mr. Oliver always wore a hunting-shirt and a large wool hat, was very proud of his costume, and was never known to appear in any other on any occasion. A Dunkard and very jovial, there is hardly an old citizen but what, when his name is mentioned, will laugh and relate some joke played by him.

When McCullum first built his tavern on Main Street, and was getting settled, he found himself one Saturday morning very much in need of hay. On making inquiry as to where he could probably get a load without delay, he was referred to "Uncle Jimmie Oliver." Uncle Jimmie said, yes, it was Saturday, and a busy time, but he would bring the hay in in the afternoon, which he did, and on driving to the tavern McCullum commenced, "Well, old man, what do you ask for this load of hay?" The price was named, and McCullum said he would give so much for it, when Uncle Jimmie replied he would not give four cents, and, turning to his driver, George Weaver, said, "George, drive to Alexander Grimes's and put this hay in his barn." As the man drove away, Uncle Jimmie turned to the inn-keeper and remarked very pleasantly, "It is getting colder." McCullum asked in amazement where the man was going with the hay, and why it was not being unloaded in his barn. Uncle Jimmie quietly replied, "That hay is gone; old Alexander Grimes gets it." On Monday Uncle Jimmie met Mr. Grimes, who said that he had not bought any hay, but the man had put a load in his stable on Saturday. "Well," said Uncle Jimmie, "I know you didn't buy it, but the hay is good, isn't it? Your horses will eat it. It is all right; it don't cost you anything; I make you a present of it." His friend, and afterwards his executor, Henry Stoddard, was out at the farm one afternoon. As they walked about, Mr. Stoddard was very much interested, making inquiries as to the times of planting clover, timothy, wheat, etc., and how to prepare the soil. Uncle Jimmie willingly gave him all the information he could on the subject. Soon after, on entering Mr. Stoddard's office, he was presented with a bill for five dollars for legal advice relating to a division fence. Uncle Jimmie at once sat down and drew up a bill for five dollars for advice on farming, which balanced the account. One day Dr. Steele asked Uncle Jimmie to send him a load of wood that would *kindle* easily, and Uncle Jimmie sent him a load of buckeye. In a few days the Doctor met him and asked what kind of wood that was. Uncle Jimmie replied, "Oh, you wanted wood to *kindle* easily, so I sent it." Buckeye has a peculiar bark that, when dry, at the touch of flame, will fizz, but die out, and it is almost impossible to burn it. Owing to this peculiarity it was almost universally used for backlogs. There is no doubt that this little joke cost Mr. Oliver considerable wood in the end. He at one time suspected a neighbor, a "new emigrant," of stealing his corn, so one morning asked the man if he was too busy to help, as the corn was being stolen, and he wanted to fix a trap to catch the thief. The two men worked busily for some hours, fixing the trap. After the neighbor departed Mr. Oliver quietly moved the trap to a different location, and the next morning found his suspicions verified. The man begged to be let out, saying that he would never do such a thing again. Mr. Oliver released him, took him to the house for breakfast, forcing him to eat a hearty meal, then loaded two bags of corn on his shoulders and sent him home with the promise that he would never mention his name if the offense was not repeated.

Mr. Oliver died January 17, 1846, at the age of sixty-four years, and is buried on the road running north from the Soldiers' Home. James Oliver Arnold, of Dayton View, is his oldest grandson.

John Neff removed with his family to Dayton in 1801, from Shenandoah County, Virginia. He entered one thousand eight hundred acres of land in Harrison Township, extending two miles along the bank of the Great Miami River, and adjoining the park now known as Idylwild. He had nine children—five sons, Christopher, Henry, Abraham, Daniel, and John, and four daughters, Elizabeth, Esther, Barbara, and Mary. As his children came of age, he gave each of his sons two hundred acres of land, and his daughters each one hundred acres. Mr. Neff died in 1847, and his wife in 1879, in the ninety-fourth year of her age. They are both buried at Beardshear's Chapel. Abraham, the third son of John Neff, was a soldier in the War of 1812. He was married in 1808 to Mary Spruce, and was the father of the late Lewis Neff, better known as Squire Neff, who was born in 1810. Mary married George Beardshear, who came to Dayton from Virginia about 1805. They settled on the hundred acres given Mrs. Beardshear by her father, and their seven children are all living in the same neighborhood. Barbara married

Martin Houser, who came from Virginia about 1805, and settled on Section 25, near Peach Tree Bend, a short distance south of J. McLain Smith's farm. They had eight children. Mr. Houser died February 23, 1842. His wife died January 8, 1844.

Henry Leatherman came here first in 1803. In 1819 he bought the right of way through the Hamer land, dug a race from Mad River to where Harbine Street crosses the Hydraulic, and built a sawmill. Two years ago one of the sills of that mill was dug out of the mud perfectly sound. In 1820 Mr. Leatherman and Elisha Brabham built the red mill on the foundation of the Cooper mill, which burned that year. This mill was torn down in 1837, when Messrs. Grimes and Davies changed the bed of Mad River, to make room for the extension of the canal basin. In 1825 George Kniesley bought sixty acres of the Hamer property, and erected a mill on the north side of the Springfield road. In 1843-44 H. G. Phillips, Daniel Beckel, and Samuel D. Edgar bought the Kniesley and Leatherman interests and built the Upper Hydraulic. I understand that Mr. Leatherman went to California and died there in 1859.

Gilbert Kennedy, born in Glasgow, Scotland, on coming to this country settled first in Pennsylvania. In 1803 he came to Dayton on horseback, bought land on Stillwater, and in 1807 cut his way through from Ebenezer Church. On reaching his land, he chopped down a large oak tree, built a tent against it, and lived there while building his house. At that time there were only two cabins between his place and town. Mr. Kennedy kept bachelor's hall until 1812, when he married Nancy Kerr, who lived at the foot of the hill this side of the Kennedy homestead. They had six children,—four sons and two daughters,—two of whom, John and Joseph, are still living, Joseph on the home farm.

Isaac Spining, born in Elizabeth, New Jersey, came to Ohio with his brothers, Mathias and Ichabod, about the year 1796. Mathias settled near Lebanon, and Ichabod, in 1805, made Cincinnati his home. In 1801 Isaac Spining came to Dayton, and in 1803 was appointed one of the first two associate judges in Ohio. The following is a copy of his commission:

"EDWARD TIFFIN, *Governor, in and by the authority of the State of Ohio, to all who shall see these presents, Greeting.*

"KNOW YE, that we have assigned and constituted, and do by these presents constitute and appoint, Isaac Spining Associate Judge of the Court of Common Pleas for the County of Montgomery, agreeable to the laws, statutes, and ordinances in such cases made and provided, with all the privileges, immunities, and emoluments to such office belonging or in any wise appertaining, for and during the space or term of seven years from the 6th day of April in the year of our Lord one thousand eight hundred and three, if he shall so long behave well.

"In witness whereof, the said Edward Tiffin, Governor of the State of Ohio, hath caused 'the great seal of the State of Ohio' to be hereunto affixed, at Chillicothe, the 8th day of April, in the year of our Lord one thousand eight hundred and three, and of the independence of this State the first.   By the Governor,
(SEAL.)   (Signed,)   "EDWARD TIFFIN."
[Private seal, no State seal being yet procured.]

Mr. Spining took his oath of office before John Ewing on the 10th day of May. Judge Spining and his brothers were Revolutionary soldiers, and when he died, December 24, 1825, after having served as associate judge for twenty-two years, having continued to "so long behave well," he was carried to the grave by six Revolutionary soldiers. Mr. Spining married Catharine Pierson, of Morristown, New

Jersey. They had several children. One of the daughters married Dr. Job Haines; another married Dr. Monfort. One son, Pierson, married Mary Schooley, and was the father of Mrs. Mary Wade, Mrs. David Stewart, and Miss Lizzie Spining, of this city. George B. Spining was the father of the Rev. Dr. George Spining, a noted minister of the Presbyterian Church.

Charles Spining was born in Elizabethtown, New Jersey, on February 7, 1793, and was but three years old when his father brought the family across the mountains to Ohio. In a letter which he wrote to Mr. George Kemp, some years ago, but which is not dated, he says he was eight years old when his father moved to Dayton. Until 1815 they raised all their own flax and wool, spun, and made most of the clothing for the family. In 1825 Mr. Spining married Jane Perlee, of Springfield. He devoted part of his time to mercantile pursuits, but later moved to the farm. As old age crept on, he transferred the farm to his son George and came to make his home with his daughter Jennie, Mrs. Frank Mulford. Here he died on May 31, 1879, at the advanced age of eighty-six years, in full possession of his mental faculties.

One of the prominent men of this period was John Whitten Van Cleve, who was born in Dayton June 27, 1801. He was from boyhood a student, beginning Latin when but ten years of age. When sixteen he was admitted to the Ohio University at Athens, and, owing to his unusual knowledge of Latin and Greek, was employed as a teacher of those languages before he graduated. He had a remarkable memory, and mastered the higher mathematics without difficulty. Mr. Van Cleve was an artist, painting many of the native flowers. He engraved many a picture of Dayton, and illustrated the songs which he wrote to be used in the

Log Cabin, a campaign paper issued in 1840 in the interests of General Harrison, whom he greatly admired. He spent much of his time wandering over the county, hammer in hand, seeking geological specimens, especially the fossils which crop out in the blue limestone, and prepared a number of engravings himself. These were published in the Indiana Geological Reports. The originals are now in the Dayton Public Library. Mr. Van Cleve was a musician, and could play on a violin (which he also made), piano, and other instruments. He was president of the first musical society organized here, in 1823, called the Pleyel Society. He was interested in horticulture, devoting much care and attention to his farm, now city lots, just north of my father's farm, in the southeastern part of the city. He at one time planted ten acres in peaches, which, unfortunately, did not thrive, and was the first to plant the osage orange as a hedge, but did not live to trim it. He was one of the organizers of the Horticultural Society of Montgomery County, and was probably the first secretary, as the minutes are decorated with some of his work—a peach on a branch, with a cluster of leaves, done in water-colors.

With all his accomplishments, love of nature, and outdoor life, Mr. Van Cleve was also a practical business man. He could use his father's compass and chain as well, perhaps, as any surveyor or engineer of his day, and served as town engineer for several terms. On returning from college he entered the office of Judge Crane, and was admitted to the bar in 1828, but never practiced, and at once bought an interest in the Dayton *Journal,* which he edited until 1834. During this time, as Whig, he served as Mayor for one term. In 1834 he formed a partnership with Augustus Newell in the drug business, furnishing the capital and allowing Mr. Newell to conduct the business. In this he continued until 1851, when, having accumulated enough to live on comfortably, he retired from business.

To Mr. Van Cleve's untiring energy and love of the beauties of nature, we owe our Woodland Cemetery, the third rural cemetery to be opened in the United States. One of the most attractive spots to him around Dayton was the highest point of the hill, where the rustic lookout now stands. Many a time have I, when hunting squirrels, long before the ground was suggested by Mr. Van Cleve as a cemetery, seen him there by himself, looking over the town in the valley below. When, in 1840, Mr. Van Cleve suggested that a corporation be formed to purchase forty acres for a cemetery, people thought him visionary,—that the forty acres would never be filled, but, as in many other instances, for the good of Dayton, he had his way. "The cemetery was laid out, the roads run, the platting done, the accounts kept by this skilled surveyor and bookkeeper, and all the duties of a superintendent performed by him without compensation, during the earlier years of its history." He continued president of the Association until his death.

Mr. Van Cleve was a great lover of the forests, and knew the name of every tree and plant in Montgomery County. He assisted in planting the trees on each side of the levees, and himself planted the elms in front of the Courthouse, on Main and Third streets, caring for them until his death. There they remained, an ornament to the town, and a memorial of John W. Van Cleve, until the paving of the streets seemed to make their removal necessary. He made a complete herbarium of the plants of the county, which at his death was given to Cooper Seminary, but it was evidently not appreciated, as no particular care was taken of it. What remains can now be found in the museum at the Public Library.

In 1841 Mr. Van Cleve purchased one rod of land from Robert W. Steele's southern boundary, and I purchased a rod from S. D. Edgar's northern boundary, adjoining, which, by jointly grading and graveling, formed a good road from our farms to what is now Wayne Avenue, thus making an outlet to town. Shortly after this was completed, several young ladies suggested a quilting at my mother's. The quilt was patched and framed, and the time set for the quilting, which came off in good style. Among the guests was a young man, something of a wag, a sign-painter by trade, who, in consequence of the fact that neither Mr. Van Cleve, Samuel D. Edgar, nor myself was married at that time, wrote a sign, "Bachelor's Alley," nailed it to a fence-rail, and set it up. The sign remained there for a long time, and the lane continued to be called Bachelor's Alley until about two years ago, when Council officially named it Lathrop Avenue.

In 1833 Mr. Van Cleve delivered a lecture on Dayton, in which he made the statement that it had grown to be a place of four thousand inhabitants, and gave the following description of the town as it was in 1800:

"While the inhabitants all lived on the river bank, it was no uncommon thing for strangers, on coming into the place, after threading their way through the brush until they had passed through the whole town plat, from one extremity to the other, and arrived at the first few of the cabins that constituted the settlement, to inquire how far it was to Dayton. They were, of course, informed that they had just passed through it and arrived in the suburbs. The fact seemed rather ridiculous, and it was very natural for them to think that the projectors of the town had calculated much too largely in laying it out upon so extensive a scale. The inhabitants themselves, indeed, partook of the same opinion. The lots on the east side of Main Street, opposite the Court-house, were considered so far out of the way that it was not thought probable that the town would extend much beyond them, and they were accordingly appropriated for a graveyard, and remained so till 1805, when the present burying-ground [on Sixth Street] was selected, which has been used by the town and county ever since."

Mr. Van Cleve never married. He died at his lodgings at the Phillips House on September 6, 1858, universally mourned.

CHAPTER IV.

MONTGOMERY SEPARATED FROM HAMILTON COUNTY.

ALL local officers had, up to this time, been appointed by the courts, but as the population of the township had increased rapidly other officers were required, and it was decided that they should be elected by the citizens. The first election was held on the first Monday in April, 1802, according to the following order issued by the Court:

"TERRITORY OF THE UNITED STATES NORTHWEST OF THE RIVER OHIO. } HAMILTON COUNTY.

"*The United States to Jerome Holt, of Dayton Township, Greeting:*

"You are hereby required to give notice to the inhabitants of said township, in three of the most public places thereof, at least ten days before the first Monday in April next, that they may and shall convene on said day at the house of George Newcom, in the township aforesaid, and then and there proceed to elect by ballot a Chairman, Town Clerk, three or more Trustees, or Managers, two or more Overseers of the Poor, three Fence Viewers, two Appraisers of Houses, Lister of Taxable Property, a sufficient number of Supervisors of Roads, and one or more Constables, agreeable to a law entitled 'An act to establish and regulate town meetings.' And of this warrant make due return. By order of the Court.

"In testimony whereof, I have hereunto affixed the seal of our same Court of General Quarter Sessions of the Peace, at Cincinnati, this second day of March, in the year of our Lord 1802.
(SEAL.)   "JOHN S. GANO, *Cl'k*."

There was no record of this election kept, so the names

of the officers are not known, but they served until the organization of the county, in 1803.

On March 24, 1803, by act of the Legislature, Hamilton County was divided and Montgomery County formed, named in honor of General Montgomery, who fell at the battle of Quebec. It included all of the present counties of Preble, Miami, Darke, Shelby, Mercer, Van Wert, Paulding, and Defiance, nearly all of Allen, Putnam, and Henry, and about one-half of Lake County. It was divided into four townships, of which Dayton Township was one.

Dayton Township consisted of all the territory north of Washington Township to the north line of the seventh range of townships, and east of the Miami River to the Greene County line, including in all about six thousand three hundred square miles.

On April 5, 1803, the Legislature appointed Ichabod B. Halsey, Bladen Ashby, and William McClelland as commissioners to locate a county-seat. Dayton was selected by the commissioners. The seat of justice was fixed by an act of the Legislature that went into force on May 1, 1803, at the house of George Newcom, of Dayton.

There were in Montgomery County at the time it was formed five hundred and twenty-six white male inhabitants over twenty-one years of age, and in the State at that time fifteen thousand three hundred and fourteen.

The first election held in Montgomery County after its organization, on March 24, 1803, was to elect a member of Congress. There were three candidates—Jeremiah Morrow, William McMillen, and William Goforth. Three hundred and seventeen votes were cast, of which Jeremiah Morrow received one hundred and seventy-five, William McMillen one hundred and thirty-nine, and William Goforth three.

MONTGOMERY SEPARATED FROM HAMILTON COUNTY

The second election was held on the second Tuesday of October of the same year, for sheriff and coroner. George Newcom was elected sheriff and James Miller coroner.

On April 2, 1804, an election was held for three county commissioners, at which there were twelve candidates. Edmund Munger, John Dover, and William Browne were elected, the first commissioners of this county. The first session of this board was held at Newcom's Tavern, June 11, 1804. Lots were drawn for the length of time each member should serve, the result being that William Browne served three years, Edmund Munger two years, and John Dover until the next October election.

The revenue from the tax duplicate for 1804 amounted to $373.96, the highest tax from any one person being $71.80, and the lowest fifteen cents.

After the county was erected, and Dayton made the seat of justice, George Newcom, as sheriff, had to provide in some way for the prisoners who were by the court committed to jail, no jail having at that time been built. Newcom was an Irishman, of ready wit, and immediately put to such use a dry well at the rear of his house for white prisoners. The Indians he would buck and chain to his corncrib.

On August 9, 1804, the county commissioners advertised, by posters nailed to the trees, for bids for a jail building thirty by sixteen feet, of round logs. The logs were to be straight, and the corners fitted so that the logs would touch all along, with a log partition, dividing the building into two rooms. The floors were to be hewed logs, closely laid, and covered with heavy oak plank, fastened down with wooden pins. The ceilings were also to be covered with heavy plank. One room had one window of four lights, four-by-five glass, and the other had two windows of four-by-six glass. The windows had iron bars across, and heavy oak shutters with iron hinges. The doors were made of two-inch oak plank, double thickness, the doors and shutters being fastened with large locks in wooden cases on the outside. The contract for building the jail was sold at auction on September 28, 1804, to the lowest bidder, David Squier securing the contract at $299. The building was erected on Third Street, near where our present jail stands, and was completed and accepted by the county commissioners in December, 1804.

In 1811 this jail was removed to give place to a building combining jail and dwelling-house. The building, two stories high, eighteen by thirty-two feet, was to be built of stone, with shingle roof. A hall through the center divided it, the sheriff's residence being on the west side and the prisoners' quarters on the east side.

The contract for this building was sold at auction from the Court-house steps on July 27, 1811, to James Thompson, the lowest bidder, for $2,147.91. He was about two years and a half in doing the work, the building being completed and accepted by the commissioners in December, 1813. The entrance was from Third Street. There were three cells on each floor. Those on the second floor, being better furnished and less like a prison, were used for women and minor offenders, one being called a debtor's cell, as in those days a man was imprisoned for debt. The walls and floors of the six cells were covered with a layer of heavy oak plank, driven full of nails, and then covered with a second layer of plank. The window of the front cell faced the street, and through its bars a prisoner could easily converse with the passers-by, and small articles could be passed back and forth. One morning the sheriff found that four prisoners had escaped

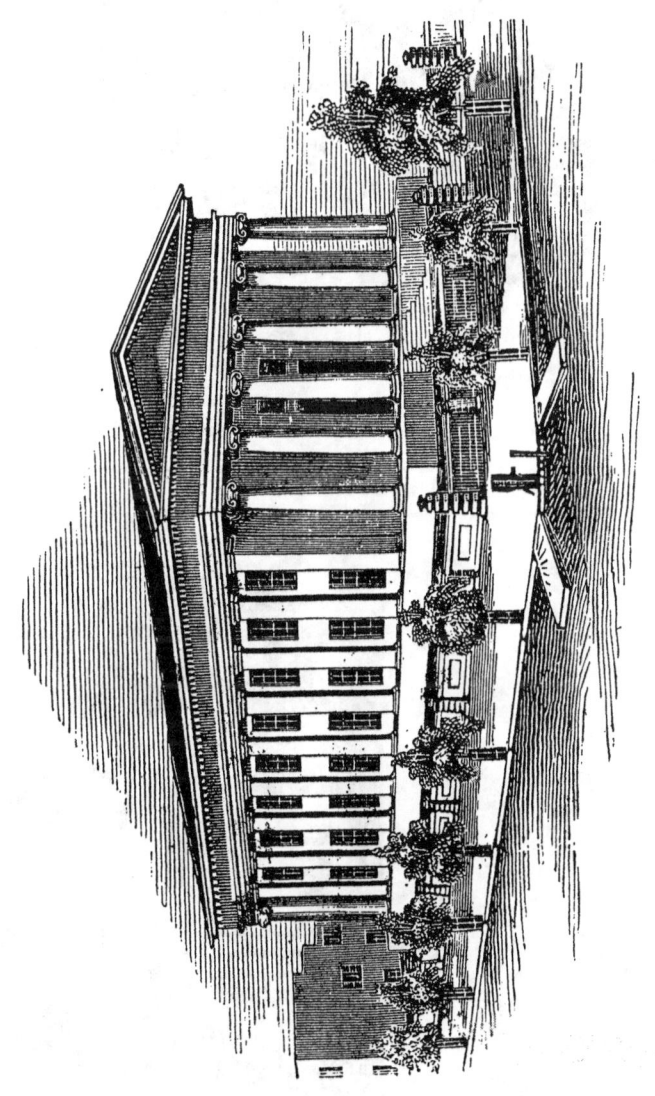

COURT-HOUSE IN 1858.

MAIN STREET, LOOKING NORTH FROM BELOW THIRD STREET.

MONTGOMERY SEPARATED FROM HAMILTON COUNTY

during the night by cutting through the floor and tunneling under the wall. It was then decided at once that a new building was needed, and during 1834-35 a one-story structure of heavy cut stone, containing four cells, with stone floors and arched brick ceilings, was erected in the rear of the jail, and used as the county jail for ten years.

The first term of court was held in the Newcom Tavern, in 1803, but in 1805 the county commissioners rented rooms in Hugh McCullum's new tavern, at the corner of Main and Second streets, for court purposes, at an annual rent of twenty-five dollars. The fall term of court in 1805 was held in the new quarters, and they were used until the first brick Court-house was completed, on the northwest corner of Main and Third streets.

In 1804 the county commissioners sent advertisements to Cincinnati and to Lexington, Kentucky, for proposals to build a brick Court-house, thirty-eight by forty-two feet, two stories high, the first floor to be used as a court-room, the jury-rooms to be on the second floor. The contract was let February 3, 1806, and the house was occupied in the winter of 1807-08 for court and religious purposes, the commissioners having borrowed money of the trustees of the First Presbyterian Church with the understanding that until it was paid back the congregation could hold their services in the Court-house, and neither rent nor interest was to be charged. There were no locks on the doors of this building for four years after it was completed. The furniture in the court- and jury-rooms consisted of a few three-legged stools and a bench. At first the jurors were not furnished with seats, and it was not until 1811 that tables were placed in the building. In 1815 the commissioners built a cupola on the Court-house, and the next year a bell was hung.

This building, with the jail, was sold at auction in October, 1845, for $864. The new jail, now the City Work House, was built on the corner of Main and Sixth streets, and when it grew too small the present brownstone edifice, combining sheriff's residence and jail, was erected on Third Street, on the site of the original stone and log jail. The Court-house then erected still stands, in its Grecian majesty and simplicity, a monument to its unknown architect. In the Odell Directory M. E. Curwen gives the following description:

"In the spring of 1847 were laid the foundations of the Dayton Court-house the most elegant and costly building of the kind in the State of Ohio. It is constructed of a species of compact white limestone, which abounds in the vicinity, and which is well known, from its extensive use in the building of canal locks, the Cincinnati Catholic Cathedral, and other buildings, as the Dayton marble. The building is fire-proof throughout, and is covered with a marble roof. The only wood used in its construction is for the inner doors, furniture, and window-sashes. Rising by a flight of eight marble steps, you reach the broad terrace on which the building is erected; advancing about six paces, you rise, by another flight of steps, to the floor of the portico, nearly on a level with the windows of the second story of the buildings on the opposite side of the street. The entrance into the main hall, which is thirty-eight feet long and eleven wide, is by two massy, ornamented doors of iron, each of which is more than two thousand pounds in weight. On the right of the hall are three rooms, with groined ceilings, which are used as the clerk's office, the middle one being the principal business room. On the left are the sheriff's and recorder's offices. The hall leads to the rotunda, twenty feet in diameter and forty-two feet high, ornamented with a dome, the eye of which lights the hall below. Around this rotunda a circular flight of geometrical stone stairs leads to the gallery of the court-room on one side, and to the offices of the treasurer of the county on the other.

"Immediately in front of the principal entrance, at the west of the rotunda, is the court-room. It is one of the striking effects of perfect proportion in architecture to diminish the apparent size of a building. For this reason the stupendous magnitude of the grand altar of St. Peter's at Rome loses half of its effect, and seems to the casual visitor too small for the building, until he reflects that it is of the same height as the Capitol at Washington. Spectators who enter the Dayton court-room for the first time often remark how small it seems. Yet the gallery alone is spacious enough to afford seats for more than two hundred persons.

"The room is in an elliptical form, the shorter diameter being forty-two and the longer fifty-two feet in length. A light gallery of iron, at the height of sixteen feet from the floor, supported by brackets and surmounted by an iron railing, surrounds the room. The whole is lighted by a handsome dome, the eye of which is forty-three feet from the floor. The court-room is ventilated by openings, invisible from below, around the eye of the dome. While it was building, great fears were entertained that, as in the dome of the Capitol at Washington, the reverberation would be so great that the room would be useless for the purpose of a court. These fears were, however, unfounded. The utility of the building has not been sacrificed to a showy appearance, and no room could have been constructed better adapted to the purpose for which this was designed."

This old Court-house is now used for the Probate Court, and for the storage of papers and documents. The Rev. Mr. Clayton drove a team and hauled stone for the building. John Carey, the contractor, afterwards moved to Sidney, Ohio.

On July 27, 1803, Hon. Francis Dunlevy opened the first court in Dayton in the upper story of Newcom's Tavern. Following are extracts from the first appearance docket of the first term of the Court of Common Pleas, of Montgomery County:

"THE STATE OF OHIO, } ss.
  "MONTGOMERY COUNTY.

"COMMON PLEAS.

"Term of July, Anno Domini one thousand eight hundred and three.
"Present, the Honorable Francis Dunlevy, Esquire, President 1st Circuit.
"Benjamin Archer,
"Isaac Spining, and } Esquires, Associate Judges.
"John Ewing,
    "Benjamin Van Cleve, Clerk, P. T.
    "George Newcom, Esq., Sheriff.
"Daniel Symmes, Esq., prosecutor, p. t., in behalf of the State.

"Came a Grand Jury, to wit: John McCabe, foreman, and present for assault and batteries Jeremiah York, Peter Sunderland, and Benjamin Scott."

At the second term of court, which was held in November, 1803, there was considerable business transacted, and the following are extracts from the docket, the same judges presiding:

"George F. Tenney, Esquire, sworn and admitted to practice as an attorney at law in this court."

MONTGOMERY SEPARATED FROM HAMILTON COUNTY 85

"Letters of Administration are granted to Hannah Davis, relict of Thomas Davis, deceased, late of the State of Delaware. The securities are Owen Hatfield and William Hatfield, bound in $1,500 to the State of Ohio."

"Letters of Administration are granted to Abigail Bigger and James Bigger on the estate of Joseph Bigger, deceased. The securities are James Petticrew and Jacob Long, bound in $500 to the Governor of the State of Ohio."

"Upon application and proper vouchers being produced to the court, licenses are granted to the Reverend Jacob Miller and the Reverend William Robinson, ministers of the Gospel in this county, to perform the rites of marriage agreeable to the law within this State."

"Allowed by the Court to Arthur St. Clair, Esquire, for prosecuting the pleas in behalf of the State at the late term of the Supreme Court and at this term of the Court of Common Pleas, thirty dollars."

"It is ordered by the Court that a permanent clerk be appointed at our next term."

The third term of court was held in June, 1804, and the following are extracts from the docket:

"Came a Grand Jury, to wit: John Gerard, James Gillespie, James Thompson, James Russel, Nathaniel Knotts, James Miller, Sr., Edmond Munger, John Bradford, James Scott, Michael Moyer, John Noop, Shadrach Hudson, and John Mikesell; found no bills."

At this term the case of the *State* v. *Benjamin Scott* came up, the defendant pleading "not guilty." The jurors were George Koons, Joseph Kingry, Benjamin Bowman, William Mason, Benjamin Iddings, George Yount, Alexander Snodgrass, Barney Blue, John Vansel, John McKabe, Robert Edgar, and Henry Atchisen. A verdict of "not guilty" was rendered, and judgment of acquittal was entered.

The above are the first recorded names of the grand and petit juries.

On this same docket we find the following:

"An inventory exhibited and filed of the estate of Joseph Bigger, deceased."

"An inventory of the estate of Thomas Davis, deceased, was exhibited and filed."

"Richard S. Thomas was sworn and admitted to practice as an attorney at law in this court."

"Allowed by the Court to Arthur St. Clair for prosecuting the pleas at this present term, $20."

It was customary in those days to bind out orphan children and poor children to those who were able to take care of them, and accordingly we find the following entries:

"Ordered that Thomas Coppock be appointed guardian to 5 orphan children now under his care; namely:" (The names are not given.)

"Ordered that Daniel C. Cooper be appointed guardian to Thomas Adams and Nancy Adams, orphan children, who lately lived with Ralph French."

"Adjourned without day."

In 1804 Dayton received valuable acquisitions to its population in Colonel Robert Patterson, Joseph H. Crane, Luther Bruen, Captain Hugh Andrews, Henry Brown, and others.

Luther Bruen, a son of Jabez Bruen, a Revolutionary soldier, and Abigail Spining, sister of Judge Isaac Spining, came to Ohio with his father, on horseback, at an early day. The rest of the family came by boat down the Ohio River to Cincinnati, and settled on Mill Creek, about nine miles from Cincinnati, on a farm of one hundred acres, purchased from one of Mrs. Bruen's brothers, who had come west as early as 1797. Luther was the fourth in a family of eight children, having three older and three younger sisters, and one brother, Isaac, some eight years his junior, who died on the farm in 1866, aged seventy-five years. Luther Bruen was born September 8, 1783, and spent the last two years of his minority in learning to make shoes in Cincinnati. In August of 1804 he went to Yellow Springs for his health, and on leaving there for home, decided to stop in Dayton to visit his uncle, Isaac Spining. While visiting there he made shoes for all of his uncle's family, and was finally induced to settle in Dayton. In December, 1804, he built a little shop, where he lived and worked, and evidently prospered, for in 1806 he began to acquire land.

On July 9, 1807, Mr. Bruen married Priscilla Owings, who died March 11, 1809, at the birth of a daughter, Priscilla, who afterwards became Mrs. Samuel Brady. On June 4, 1810, Mr. Bruen married Susan Barnett, daughter of John and Elizabeth Barnett, who lived near Miller's Ford, south of Dayton. Their children were David H.; Isaac Spining, who died in infancy; Eliza, who married Robert G. Corwin, of Lebanon, Ohio, and died March 27, 1894, in her seventy-sixth year, and Luther. Mr. Bruen's second wife dying September 11, 1843, he married, on May 2, 1844, Susan D. Howell. One daughter was born to them, Susan Eleanor Seely, who married John Morgan, of Cincinnati. Mrs. Bruen died December 4, 1868. Mr. Bruen died July 1, 1849, of cholera.

David H. Bruen, the oldest child of Luther Bruen and Susan Barnett, was born in Dayton, October 20, 1811, and died January 19, 1853. He graduated at Miami University, Oxford, Ohio, September 24, 1834, with the degree of Bachelor of Arts. He was a respected member of the Dayton bar, and was connected at one time with the Dayton Bank. He never married.

Luther Barnett, the youngest child, was born in Dayton

September 14, 1822. He entered Miami University in October, 1840, as a junior, and remained there a year. About the first of 1843 he went to Lebanon, Ohio, to study and practice law with his brother-in-law, Robert G. Corwin, staying there until the spring of 1845, when he went to Cincinnati and opened an office for himself. In 1849 he visited Detroit, Chicago, Milwaukee, Madison, Galena, and St. Paul, in search of an opening, but found all the places crowded with lawyers. While on this trip he received an appointment to a position in one of the departments at Washington, District of Columbia, and assumed his duties about December 1, 1849. In March, 1852, he purchased an interest in the Cincinnati *Gazette*, and was junior editor until sometime in 1856, when he opened a law office in partnership with Robert G. Corwin in Dayton, and practiced law until 1861. He was then made one of the majors in the Twelfth Regiment United States Infantry, a regiment raised by President Lincoln and officered by civilians. Major Bruen assumed his duties July 4, 1861, at Fort Hamilton, Long Island, being ranking officer for some time. Later he was ordered to join the Army of the Potomac, in Virginia. While in command of his regiment at Spottsylvania Court-house, May 13, 1864, he was wounded by a fragment of shell, and died from the effects of the wound June 21, 1864, at Douglas Hospital, Washington, District of Columbia.

On December 8, 1853, Mr. Bruen married Augusta Forrer, daughter of Samuel and Sarah Forrer, of Dayton, and Mrs. Bruen and four children—Sarah H., Frank, Robert L., and Mary H. Bruen—are still living.

Henry Brown, whose ancestors emigrated from the north of Ireland about 1740, was born near Lexington, Kentucky, in 1770, and in 1793 was military secretary for Colonel

MONTGOMERY SEPARATED FROM HAMILTON COUNTY 89

Preston, who commanded a regiment in General Wayne's army. Mr. Brown was afterwards interested in forwarding supplies to the army, and in 1795 entered into partnership with John Southerland, at Hamilton, Ohio, their principal business being to trade with the Indians for furs, peltries, etc. In 1799 Mr. Brown took a stock of goods to Fort Laramie, following up the retreating Indians.

In 1804 he removed his business to Dayton, and it is said that in 1808 he built the first two-story brick residence in Dayton, on lot 110, just north of the Court-house. The house, as was usual in those days, was built about three feet above the street level, so as to be above high water. In the front room Mr. Brown had his store. Henry Herrman opened a store in that room about 1829, and in 1863, when Major Bickham took charge of the *Journal*, he opened his office in this building, and occupied it a number of years.

In 1810 Mr. Brown was appointed agent in charge of Indian supplies to be distributed under the direction of Colonel John Johnston, Indian agent. On February 19, 1811, he and Kitty Patterson, daughter of Colonel Robert Patterson, were married by the Rev. James Welsh, pastor of the First Presbyterian Church. Miss Patterson was born at Lexington, Kentucky, March 7, 1793. They had three children—Robert Patterson, Henry L., and Eliza J. Mr. Brown died May 19, 1823.

Mrs. Brown was for many years an active Christian worker, and it was at her home, on April 12, 1815, while she was confined to her bed by sickness, that several ladies met and organized the Female Charitable and Bible Society of Dayton, the first organization of that kind effected here. Mrs. Brown married Andrew Irwin, and had one son— A. Barr Irwin. Mr. Irwin died, and in 1836 Mrs. Irwin married Horatio G. Phillips, who died in 1859. Mrs. Phillips died in 1864. They had no children.

Robert Patterson Brown was born December 6, 1811, and married Sarah Galloway, of Xenia, October 31, 1837. He was a lawyer, and served for some time as associate judge. He died in Kansas City, May 4, 1879. They had three children—Mary (Mrs. Campbell), Henry, and Charles.

Henry L. Brown was born December 2, 1814. He married Sarah Bell Browning, of Indianapolis, Indiana, February 7, 1837. He was for many years an active merchant in Dayton, and at one time had his store and residence on the corner of Third and Main streets, where the Phillips House now stands. Mr. Brown was an elder and active worker in the First Presbyterian Church. His wife died October 15, 1858. He survived her twenty years and a little over a month, dying November 25, 1878. They had eight children—Fannie (Mrs. L. B. Evans), Ashley, Katie (Mrs. Noel), Hattie (Mrs. Dr. Telfair), Sarah Bell (Mrs. Daring Whitmore), Harry, Edward, and Robert, all of whom are still living.

Eliza J. Brown was born October 29, 1816, and on September 16, 1835, married Charles Anderson, a young lawyer who came to Dayton in 1835 when but twenty-one years of age, having been born in Louisville, Kentucky, June 1, 1814. Although born and reared in a slave State, Mr. Anderson was opposed to the system of slavery. He was living in Texas when the War of the Rebellion broke out, and was imprisoned for expressing antislavery sentiments, but effected his escape and returned to Dayton. He soon after went to the front as colonel of the Ninety-third Ohio Regiment, of which Hiram Strong was major. Owing to a wound which he received at the battle of Stone River, he was compelled to leave the army, and was soon after elected Lieutenant-Governor of Ohio. On account of the death of Governor Brough, he was serving as Governor of Ohio at the close of the War. He afterwards removed to Kentucky, where he died in the fall of 1895. His wife and three children—Kitty, Latham, and Bell—are still living.

Judge A. Barr Irwin married Jane Schenck, daughter of Admiral Schenck. He was for many years one of the prominent merchants in Dayton, in partnership with Henry L. Brown. He afterwards moved to Kanawha, Kentucky, where he received the appointment of judge. They had four children—Eliza Schenck, Sarah Crane, Catharine Patterson, and Woodhull Schenck, all of whom are still living.

Captain Hugh Andrews, of Scotch-Irish extraction, was the son of James Andrews and Jane Strain (widow of John Strain), and was born August 31, 1764, in Hanover Township, Dauphin County, Pennsylvania. He won his title of captain as the commander of a Light Horse Company in Pennsylvania. Captain Andrews was twice married—first to Miss Spear, of Hanover Township, Lebanon County, Pennsylvania. They had three children—John, Isabella, and Margaret, all of whom lived and died in Logan County, Ohio. His second wife was Elizabeth Ainsworth, whom he also married in Hanover Township, Lebanon County, Pennsylvania, where, too, his son Samuel went for his wife, Margaret Ramsey, in 1831. By Captain Andrews's second wife he had five children—Nancy, Samuel Ainsworth, James, Hugh, and Eliza, the first three of whom— Nancy (afterwards Mrs. Shaw), Samuel, and James—lived and died here in Dayton, each having attained nearly eighty-eight years, and leaving numerous children and grandchildren, who are well known in the community.

Hugh died near Muncie, Indiana, and Eliza (Mrs. Stevens) lived and died in Greene County.

Captain Andrews first came to Ohio on a prospecting tour in 1797, by flatboat down the Ohio River to Cincinnati, and thence through the woods to Dayton, where there were then only about a dozen houses. After buying considerable land in this vicinity, he returned to Pennsylvania, and in the spring of 1804 emigrated with his family (Samuel being then an infant) and settled about six miles northeast of where the Court-house stands. He died in May, 1811, and was buried in the old graveyard on Fifth Street, near the Union Depot.

Nathan Worley was born in Virginia, January 7, 1773, and on March 2, 1791, married Rachel Greer, of Fayette County, Kentucky, coming to Dayton in 1804. Being an earnest worker among the Newlights, in 1815 he was regularly appointed to the work of the ministry, in which he continued until his death, April 9, 1847.

Joseph H. Crane was born in Elizabethtown, New Jersey, August 31, 1772. His father was a major in the Revolutionary War, and lost a leg in that struggle for liberty. Mr. Crane read law and was admitted to practice in his native State. In the spring of 1804 he came to Dayton, opened an office, and commenced the practice of law. On July 16, 1809, he married Julia Ann Elliott, daughter of Dr. John Elliott, born in February, 1790. Two of their sons, William and Joseph G., were members of the Montgomery County bar. Mr. Crane was nominated by the Whigs and elected September 6, 1809, to the Eighth General Assembly, which convened at Chillicothe the first Monday of December, 1809. In 1812 he enlisted in Captain Steele's company and marched to the front, where he was promoted to the rank of sergeant-major. He served as prosecuting attorney for the First District Circuit Court from 1813 to 1816, and in 1817 was appointed presiding judge to succeed Judge Dunlevy. He held that office until 1828, when he was elected to Congress, and served as the Representative of this district for eight years, after which he resumed the practice of his profession. In 1838 he was again appointed prosecuting attorney and served one year.

Judge Crane formed a law partnership with Colonel John H. James, of Urbana, which continued until 1831 as Crane & James, at which time Robert C. Schenck was admitted to the firm, and the name changed to Crane, James & Schenck. In 1834 this firm was dissolved by mutual consent, and Judge Crane became associated with Edward W. Davies, and in 1837 his son William was taken into the firm, where he remained until his death. The law firm of Crane & Davies continued until the death of Judge Crane, in November, 1851.

Judge Crane was the chairman of the meeting at the organization of the Montgomery County Bible Society, on August 21, 1822. His wife had been one of the organizers of the Female Bible Society in 1815. He was loved and venerated by the older citizens, and looked up to by the bar as an able lawyer and an honest man. He was a noble Christian gentleman, a devoted member of the Episcopal Church. His portrait, painted by Charles Soule, Sr., is in the Law Library.

Joseph G. Crane, born October 17, 1825, married Sarah Schenck, daughter of Admiral James F. Schenck. He was a soldier in the late War, serving on the staff of General R. C. Schenck. At the close of the War he was commissioned captain, with the brevet of colonel in the regular army, and was made mayor of Jackson, Mississippi, in

1868. While acting in this capacity, he was killed in the street by the noted ex-Confederate officer, Colonel Yerger, on June 8, 1869.

Colonel Robert Patterson was born March 15, 1759, near Big Cove Mountain, Pennsylvania. At the age of fifteen, in 1774, he served six months with a company of Rangers of the frontiers of Pennsylvania. In the spring of 1775 he, with three other men, started west to Fort Pitt, and in October of that year, in company with eight or ten other persons, started in boats down the Ohio River for Kentucky. In 1776 they built a fort north of the Kentucky River and named it McClelland's Station, for one of the party. In the month of April, 1777, he and his company built a cabin near a big spring, now in the city of Lexington, Kentucky. While there, he with his ax blazed the trees around a large tract of land, which he subsequently, in 1779, entered under the laws of Virginia, and laid out the city of Lexington, Kentucky.

Their supply of ammunition was nearly exhausted, and a company of seven volunteered to return to Fort Pitt for supplies. Their trip up the river was made in a canoe. They reached the mouth of the Kanawha River safely the night of October 12, 1776. They camped on the north side of the river, and, contrary to custom, built a fire, and in the night, while asleep, were attacked by a party of Indians. The Indians fired on the sleeping whites and killed one, wounded four, took one prisoner, and one, Mitchell, was unhurt. Patterson had his right arm broken and was wounded by a tomahawk in his right side. He escaped into the bushes. While running, his broken arm swung between two saplings, and he had to stop to extricate it. At daylight the warriors assembled at the camp, and found five of the company. They had saved one rifle and some ammunition. Their boat had been stolen by the Indians, so they concluded to continue their journey on foot. They dressed the wounds as best they could and started. They found one of the five, named Wernock, unable to travel. He felt he must die, and desired the other four to go on and leave him. They tried to carry him, but finding they could not do that, they finally filled a camp-kettle with water and set it beside him, and started on their journey. After going a short distance, they gave out near a small stream of water, and concluded to camp there and send Mitchell back to the wounded man, while Perry was to take the rifle and reach the first settlement up the river and bring relief. Mitchell returned to Wernock and found him dying. He stayed with him until all was over, then returned to Patterson and Templeton, and that day moved them some distance up from the river, into a deep ravine, although Patterson could not move about much, owing to the tomahawk wound in his right side. Mitchell found a projecting rock near, and removed the camp to that place, where they were protected from the rain. They lived on wild grapes and papaws. The broken arm was very painful, and, undertaking to dress it, they found the splints and shirt cemented together with blood, so that it was almost impossible to remove them. They finally did get them off, and dressed the arm with oak leaves, making it more comfortable. The wound in his side was more difficult to dress, and little could be done for it. Mitchell was constantly on the river bank watching for boats going down the river; but none appeared until the 20th of October, 1776, when he was rejoiced to see his brave friend Perry with Captain John Walls and troops from the Fort of Grave Creek. The wounds of Patterson and Templeton were then dressed, and they were taken on board the boats and supplied with nourishing food. The Captain then had the bones of Wernock and McNutt buried (the wolves having eaten all the flesh off of them), and they all then started up the river in boats to Grave Creek. Patterson was nearly a year under the surgeon's care at his home in Pennsylvania.

In September we find him again with his rifle in hand, on his way to Kentucky. In 1778 he was with Colonel George Rogers Clark in the Illinois campaign, and was promoted to the rank of ensign of the company. In March, 1779, he was detailed with twenty-five men to establish a garrison north of the Kentucky River (now the center of the city of Lexington, Kentucky). The stockade included the big spring found by him in 1777, where the men that were with him cleared a patch of ground and planted corn in it. While there, he blazed a tract of land, which he afterwards entered and upon which he laid out the city of Lexington.

In 1779 he and his company joined Captain Levi Todd, as a part of his force to march against old Chillicothe, Little Miami, and old Piqua on Mad River. In the winter of 1779 he returned to his old home in Pennsylvania, and on the 20th of March, 1780, married Elizabeth Lindsay, of Franklin County, Pennsylvania, and returned to Kentucky shortly after. Later in 1780, as captain of a company, he was with the expedition of General George Rogers Clark against the Shawnees in the vicinity of Springfield.

April 7, 1781, Thomas Jefferson, Governor of Virginia, commissioned him captain of Virginia volunteers. August 19, 1782, he, with his company, was in the battle of Blue Licks, which proved disastrous to the whites. During the retreat, one of his men, Aaron Reynolds, on horseback, overtook Captain Patterson walking and almost exhausted. He dismounted and helped the Captain on his horse and

MONTGOMERY SEPARATED FROM HAMILTON COUNTY

started on on foot. Reynolds was soon captured by three Indians. Two of the Indians left the prisoner with the other and started to find some other of the defeated troops. Reynolds watched his opportunity and knocked his captor over and escaped. Patterson also escaped, and presented Reynolds with two hundred acres of land for his generous act. There was great rejoicing on his return to the camp after that disastrous defeat. Again, in the fall of 1782, we find Captain Patterson and his company in Colonel Logan's regiment in Clark's expedition against the Indians at Piqua, Laramie, and Portage. On returning, they camped a few days at the mouth of Mad River. In 1783 he built a log house on one of the lots in Lexington, and moved his family from the stockade, and subsequently erected a substantial stone house, instead of the log cabin, within the stockade and moved there.

In 1783 he was elected justice of the peace for Fayette County, and in July, 1785, was chosen delegate to a convention that met in Danville. August 8 that convention petitioned the Virginia Legislature for the separation of Kentucky, so as to form a separate State of the United States. In September, 1785, Governor Patrick Henry commissioned him as colonel, and in the fall of 1786, with his regiment, he marched under Colonel B. Logan against the Indian towns on Mad River. This expedition burned eight of the Shawnee towns and destroyed a large amount of provisions. In a skirmish November 5, he became engaged in a hand-to-hand fight with a savage chief, who, to ward off the thrust of Colonel Patterson's sword, struck his right hand with his gun, breaking two of the bones. This encounter caused his old wound in the side to break out afresh, and it never afterwards healed, but remained a running sore for forty years or more.

Mathias Dennison, having bought land on the Ohio opposite the mouth of the Licking, came west to Lexington, and on August 25, 1788, entered into an agreement with Colonel Patterson and John Filson to effect a settlement on his land, and after a rough passage from Limestone, Kentucky, landed and commenced to erect cabins on Denman's land. In 1790 Colonel Patterson was a delegate from Fayette County to the Virginia Legislature; in 1791, with his regiment, he was in St. Clair's defeat, where he suffered in the retreat as did others, but returned safely, and in 1792 he was representative from Fayette County in the first Legislature of Kentucky.

In 1803 he bought from D. C. Cooper his farm two miles south of Dayton, and moved his family there in 1804. On this land was a large spring subsequently called Wade's spring (now owned by the Southern Ohio Asylum), which gave water enough to run a corn-mill and woolen factory on Warren Street, and a sawmill on Main Street. There is a large sulphur spring on the same land owned by St. Mary's Institute. Sixty or seventy years ago this spring was a great resort for the young people of the vicinity. Colonel Patterson named this branch and farm the "Rubicon."

In the War of 1812 he had charge of the transportation from Fort Meigs north to the army. He subsequently lived quietly at home in a comfortable brick house that he built on ground high enough to overlook the farm, enjoying the comforts of a well-spent life, in which he earned distinction for himself and his family, until August 5, 1827, when he died, aged sixty-eight years and six months. His faithful wife, Elizabeth Lindsay, survived him six years and died October 23, 1833. They are buried in our beautiful Woodland Cemetery. Their family were all born in Lexington, Kentucky, and consisted of two children who were born and died in the stockade in Lexington, Kentucky; Margaret, born June 9, 1786; Elizabeth, born January 27, 1788; Francis, born April 6, 1791; Catherine, born March 7, 1793; Jane, born May 25, 1795; Harriet, born March 25, 1797; Robert L., born May 27, 1799; Jefferson, born May 27, 1801.

Jefferson, who was three years old when the family came to Dayton, was raised on a farm. On February 23, 1833, at the age of thirty-two, he married Julia Johnston, daughter of Colonel John Johnston, the Indian agent, at Piqua, Ohio. They started on their wedding trip to Dayton on horseback, but were intercepted by John Shellabarger, with a four-horse carriage, some distance out of town and brought in with great glee. "Uncle Jeff" being a great favorite, every one wanted to greet him and his young bride, and old Jim Elliott, according to his custom of giving a rolling-pin to every bachelor who got married, had one ready for the bride to roll out the biscuit for breakfast. Mr. Patterson was for some years a merchant on Jefferson Street, and in 1840 moved to the Rubicon farm, and remained there until his death. He was a noted farmer and horticulturist. Mrs. Patterson is still living. They had five children—Robert, Stephen J., John H., and Frank J. Patterson, and Julia, now Mrs. J. H. Crane.

In 1804 David McConnaughey, a native of Westmoreland County, Pennsylvania, when twenty-one years old, made a trip with his brother Francis on a flatboat to New Orleans. His brother died in Louisiana. David was also very sick with ague, and the Indians took some care of him, so that he partially recovered. On his best days, between the spells of fever, he endeavored to walk home. One day he found a silver half-dollar in the road, with which he purchased ague medicine. Finally he reached Dayton with fifty cents in his pocket, which he had earned on the way, and stopped at the Newcom Tavern. Having a knowledge of distilling, he engaged with Mr. Newcom to run his still-house on the Newcom farm, near the location of the Davis Sewing Machine Works. While engaged in this way he earned enough money to purchase a hundred and sixty acres of land in Bethel Township, Miami County, the Dayton and Brandt pike now running on the east side of the farm. In 1811 he married Anna Grimes, moved to a cabin on his farm, and was soon afterwards drafted in the War of 1812. He served part of his time, and then his brother Robert came and served as a substitute. Mr. McConnaughey continued to live on his farm until his death in February, 1847. His wife died in April, 1863. They had eleven children, eight sons and three daughters,—Maria, Francis, William, Isabel, James (who was killed at Vicksburg Landing in 1863), Samuel, John C., Robert, David, Margaret, and Thomas H.

John C. McConnaughey married Elizabeth Keplinger, and continued to farm the old home place until, in 1893, he retired. He still owns the farm. They had five sons and six daughters, all of whom are still living.

Aaron Baker, who came here at an early day, and was elected justice of the peace, was married four times. His first wife was Hannah Maxwell. They had four children— two who died young, Eliza, who married Moses Simpson, and David C. Baker.

David C. Baker married Sophia Van Cleve, daughter of Benjamin Van Cleve, and had four children—Mary Sophia, Clara, Charles, and David. His wife died, and he then married Sophie Sourby, and had five children—Harriet, Axia Green, Aaron, Hannah, and Mahala. David afterwards moved to Portland, Indiana, and died there in 1895.

Philip Gunckel was born in Berks County, Pennsylvania,

April 7, 1766, and learned the trade of milling. In 1793 he married Katarina Schaeffer, born July 12, 1766, also in Berks County, Pennsylvania. In 1796 he moved his family to Center County, Pennsylvania, built a mill, and became proprietor of Millheim, Pennsylvania. In the year 1803 Mr. Gunckel and several of his neighbors made a trip to and down the Ohio River, in search of a location for a colony, but not finding a satisfactory place returned home. In 1804 twenty-four families from Berks and Center counties arranged to start west in wagons in two companies to meet at Pittsburg, and from there to travel in company with Philip Gunckel as leader, he probably being the only one that could speak English. The party, with their horses, wagons, and effects, were loaded on flatboats at Pittsburg, and reached Cincinnati in safety on June 20, 1804. After a short stay they again took up their march northward to Hole's Station, where they camped for about two weeks, living in their wagons as best they could, while the men prospected for unoccupied land. All the desirable locations on the east side of the river had been taken, but at the forks of the Great and Little Twin creeks Mr. Gunckel finally found the mill site he was in search of, together with good land for farming purposes. The few squatters were soon bought out, and all the land wanted was purchased of the Government by the settlers. This was a strong colony, both as to numbers and money. They built good, warm cabins, and hunting parties were kept out during the winter, all sharing in the supplies brought in, while those at home were kept busy clearing the land and building cabins. Mr. Gunckel built a two-story log house the first winter, and had the best house in the settlement.

Although the colony was composed of quiet, peaceable Christian people, nearly all in some way connected, they very soon found it necessary to have some one to decide points of law, and on December 9, 1804, Mr. Gunckel was elected justice of the peace for German Township. Mr. Gunckel was never known to use profane language, and his even temperament and high standard of morals gave tone and character to the colony. He was soon recognized as one of the most influential men in the county, was referred to in all matters of public improvement, and "was ready and active in all movements for the good and prosperity of the community." It is said he was quite a musician.

In the year 1805 Mr. Gunckel commenced building a saw- and grist-mill, completing the grist-mill in 1806. The same year he purchased land of James Hatfield and Robert Hardin and laid out the town of Germantown, donating lots for school, church, and graveyard purposes on his plat. On October 17, 1806, Mr. Gunckel was elected to represent Montgomery County in the General Assembly, which met at Chillicothe in December, and he and General Munger were chosen to represent Montgomery and Preble counties at the Assembly which met December 5, 1808, at Chillicothe. The General Assembly of 1816 appointed Mr. Gunckel associate judge of the Circuit Court for Montgomery County, and he served for fifteen years.

Mr. and Mrs. Gunckel had eight children, six of whom — John, Michael, Catharine, Philip, Jacob, and Sarah — were born in Pennsylvania, and Daniel P. and Elizabeth were born in Germantown. Mr. Gunckel and his wife were members of the German Reformed church of Germantown, having been instrumental in its organization, and contributing freely of their means to its prosperity, as well as to other church organizations in Germantown. Mrs. Gunckel died at Germantown, August 2, 1836. After her death Mr.

Gunckel was twice married, his last wife surviving him. He died May 24, 1848, in his eighty-third year. Judge Philip Gunckel was the grandfather of Hon. Lewis B. Gunckel, of this city, and great-grandfather of O. I. Gunckel, secretary of the Columbia Insurance Company.

Lewis B. Gunckel was born in Germantown, Ohio, October 15, 1826, and has been a citizen of Dayton since early manhood. In 1860 he married Catharine Winters, a daughter of Valentine Winters, and has had four children —Winters, Katharine, Lewis W., and Percy, the second and third of whom survive, and are now living in the city. Mr. Gunckel was Representative in Congress from the Third Ohio District from 1872 to 1874, a member of the Board of Managers of the National Soldiers' Home for the first twelve years of its existence, and was chiefly instrumental in securing the location of the Central Branch near this city.

John Martin Shuey, second son of Lewis Henry Shuey, was born June 20, 1750, in Bethel Township, Lancaster County, Pennsylvania. His grandfather, Daniel Shuey, and his father, came to America from the Palatinate, Germany, in 1732, landing at Philadelphia. They were probably of Huguenot descent. John Martin's father was a member of the Committee of Inspection of Lancaster County elected to coöperate with the Continental Congress in the years preparatory to the Revolution, but died before the Declaration of Independence was signed. John Martin married Margaret Elizabeth Conrad, and had ten children—John, Catharine (Mrs. Spitler), Christiana (Mrs. John Zeller), Martin, Barbara (Mrs. Michael Gunckel), Margaret (Mrs. John Moyer), Henry, Mary (Mrs. John C. Negley), Eve (Mrs. Dodds), and Adam. In 1805 he moved, with all but the first two of his children, to the Miami Valley, settling near Germantown. His party came by way of Pittsburg, floating down the Ohio River in a flatboat to Cincinnati. Some years later he removed to a farm on the east bank of the Miami, about two miles north of Miamisburg. The house he then occupied is still standing. Mr. Shuey died in February, 1829. His descendants in Dayton and Montgomery County are very numerous.

Martin Shuey, the second son of John Martin Shuey, was born September 28, 1785, in Dauphin, now Lebanon, County, Pennsylvania, and came with his father to Ohio in 1805. In the latter year he was chosen lieutenant of militia. In 1810 he was elected captain of his company and placed in command of the Eighth Military District of Ohio. He served through the War of 1812; in 1815 was elected major, in 1816 colonel, and in 1818 was promoted to the position of brigadier-general. The military district which he commanded embraced Forts Brown, Winchester, Laramie, St. Mary's, Amanda, and Jennings. In 1826 he resigned his military position. Mr. Shuey married Margaret Shuperd in 1808, and had eleven children. In 1820 he moved to Indiana, in 1829 to Illinois, and in 1859 to California, where his descendants are now quite numerous. He died February 12, 1876, at the age of more than ninety years.

Adam Shuey, the youngest son of John Martin Shuey, was born September 21, 1799, in Lebanon County, Pennsylvania. In 1805 he came with his parents to the Miami Valley. In 1819 he married Hannah Aley, a daughter of Isaac Aley, of Montgomery County, formerly of Washington County, Maryland, and had four children—a daughter who died in infancy, Mary, Catharine, and William John. Mr. Shuey was a builder and cabinet-maker, and a number of houses erected by him in Miamisburg are still standing.

He was the first postmaster of Miamisburg, serving from 1820 to 1832. In the latter year he was elected assessor of Montgomery County on the Whig ticket, and was twice reëlected. At that time there was only one assessor for the whole county, and he repeatedly visited every house in the county. In 1836 he moved to Springfield, Ohio, and was for six years a commissioner of Clark County. He also occupied other public offices. In 1854 Mr. Shuey became a citizen of Dayton. He died in this city April 22, 1882, at the age of over eighty-two years.

Rev. William John Shuey, the only son of Adam Shuey, was born in Miamisburg, Ohio, February 9, 1827. He has long been a resident of Dayton, and for the last thirty-two years has been the publishing agent of the United Brethren Publishing House. He has in his possession a wall clock made in Reading, Pennsylvania, in 1774, which his grandfather, John Martin Shuey, brought down the Ohio in 1805. In 1848 he married Sarah Berger, of the vicinity of Springfield, Ohio, and had four children—Albert L., Edwin L., William A., and Lincoln C., of whom the second and third are still living and are citizens of Dayton.

Among the other descendants of John Martin Shuey now living in Dayton are Hon. Lewis B. Gunckel, son of Mrs. Barbara Gunckel; John Dodds, son of Mrs. Eve Dodds; Oliver I. Gunckel, Herbert H. Weakley, Thomas Jefferson Weakley, George Willis Weakley, and Edward L. Rowe, grandsons of Mrs. Barbara Gunckel; Webster W. Shuey, grandson of Henry Shuey; Mrs. A. C. Marshall and Anna V. Zeller, granddaughters of Mrs. Mary Negley.

CHAPTER V.

THE TOWN OF DAYTON INCORPORATED.

ON February 12, 1805, the Legislature passed an act incorporating the town of Dayton. The act provided "that such part of the township of Dayton in the county of Montgomery as is included in the following limits, that is to say, beginning on the bank of the Miami where the sectional line between the second and third sections, fifth township, and seventh range intersects the same; thence east with said line to the middle of Section 33, second township, seventh range; thence north two miles; thence west to the Miami; thence down the same to the place of beginning, shall be and the same is hereby erected into a town corporate, which shall henceforth be known and distinguished by the name of the town of Dayton."

The "town of Dayton" was to be governed by a board of seven trustees, a collector, a supervisor, and a marshal, to be elected by the freeholders who had lived in the town for six months previous. The trustees were to choose one of their number as president and recorder, and were also to elect a treasurer, who need not be a member of the board of trustees. The board thus organized was to be known as "The Select Council of the Town of Dayton." The president of the Council was also to be Mayor of the town. The term of office of the first trustees was to expire in one and two years, so the entire board would not go out of office at the same time. All expenditures were to be authorized by vote of the freeholders and householders. The total expense of the town for the first year was seventy-two dollars. The Select Council thought to raise this by taxation, but at a meeting of the voters,—in all, just thirty,—it was decided not to do so by a vote of seventeen to thirteen. The clause in reference to expenditures being authorized by vote was repealed in the winter of 1813-14. The first election of the town was held on the first Monday of May, 1805, at which the proper officers were elected.

For ten years the meetings of Council were held at the residences of the different members. Any member thirty minutes late was fined twenty-five cents. One of the first acts of the Select Council in September, 1806, was to pass an ordinance prohibiting "the running of hogs and other animals at large upon the streets of the town," but it was not enforced until the following year. In later years for a long time it was not enforced at all.

The year 1805 was a memorable one in the history of Dayton, as, besides receiving its charter, it was first threatened with extinction by a great overflow of the Miami and Mad rivers. In March, owing to a thaw of the deep snows and heavy rains on the head-waters of the Miami and Mad rivers, the water rose rapidly, overflowed the banks at the head of Jefferson Street, and just west of Wilkinson Street, covering nearly all of the town plat, excepting a small section bounded about by Water, Wilkinson and Perry, Third, and Main streets. The people were much alarmed, thinking that the town would be entirely washed away, and also fearing that the same trouble would occur each year, thus making it impracticable to plant the crops much before June. Mr. Cooper proposed to vacate the ground and lay out a new plat on the hill east of town, in the neighborhood of Hickory and Eagle streets, pledging himself that every property holder should have a lot in the same location, and of the same size that they then owned, but several of the prominent citizens were much opposed to the project, and it fell through.

The same thing has occurred several times since, in 1832, 1847, and 1866. In 1847 the levee broke near the north end of Wilkinson Street, and the water carried a large sycamore tree to Second Street, lodging it against a brick house near Roe. In 1866 the levee gave way east of town. The water was over a foot deep on the first floor of the Beckel House, all the cellars on the east side of Main Street from Second Street south were full, and there were about four inches of water on the first floor of the Phillips House.

In June of this year the county commissioners fixed the following rates for licenses: Doctors and lawyers, each, per year, $3; taverns, in Dayton, each, per year, $9; taverns on the road between Dayton and Franklin, $6; taverns at all other places, $5. For ferry-boats the fees were fixed as follows: Each loaded wagon and team, 75 cents; each empty wagon and team, 50 cents; each two-wheeled carriage, $37\frac{1}{2}$ cents; each man and horse, $12\frac{1}{4}$ cents; each person on foot, $6\frac{1}{4}$ cents.

There were then two ferry crossings,—bridges at that time being unknown here,—one at the foot of First Street, on the road to Rench's Mill, now Salem, which was used until the red toll-bridge at Bridge Street was completed in January, 1819. The other ford was at the foot of Fourth Street, on the road to Eaton, and also to Gunckel's Mills, now Germantown.

At this time the industries of Dayton received quite an impetus. Many improvements were made, and many who proved to be valuable citizens came to make Dayton their home.

The first brick house was built in 1805, for a tavern, by Hugh McCullum, on the southwest corner of Main and

Second streets. It was two stories, the first floor being three feet above the street, so as to be above high water. After it was completed, the county commissioners rented the second story for court purposes, until the Court-house would be completed, for which they paid twenty-five dollars per annum. As a tavern it was well known and popular. A belfry on the Second Street wing contained a bell, which served "mine host" in several ways. One was to call the hostler. When a traveler would arrive and signify that he desired to have his horse put up, the bell would be rung, and every person in hearing would run to see the new arrival. The second and no less important duty was to call the guests to meals. On such occasions there were always two bells rung, about ten minutes apart, the first as a warning that it was time to get ready, and the second the signal for a grand rush to the tables. Ladies were always seated before the second bell rang. Everything was on the table, and the guests helped themselves, except that the host usually carved the meat—roast pig, venison, and wild turkey. Mr. McCullum's sign was a picture of the capture of the English frigate *Guerrière* by our frigate *Constitution* in the War of 1812. The boys never tired of looking at it. This building was used as a tavern until 1870, the various landlords being A. Houk, C. Smith, L. Eichelberger, and L. Lindsley. Philip Kemper leased it, lowered the floors, and converted it into a business house. In 1880 the Firemen's Insurance Company bought the property and erected the large building now used for offices and by the Dayton Gas Light and Coke Company. The property is now owned by J. K. McIntire.

Colonel John Grimes, an officer of the War of the Revolution, was a son of Samuel Grimes, of Lancaster County, Pennsylvania. He moved from Kentucky to

Chillicothe, Ohio, in 1804, and in 1808 had a tavern on the east side of Main Street on the south side of the alley between Water and First streets. The bell in the belfry rang twice for meals, as was the custom at taverns in those days. As Mad River could not be conveniently crossed by ferry, the first meeting to discuss the building of a free bridge over Mad River was held at Colonel Grimes's tavern on January 27, 1816. The project fell through, and a bridge at Taylor Street was built the next year by the county. The old tavern was moved twice—first, to where the First Baptist Church now stands, and, second, to the north side of West First Street, next to the Boulevard.

Colonel Grimes was married before coming to Dayton to Susanna Martin, daughter of Alexander Martin, of Lancaster County, Pennsylvania, who died December 14, 1827, at the age of sixty-six years. Colonel Grimes died May 13, 1836, at the age of eighty-one years. They had three sons— Samuel, Alexander, and John—and one daughter—Eliza.

Alexander Grimes was born April 27, 1790, at Marysville, Kentucky. He married, first, Belle Frances Burnett, and had one son—William Burnett Grimes. Mr. Grimes was a merchant, in partnership with Steele and Peirce, under the firm name of Alexander Grimes & Company. They dissolved partnership in 1817, and Mr. Grimes was afterwards county auditor, commissioner of insolvents, and cashier of the Dayton Manufacturing Company, the first bank in Dayton, at a salary of $550 per annum. Mr. Grimes and Mr. Edward W. Davies, as trustees of the estate of David Zeigler Cooper, changed the bed of Mad River, opening the way for the extension of the canal basin from First Street to its junction with the canal at the east end of the Car Works, and throwing into the town much valuable real estate. Mr. Grimes was a

THE TOWN OF DAYTON INCORPORATED 111

public-spirited citizen, always foremost in any enterprise for the good of Dayton. When the citizens subscribed one hundred and fifty thousand dollars to build the Mad River Railroad from Dayton to Springfield, he was appointed custodian of the funds, and the first receipts were signed by him. In 1827 Mr. Grimes was elected to the State Legislature, and again in 1830 by the Whigs. In 1820 Alexander Grimes married Marie Antoinette Greene, a sister of Charles Russell Greene. He died January 12, 1860, and Mrs. Grimes died February 26, 1875, at the advanced age of ninety-four years. They had two children: Susan (Mrs. Marcus Eells), who is now living in California, and Charles Greene Grimes, born January 28, 1828, married Mary Isabel Keifer, daughter of Daniel Keifer, of this city, and died December 11, 1895, leaving one son — Edward Grimes.

Eliza Grimes, in 1830, married Samuel Bacon, a cabinetmaker, who died November 5, 1832. Their one daughter, Anner, was born November 18, 1832, and in 1852 married David Carroll, of this city. She is the great-granddaughter of Elder William Brewster, who came over in the Mayflower, and died in Plymouth, Massachusetts, April 10, 1644. Mrs. Bacon remained a widow until her death.

Colonel David Reid, to avoid the tax of ten dollars assessed by Council on "taverns," kept a house of "private entertainment," without bar, in a long, two-story frame house on Main Street, the property now owned by the First Baptist Church. Colonel and Mrs. Reid were very dignified. He would open the door and say, "Gentlemen, dinner is ready." The ladies were always seated first. When all were seated, Colonel Reid would stand at the head of the table, knife and fork in hand, and say, "We have roast beef, roast venison, pork, etc.; send up your plates and be served." I can see him yet. In 1830 John W. Van Cleve, R. A. Thruston, R. C. Schenck, my oldest brother, Robert, and myself, with many others, were boarding there. Mr. Van Cleve was then living on vegetables, on account of his corpulency. Josiah Foutz, who recently died, then about thirteen years of age, lived there as a lad of all work.

Tavern signs were usually hung on an arm mortised into a post set in the ground like a telegraph post, thus:

After the War of 1812, Colonel Reid had painted on his sign a portrait of Captain Lawrence, with his brave words, "Don't give up the ship," and underneath that in small letters, "Reid's Inn." We all considered this *very fine*.

Daniel Kiser had a tavern in a frame house on the corner of Jefferson and Sixth streets, with a sign hung like this illustration. These signs would swing and squeak in the wind, so the belated traveler, on a dark night, would know before he could see it that a tavern was near. I believe this sign is still in Harrison Kiser's possession.

General Fielding Loury was born in Spottsylvania County, Virginia, March 13, 1781, emigrated to Cincinnati in 1802, and came to Dayton in 1806. He was a surveyor by profession, and laid out the town of Staunton, Miami County, naming it after Staunton Academy, in Virginia, where he was educated, to compete with Troy for the county-seat. General Loury was twice married—in 1811 to Ann Smith, daughter

THE TOWN OF DAYTON INCORPORATED

of Hon. John Smith, the first United States Senator from Ohio. They had four daughters—one who died young, and Mary B., Harriet S., and Ann E. In 1808 or 1809 General Loury was a member of the Legislature, while Chillicothe was still the capital of the State; in 1812 he served at Detroit as Indian agent, and in 1816 and 1835, as a Jacksonian Democrat, he was again sent to the Legislature. In January, 1823, he married Mrs. Sophia Greene Cooper, the widow of Daniel C. Cooper, and had one son—Fielding Loury, Jr. General Loury died in Dayton October 7, 1848, his death resulting in a few hours from a fall down stairs.

Mary B. Loury married Samuel Hiley Davies, a brother of Edward W. Davies. Harriet Loury married Lewis Huesman, who came to Dayton from Germany at an early day, and Ann E. Loury married John Howard, all of whom are deceased.

John Howard was born in Belmont County, Ohio, October 5, 1813, graduated at Kenyon College, Gambier, in 1838, in 1839 came to Dayton, read law in the office of Odlin & Schenck, and was admitted to the bar in 1840. He died in Dayton May 8, 1878, leaving two children—John, who married Annie Keifer, daughter of Daniel Keifer, and Eliza, who married Samuel W. Davies, of this city.

Fielding Loury, Jr., was born in Dayton October 9, 1824, and was educated at Kenyon and Woodward High School, Cincinnati. He was commissioned by Abraham Lincoln in 1861, entering the Union service as captain on the staff of General Schenck, and resigning at the end of the Rebellion, leaving a splendid record for indomitable bravery and strictest integrity, with the rank of lieutenant-colonel. In 1847 Colonel Loury married Elizabeth Richards Morrison, the oldest daughter of Joseph Morrison, of "Old Kas-

kaskia," Illinois. In 1874 he was commissioned postmaster of Dayton by President Grant, and reappointed in 1878 by President Hayes. He died in 1882. Mrs. Loury and their four children, Sophia, Mrs. Anna Dana, Mrs. Elise L. Smith, and Charles G., are still living.

David Squier was born in Westfield, New Jersey, in 1777, came to Dayton at an early day, and in November, 1805, married Sally Gard. They had three daughters—Phœbe, Eliza, and Julietta. Mr. Squier owned a fifty-acre lot lying on both sides of Wayne Avenue. In 1814, when only thirty-eight years old, David Squier died, and his widow afterwards married Maxwell Potter, whose son Benjamin had married Phœbe Squier. Eliza Squier married Philip Landis, and Julietta married Sutton Van Pelt.

Timothy Squier, son of Ellis and Rebecca Squier, was born in Essex County, New Jersey, September 25, 1786, and moved to Ohio with his father's family in 1796. Mr. Squier enlisted in the War of 1812 from Dayton with General William Henry Harrison. Having purchased the David Squier fifty-acre lot, he erected the house now owned by S. N. Brown. In 1815 he married his second wife, Rebecca Tucker, born in Springdale, Hamilton County, Ohio, April 16, 1798. They had three daughters—Harriet Ann (Mrs. David Benedict Groat, of New York City), Samantha (Mrs. William B. Stone), and Mrs. Mary Winters. Mr. and Mrs. Squier moved to Porter County, Indiana, where Mr. Squier died, May 1, 1860. Mrs. Squier died at the home of her daughter, Mrs. Mary Winters, at Lafayette, Indiana, March 7, 1868. Mr. Squier, while living in Dayton, was one of the prominent men of the place.

Matilda Owens, daughter of John and Deborah Owens, came to Dayton before 1805. She was one of the first

THE TOWN OF DAYTON INCORPORATED 115

Methodists in Dayton, and joined the class of which William Cottingham was leader, when seventeen years old. After her father's death Matilda and her mother lived in a cabin on the lot on Third Street where Mr. John H. Winters now lives.

William Roth owned the west two-thirds of the original lot number 127, on which he had two cabins, and a ropewalk along the west side of his lot. He married Matilda Owens, pulled down the old cabins, and built the two brick houses that are still standing on the lot, now owned by his daughter, Miss Carrie Roth. After her marriage Mrs. Roth was confirmed in the Episcopal church, soon after its organization, and Miss Roth has in her possession the following receipt:

"Received of William Roth $3.00, being pay for his seat in meeting-house.   JAMES HANNA.
"March 15, 1821."

Matthew Patton was born in Rockbridge County, Virginia, August 22, 1778, and when sixteen years old moved to Lexington, Kentucky. While there he married Margaret Hamilton, moved to Dayton in 1805, and built a cabin on the southwest corner of Main and Third streets. Soon after coming here Mrs. Patton took sick, it is said from washing on a Friday in April, when it was so cold that a cup of water thrown up by Mr. Patton froze before reaching the ground. She died in two weeks. On October 20, 1808, Mr. Patton was married to Elizabeth Ludlow, a niece of Israel Ludlow. Mr. Patton was for many years the village cabinet-maker, and was also the first undertaker in the town. In 1815, when the Moral Society was organized, he was one of the managers, and in 1827 he was appointed one of the first fire-wardens. He was an early elder in the First Presbyterian Church, but in 1836, at the time of the old- and new-school division, went to the Episcopal church, and was confirmed there under the Rev. Ethan Allen. When the Park Presbyterian Church was organized Mr. Patton and his family united with it. Mr. Patton died December 24, 1856, in his seventy-eighth year. His wife died April 19, 1872, in her eighty-fifth year. They had ten children—nine girls and one boy, William Patton. Three of the children are still living—Mrs. Hugh Wilson, of Greenfield, Indiana, and Miss Belle and Captain William Patton, of this city. Captain Patton was sheriff of the county for two terms.

Joseph Peirce, the son of Isaac and Mary Sheffield Peirce, was born in Rhode Island in 1786. In 1805, when nineteen years of age, he moved to Dayton, and on December 2, 1807, went into partnership with James Steele in the general merchandising business, in which he continued until his death in 1822. In 1812 he was sent to the State Legislature, and in 1814 was elected president of the Dayton Bank. On November 10, 1810, Mr. Peirce married Henrietta, daughter of Dr. John Elliot. Mr. and Mrs. Peirce had four children—David Zeigler, Mary Ann, Jeremiah Hunt, and Joseph Crane. David Zeigler Peirce married Eliza J. Greene, daughter of Charles R. Greene. Mary Ann Peirce, in 1829, married Edward W. Davies, who came here in 1826.

Jeremiah Hunt Peirce, born in Dayton on September 8, 1818, received his early education in the Dayton schools, graduated at Miami University in 1835, and joined the engineering corps on the Miami and Erie Canal in 1836. In 1846 Mr. Peirce married Elizabeth Forrer. They had eight children—Samuel Forrer, Henrietta Elliot Parrott, Edward, Sarah Howard, Mary, Elizabeth Forrer, John Elliot, and Howard Forrer. Of these

THE TOWN OF DAYTON INCORPORATED 117

three—Samuel Forrer, Edward, and Mary—are dead. Mrs. Peirce died January 16, 1874. Mr. Peirce on October 5, 1882, married Mary Forrer, who is still living. Mr. Peirce died May 6, 1889.

Joseph Crane Peirce married Louise, daughter of Dr. Edwin Smith. They had no children. Mrs. Peirce died many years ago. Mr. Peirce is still living.

Horatio Gates Phillips, son of Captain Jonathan Phillips and Mary Foreman, was born December 21, 1783. In 1803 he started west, and thought of settling in Natchez, Mississippi, but as Miss Houston, to whom he was engaged to be married, objected to going so far from her New Jersey home, he returned to Cincinnati. D. C. Cooper met him in Cincinnati and urged him to make Dayton a visit, which he did, probably in 1804, and decided to settle here. During the winter of 1805 he made the trip overland to Philadelphia, to buy goods, and to New Jersey for his bride, Eliza Smith Houston, daughter of William Churchill Houston, and great-granddaughter of the Rev. Jonathan Dickinson, the first president of Princeton College. They were married at Lawrenceville, New Jersey, April 10, 1806, and made the bridal trip across the mountains to Pittsburg on horseback, by flatboat down the Ohio River to Cincinnati, and then by wagon to Dayton. It was probably on this trip that Mr. Phillips brought the first red raspberry roots in his saddle-bags to Dayton. Their first home in Dayton was a two-story log house, at the southwest corner of First and Jefferson streets, and in the same house Mr. Phillips opened his store in 1806. He was a prosperous and progressive merchant, going east twice a year for goods. In 1809, when the baby Elizabeth was just three months old, Mrs. Phillips went east with him, making the trip on horseback, the luggage being carried by packhorse.

In 1812 Mr. Phillips built a two-story brick storeroom on the southeast corner of Main and Second streets, with his frame residence adjoining on Main Street. During the winter of 1812-13, he sent his partner and brother-in-law, George Houston, east for goods. Owing to rumors of war he bought a large stock, and Mr. Phillips, thinking he would be ruined, started a branch store in Troy, Ohio, with Mr. Houston in charge, to sell the surplus stock. As it was just at this time the Government agents commenced buying supplies for the army, instead of his being ruined there was a ready sale for the goods.

Mrs. Phillips was an active member of the First Presbyterian Church, a teacher in the Sunday school, one of the founders of the Female Bible and Charitable Association, and a leader in all charitable work. She was always delicate, but never spared herself when there was anything she could do for others, especially if they were sick and in need, and her death, on December 3, 1831, which was very sudden, was a blow to the community.

Mr. and Mrs. Phillips had several children, only three of whom—Elizabeth, Jonathan Dickinson, and Marianna Louise—lived to grow up.

Mr. Phillips was interested in all public improvements. In 1830 he, together with Alexander Grimes and Moses Smith, platted the town of Alexandersville; and he, with Daniel Beckel, J. D. Phillips, and S. D. Edgar, in 1844, purchased the water-power now owned by the Dayton Hydraulic Company, which was incorporated on March 1, 1845. In 1850 the new hotel, at the corner of Main and Third streets, was named for Mr. Phillips. He was also interested in the building of the turnpikes, and later in the railroads. Mr. Phillips was married the second time on December 16, 1836, to Mrs. C. P. Irwin, who survived him. He died November 10, 1859.

THE TOWN OF DAYTON INCORPORATED 119

Elizabeth Phillips married John G. Worthington, of Cincinnati, and afterwards moved to Washington, District of Columbia. They had two children—a son and a daughter.

Jonathan Dickinson Phillips was born December 31, 1812. He was educated at Princeton, New Jersey, was a merchant, and a public-spirited man. He took particular interest in the Public Library, was a liberal contributor to it, and, on putting up his new building at the corner of Second and Main streets, prepared a room especially for the library, charging but a nominal rent.

Marianna Louise Phillips was born in March, 1814. She married Robert A. Thruston, a graduate of West Point, a brilliant and eloquent member of the bar, and a representative in the State Legislature in 1836-37. They had four children—Jeannette, Gates P., Dickinson P., and Mrs. George W. Houk. Mr. Thruston died while still a young man, and Mrs. Thruston married John G. Lowe.

John G. Lowe graduated at Oxford in 1839, and commenced practicing law in Dayton in 1841, first in partnership with his brother Peter P. Lowe, and afterwards with Peter Odlin and Edward W. Davies. Mr. Lowe was a Whig, and took an active part in the campaign of 1840. In the last war Mr. Lowe served as colonel of the Second Regiment Ohio National Guard. This regiment, the One Hundred and Thirty-first Ohio Volunteer Infantry, was called into the field for one hundred days, during the summer of 1864. Colonel Lowe died July 30, 1892. Mrs. Lowe is still living. They had five children—Mrs. Charles Newbold, Mrs. Fowler Stoddard, Henry Clay Lowe, Houston Lowe, and Mrs. Thomas P. Gaddis.

George S. Houston, the son of William Churchill Houston, at one time professor of mathematics in Princeton College, was induced to come to Dayton about 1810, by his sister Eliza, the wife of H. G. Phillips, and was first in partnership with his brother-in-law. In 1814 he was made cashier of the Dayton Bank, holding that position until his death. He was appointed postmaster on the death of Benjamin Van Cleve, and held that office until his death. In 1820 Mr. Houston was elected recorder, and in December of that year he went into the newspaper business, as editor and proprietor of the *Watchman*, but sold out his interest in November, 1826, on account of ill health. There are few records of public meetings, after Mr. Houston made Dayton his home, of which he was not secretary. He was secretary of the Bachelors' Society until his marriage, president of the Moral Society, and a prominent member of the Methodist church. In 1815 Mr. Houston married Mary Foreman. He died on April 29, 1831, after a long illness. He left two children—George S., who moved to Philadelphia, Pennsylvania, and Eliza, who married David K. Este, a son of Dr. Charles Este, one of the early physicians of Dayton.

Charles Russell Greene, the son of Charles and Phœbe Sheffield Greene, was born in East Greenwich, Rhode Island, December 21, 1785. The family emigrated to Marietta, Ohio, in 1788, with the Ohio Company, and in 1806 Charles Russell Greene came to Dayton to go into partnership with Daniel C. Cooper, his brother-in-law. In 1813 Mr. Greene married Achsah, daughter of Henry and Sarah Anderson Disbrow. In 1822 he was appointed to succeed Benjamin Van Cleve as clerk of the Montgomery County Court of Common Pleas, which office he held until his death. He was one of the first board of directors of the Dayton Manufacturing Company and one of the first fire-wardens. On September 10, 1833, during a fire, he ordered a man by the name of Thompson into the line to pass water-buckets. The man refused, and Mr. Greene used the authority he possessed to force him to obey. The next day Thompson made complaint, and had Mr. Greene summoned before the squire. During Mr. Greene's examination Thompson struck him a blow on the head, which resulted in almost immediate death. Mr. Greene left a family of six children: Lucianna Zeigler (Mrs. J. D. Phillips), born January 10, 1819, and died June 28, 1881; Mary Sophia (Mrs. Egbert Tangier Schenck), born January 10, 1824; Eliza Johnson (Mrs. David Z. Peirce), born September 13, 1821, and died April 19, 1885; Daniel Cooper Greene, born May 8, 1814, and died March 20, 1847; Harriet Cummings (Mrs. David H. Jenkins), born December 21, 1830; and Charles Henry, who was born May 24, 1832. Charles Henry was a lieutenant-commander in the United States Navy. He married Adeline D. Piper, and died March 9, 1868. Mrs. Egbert Tangier Schenck, whose husband was a brother of General Robert C. Schenck, is now living in Downey, Iowa. Mrs. Greene for many years made her home with her daughter, Mrs. J. D. Phillips, where she died November 3, 1873.

Marie Antoinette, the sister of Charles Russell Greene, was born in Greenwich, Rhode Island, December 6, 1781, came to Dayton in 1806, and in 1820 married Alexander Grimes. She died in 1875, at the age of ninety-four years.

When John and Elizabeth Rench came here from Maryland, with their two children,—Susanna and John,—they first camped on the common (now Cooper Park). While there they made many acquaintances, among them Jonathan Harshman. They located at Rench's Mills (Salem), and on February 18, 1808, Jonathan Harshman and Susanna were married. In 1810 Mr. Rench, with his family, moved to a mill site east of town, containing twenty acres of land, with water-power, given to him and a Mr. Staley by Judge Isaac Spining, on the condition that they erect and run a flour- and sawmill. This property was afterwards sold to Jonathan Harshman, and is now Harshmanville.

John Rench, Jr., born in Huntington County, Pennsylvania, July 24, 1794, married Mary Croft in this county on February 23, 1820, and settled at the mills with his father. Mary Croft was born in Frederick County, Maryland, on March 5, 1802. In 1825 Mr. Rench, with his family, moved to town and opened a store in company with Jonathan Harshman, as Harshman & Rench, on the corner of Third and Main streets. In 1829 they opened a warehouse at the head of the basin, and in 1830 started a number of boats on the canal between Dayton and Cincinnati, and did a large business. On the death of Mr. Harshman, in March, 1850, Mr. Rench was elected president of the Dayton Bank. They had eleven children— Maria, Mrs. Elizabeth J. Langdon, Mrs. Caroline Schaeffer, Mrs. Sarah Jane Tate, David Croft Rench (who married Mary Williams), Mrs. Susan H. Dwyer, Mrs. Mary Augusta Woodhull, Joan, William H. Rench, Emily (who died in infancy), Mrs. Anna Catharine Clark, and Charles, who married first Fannie B. Long, and after her death Fannie Gilliland.

Jonathan Harshman (originally spelled Herschman), son of Christian and Catharine Harshman, was born in Frederick County, Maryland, December 21, 1781, and moved to Kentucky, but, not caring to settle permanently in a slave State, in 1805 he came to Montgomery County, Ohio, and purchased forty acres of land in what is now Mad River Township. Here he built a cabin, late in the fall hanging the door and putting in one four-light window. On February 18, 1808, he brought home his bride, Susanna Rench, born in Maryland, November 11, 1786. After his marriage Mr. Harshman set up a copper still and commenced making whisky, at which he continued until 1814, when he took the business of Rench & Staley, and moved his family to that location, now known as Harshmanville, and owned by his son, George Harshman. He also opened a store with John Rench as partner, which was afterwards moved to Dayton. Mr. Harshman was a Federalist, and a prominent Whig. He represented this county in the Twenty-fourth General Assembly of Ohio, and on May 1, 1845, was elected president of the Dayton Bank, which position he held until his death, March 31, 1850. His wife died December 5, 1839. They had eight children—Elizabeth (Mrs. Israel Huston); Catharine (Mrs. Valentine Winters); Jonathan, who married Abigail Hiveling; Mary (Mrs. George Gorman); Joseph, who married Caroline Protzman, a daughter of Colonel Protzman, who lived on the Beardshear road; George, who married Ann Virginia Rohrer; Susanna (Mrs. Daniel Beckel), and Reuben D., who married Mary Protzman, of near Alexandersville.

In 1809, when Jacob S. Brenner was nine years of age, his father, disliking slavery, emigrated from Virginia to Montgomery County, Ohio, and bought a half-section of land about seven miles north of Dayton. When Jacob became of age, his father gave him a quarter-section of land on which there was water-power, and Jacob built a flour-mill. He made two trips to New Orleans on flatboats, with a cargo of flour and pork. On one of these trips John Clark, of Tippecanoe City, was the captain. Mr. Brenner married Sarah M. Matthews, of Baltimore. They had eight children,—four sons and four daughters,—only one of whom, John L. Brenner, is living in Dayton.

William George was of Welsh descent. Old family papers, deeds, and leases show that the first William George came to this country prior to 1730, and one of his family owned the farm that is now the present site of Germantown, Pennsylvania. William George moved first to Kentucky from Pennsylvania, but preferring a free State, came to Ohio in 1803 or 1805. He purchased a tract of nine hundred acres of land across the Miami River from Dayton, where he built two mills. Some part of the tract passed to Horatio G. Phillips, and is now owned by Thomas Gaddis. William George married Ann Britton in Pennsylvania, and when they came to Dayton had a large family of children, but was so unfortunate as to lose four sons from fever soon after. He was made associate judge of the Common Pleas Court of Montgomery County, and afterwards treasurer of the county. The only children who survived him were Mary, who married William McCrery; Sarah, who married William Bomberger, and Lydia, who married David Henderson, and lived in Indiana.

Sarah George was born near Frankfort, Pennsylvania, on the 6th of July, 1793, her father moving to Dayton when she was ten or twelve years of age. She was married to William Bomberger, a citizen of Dayton, January 17, 1810. She became a member of the First Presbyterian Church at an early date, was one of the most active among the early workers in the church, and was one of the leading spirits in the organization in 1817 of the first Sunday school in Dayton, of which she was the first superintendent, and continued to be for ten years. The first year of the Sunday school's existence shows two hundred scholars on the "sere and yellow leaf" of Mrs. Bomberger's original record. Her active, faithful, Christian spirit, singularly clear judgment, and great decision of character gave her courage to undertake this great work, which she carried out successfully. In that day few women were considered eligible for any post of responsibility, and she was often heard to say that it was only her confidence that it was God's work, to be done by some one, that enabled her to do it, with the many doubts she heard expressed about it. This was only the beginning of her church work, to which she devoted her life; but with all her devotion to the cause of Christ, in the church, Sunday school, and Bible society, she never neglected her family, her home, or friends, or thought that the Sunday school could take the place of Christian home training. Bright and cheery to the close of a useful life, her light shone clear and steadfast till she entered into rest, August 4, 1859, aged sixty-six.

William Bomberger was born in Philadelphia, April 7, 1779. His parents were Quakers, and in that faith he was reared and lived until his death. When eighteen years of age he was shot by the accidental discharge of his gun while hunting, and from the effects of the wound was always a delicate man, although he lived to be seventy-seven years of age. He came to Dayton about 1806 or 1807. He was a quiet, peaceable citizen, upright, honest, and conscientious in all things. He held the office of treasurer of Montgomery County for fourteen years. He brought some means with him and bought a good deal of property in the eastern and southeastern part of Dayton, to which he retired in 1842 and spent the remainder of his life, which ended December 19, 1855. In 1810 he married Sarah George, daughter of William George, and had three children: George Wilson, who died, while Mayor of Dayton, June 6, 1848, in the thirty-sixth year of his age; Ann, who married Peter P. Lowe, and William, who married Matilda Gallup and moved to Colorado.

William G. and Augustus George, nephews of Judge William George, came here from Philadelphia, Pennsylvania, at an early day. Their first evening in Dayton was spent with their uncle's family, to meet the young people of Dayton, when Augustus played the violin.

William G. George was a surveyor, and served as county surveyor for several terms. He lived some years on a farm which he bought of Judge William George, on the north side of the Miami River, a part of which is now Idylwild.

Augustus George followed his trade of carpentering in town for some time, and in 1817 married Jane Allen Edgar. He erected a two-story frame house on the northeast corner of Main and Sixth streets, where they lived for several years. Afterwards exchanging it for his brother William's farm, he moved there, where Mrs. George died at the age of twenty-six. Her body was brought across the river in a dugout canoe for burial. Mr. and Mrs. Edgar, after her death, took Mr. George and his four little girls—Marcella, Margaret Jane, Mary, and Martha—to the Edgar homestead. Mr. George talked of returning to Philadelphia with the children, and to induce him to stay here Mr. Edgar told him of a piece of land for sale (which he was expecting to buy himself), and on November 7, 1826, Mr. George purchased of the executors of Daniel C. Cooper one hundred and eight acres of land for $487. On April 19, 1841, he sold forty acres of it to the Woodland Cemetery Association for $2,400, retaining the frontage on Wayne Avenue. In 1832 he married Anna D. Fulton. They had three children—Anna Maria, Leonida, and Augustus.

Abram Darst, born in Franklin County, Virginia, July 25, 1782, came to Dayton in 1805, bought lot 51, on the west side of Main Street, north of Second, from Benjamin

Van Cleve for seventy-five dollars, and built a two-story brick residence and store. The building is still standing, occupied now as a harness shop. On December 21, 1809, Mr. Darst married Mary Wolf, born in Lancaster County, Pennsylvania, April 2, 1787, and came to Dayton in 1807. She died December 12, 1882, at the advanced age of ninety-five years. Mr. Darst was a merchant, and one of the foremost citizens in his day. In 1827 he was appointed one of the first fire-wardens. He died February 9, 1865. There was a family of ten children—Julia (Mrs. James Perrine), Christina (Mrs. William B. Dix), Mary (Mrs. Jacob Wilt), Sarah (Mrs. W. C. Davis), Martha (Mrs. George M. Dixon), Napoleon (who married Susanna Winters, daughter of Valentine Winters), Phœbe, and John, of whom three—Mrs. Dix (in Maumee City, in her eighty-fourth year), Phœbe, and John (in Dayton)—are still living.

William Eaker came to Dayton in 1805, from Chambersburg, Pennsylvania, and opened a general store. For some time he was in partnership with George W. Smith. In connection with their mercantile business they bought a great deal of property in and around Dayton, and in dissolving partnership and dividing the property they took lot about, Mr. Eaker getting the northeast corner of Main and Second, Mr. Smith the northwest corner; Mr. Smith the southwest corner of Second and Ludlow, and Mr. Eaker the northwest corner of Third and Ludlow. They also divided several acres of land in the same way south of Fifth Street and west of Ludlow. After the partnership with Mr. Smith was dissolved, Mr. Eaker continued in business for himself on the corner of Main and old Market streets (East Second), where he carried on a thriving business, and was director in the Dayton Bank until it discontinued business in 1843.

In 1817 Mr. Eaker married Letitia Lowry, of Springfield, whose grandfather, David Lowry, took the first flatboat from Dayton to New Orleans. Mr. Eaker died in 1848. His wife survived him many years and died in 1882. Of their four children—William, Charles, Mary Belle, and Frank—the daughter only is still living.

For many years the citizens of Dayton had a story which they delighted to tell all strangers, that there was a house in town covering so many (acres) Eakers, the number varying with the occupants of the homestead at the time.

George W. Smith, when quite young, emigrated from Kent, England, where he was born, to the United States. He came to Dayton in 1804, and being a merchant was first in partnership with William Eaker, then with Robert A. Edgar, and later with his son, George W., Jr. He bought a cotton-mill of Joseph and Charles Bossom, at Smithville, now Harries' Station, and engaged in a heavy distilling business. In 1836 he built the brick building at the northwest corner of Main and Second streets, the first four-story building in the county. It was considered so high that people came from the neighboring country to see it, and many said that it would certainly fall down.

Mr. Smith was married twice—first to Miss Todd. They had two children, Mary Jane, who married William F. Irwin, of Cincinnati, and George W., who married Lucy Weston. Mr. Smith's second wife was Eliza Manning. They had five children: James Manning; Sophia (Mrs. Isaac Keirstead); Louise (Mrs. Captain Fletcher); George W., and Ann, who married William G. Sheeley, of Covington, Kentucky. James Manning Smith married Caroline Shoup, whose father, Samuel Shoup, came to Dayton when a young man, and married Harriet Umbaugh. Mrs. Smith and their one daughter are still living in Dayton.

THE TOWN OF DAYTON INCORPORATED

George Umbaugh came to Dayton from Ellicott's Mills, Maryland, in 1806, and purchased six hundred acres of land four miles north of Dayton on the Covington pike, on Stillwater, where he built a flour-mill, sawmill, and distillery. On one of his trips to the old home in Maryland, Mr. Umbaugh liberated his slaves, but brought one boy, George, back with him on horseback. George remained with him, apparently content, until he was twenty-five years old, when he brought suit to recover five thousand dollars for wages, after securing Peter P. Lowe as his attorney. Peter Odlin was the attorney for the defendant. A compromise was arrived at by which George received one thousand dollars. Mr. Umbaugh died July 22, 1850. He left two daughters — Mahala (Mrs. Bartlow) and Harriet (Mrs. Samuel Shoup).

In 1800 Henry Butt, with three or four others, came here from Maryland to see the country. His grandson, John McReynolds, tells me that "they had to leave their horses on the hill on East Third Street, and come to Dayton in a dugout or canoe." When they reached Dayton they found about half a dozen log cabins on the river bank. As a result of this visit a colony was formed in Frederick County, Maryland, coming here in 1805, and locating in and around Dayton. When they reached the hills east of town they sent a "runner" with word of their arrival to the village, and the next day the citizens turned out *en masse* to give them a most hearty welcome in the way of an old-fashioned barbecue, roast ox and all. Mr. Butt afterwards moved to Preble County. His daughter, Barbara, married Joseph McReynolds, of Dayton, and one son, John W., was a member of the firm of Beaver & Butt, so well known in Dayton for many years.

This party, in all numbering ninety-six men, women, and children, camped in their wagons on the northeast quarter of Section 27, on the Xenia road, now Oakland, until each of the families could find a location on which to settle. As each one would choose a quarter-section all the others joined with him in building his cabin, and within twenty-four hours at the farthest from the time the selection was made the cabin would be completed and the family moved in.

Peter Lehman, with his family, was the leader of this company through the wilderness of Ohio. He selected the northeast quarter of Section 27, where the company camped, built his cabin on the edge of the road, and opened a wagon-yard and tavern. The original cabin is still standing, and, I believe, is still used as a tavern. After clearing his farm and raising large crops of corn for which there was no market, he built a log still-house about fifty rods west of his house, and made whisky, which he had no trouble in disposing of. After some years he removed to town and commenced building a stone house on lot 43 on First Street, but did not live to complete it. Henry Stoddard bought the house and lived in it until about 1850, when he took down the front and used the stone in the foundation of his new residence, now owned by Joseph Gebhart. Mr. Stoddard then built a brick front to the old house, and improved it in many ways. It is now occupied by Torrence Huffman. Mr. Lehman had ten children: John, who kept a tavern on the southwest corner of First and St. Clair streets, where Cyrus Osborn now lives; Jacob, who lived on a farm on the Shakertown road; David, Peter, Catharine (Mrs. Jonathan Stutsman), Susan (Mrs. Samuel Boogher), Margaret (Mrs. Daniel Stutsman), Elizabeth (Mrs. William Cox), and Mary (Mrs. Conrad Dodson).

David Lehman, born March 11, 1771, on April 3, 1793, married Magdalena Worman, then just twenty-one years of age. They first settled on the Cox farm, Oakwood, and

THE TOWN OF DAYTON INCORPORATED 131

later located on a farm long known as the Lehman homestead, about five miles south of Dayton. Of the nine children, three—Susanna, Sophia, and Matilda—were born after the family settled on this farm.

Samuel Boogher came to Dayton on a prospecting tour in the year 1804, returned and settled here in 1806, and in 1808 married Susan Lehman. In 1826 Mrs. Boogher united with the Christian Church, under the preaching of the Rev. D. S. Burnett, and, with many others, was baptized in the river at the head of Main Street. Mr. Boogher first engaged in making road-wagons on East Second Street, and the residence which he built on the north side of Second, between Jefferson and St. Clair streets, is still standing, a part of it being now occupied by the Windsor Hotel. When the canal was opened to Cincinnati, Mr. Boogher transported large quantities of produce to Cincinnati, and owned a packet-boat running between Dayton and Cincinnati. He afterwards engaged in pump-making on the lot where Heathman's bakery now is, and continued in this business until his death, April 13, 1857. Four of their children are still living: Gideon, who moved to Kansas; Catharine and Jesse, who still live in Dayton; and Susan, now living in Salem, Ohio.

Daniel G. Boogher, son of Samuel and Susan Lehman Boogher, was born May 4, 1810, on the farm near Beavertown. He first helped his father at wagon-making, and drove a stage from Dayton to Springfield. He afterward assisted Alexander Simms in packing pork, was engaged with Henry Herrman in purchasing and shipping grain, with Foley & Babbitt in running a still-house, and had charge of a canal-boat for Robert Young Chambers prior to the opening of the Cincinnati, Hamilton & Dayton Railroad. He was popular with shippers both here and in

Cincinnati, and after the Cincinnati, Hamilton & Dayton Road was in operation he was employed by that company as transportation clerk, holding the position for nine years. He purchased produce here for the Cincinnati markets, and goods in Cincinnati for the wholesale houses here. He also carried large amounts of money back and forth, and when John Morgan was expected to raid Cincinnati several of the large dealers there urged Mr. Boogher, much against his will, to take charge of their money and secrete it about his country home for safe keeping. He then lived on a farm near the northeast corner of this county. I knew personally some of the firms that entrusted their money to him.

Jesse Boogher, son of Samuel and Susan Lehman Boogher, born February 15, 1821, has a general repair shop in the alley running from Main to Jefferson streets, between First and Second streets. He is well posted on early events in Dayton.

Catharine Boogher, born in Dayton October 14, 1839, was married to J. T. Ware by the Rev. J. C. Barnes, pastor of the First Presbyterian Church of this city. Mr. Ware died December 17, 1860. They had five children—William Harrison, Charles H. (a plumber of the firm of Ware & Moodie), George W., Edwin T., and Belle, who married Mr. Bryant. Mrs. Ware is still living, and resides on Wayne Avenue.

Lewis and Elizabeth Kemp, two of the Frederick County, Maryland, party, located on a farm near Peter Lehman's. They had nine children—George, Jacob, Isaac, Joseph, David, Samuel, Mary, Catharine, and Margaret. Mrs. Kemp died April 13, 1827, aged seventy-two years. Lewis, the father, died December 21, 1842, over eighty-two years of age.

When George W. Kemp came to town from the farm, he occupied, on Bainbridge Street, Judge Steele's old residence, moved from the corner of Main and First streets. It is said that all the oxen in Dayton were required to haul it to that location.

John Folkerth emigrated to this place from Maryland before 1804, and was elected justice of the peace soon after coming here. He had his office first in the Newcom Tavern, and afterward in the one-story brick still standing on East First Street, near Main. Mr. Folkerth held this office continuously for fifty-two years, it being his pride that he never made any canvass for the election. At the end of that time the office was secured by another man, but at the end of his one term Mr. Folkerth was again elected. He was one of the incorporators of the Dayton Academy, was the first Mayor of Dayton, and one of the founders of the Dayton Library Association in 1805. In the spring of 1809 he was elected recorder of the Select Council *pro tem.*, and at some time previous to 1817 was treasurer of the First Presbyterian Church.

Louisa Folkerth, daughter of John Folkerth, was born in Dayton July 6, 1805. On July 5, 1821, she married William Atkins, who came here from Cincinnati in 1820. He was a merchant tailor by trade. He erected a two-story brick building on the north side of Fourth, between Main and Jefferson streets, and also had a dry-goods store on Main Street, near Third. Mr. Atkins died in December, 1879. Mrs. Atkins, at the age of ninety-one, is still living in Dayton. They had nine children, of whom George Atkins and Mrs. Maria Iddings are living.

Russel Folkerth, born in 1807, had a grocery, and later a willow-ware store, in the building where the *Herald* office is now. Mr. Folkerth died in 1891.

About 1805 John Bonner, who was born in New York State July 10, 1783, settled in Montgomery County and married Elizabeth Wead. He was a devout Christian, a member of the First Presbyterian Church, and a strong abolitionist. He was a great reader, well posted on all matters of his day, and exact in all that he said and did. He died April 10, 1865, in his eighty-second year.

George Fryberger, a native of Germany, emigrated to this country about 1776, and settled in Frederick County, Maryland. In 1805 he came to Ohio, and settled on Section 21, Madriver Township. Mr. Fryberger was twice married, and had four children—George, Martin, Valentine, and Annie. He died in the year 1812.

Valentine Fryberger was born November 15, 1805, on the farm in Madriver Township. On April 14, 1831, he was married to Elizabeth Hosier by the Rev. David Winters. They had ten children. Mr. Fryberger made great improvements on his farm, on which the stone was quarried for most of the prominent buildings in Montgomery and Greene counties. For many years he and his wife were members of the Reformed church of which the Rev. David Winters was pastor. He died July 22, 1873. His wife died August 24, 1874.

In 1806 James Steele, of Scotch-Irish ancestry, came to Dayton from near Lexington, Kentucky. He, in partnership with Joseph Peirce, put up a two-story brick building on the southeast corner of First and Main streets, where they opened a general store. This house was taken down by Joseph Turner in 1865, when he built the first opera-house in Dayton. In 1812 James Steele married Phœbe Peirce. They had two sons—Robert Wilbur and Joseph Peirce. Mr. Steele was a public-spirited man, took a lively interest in education, and was for many years trustee of the Dayton Academy, on St. Clair Street. He was appointed by the Governor of Ohio as one of the trustees of Miami University, and continued to hold that office until his death.

As captain, he was in charge of the volunteer company that went to the front on receiving news of Hull's surrender, and was detailed by General Harrison to superintend the building of blockhouses along the frontier.

In 1815 Captain Steele was elected director, and in 1822 president, of the Dayton Manufacturing Company, which position he held until the company was merged into the Dayton Bank. In 1824 he was one of the electors for President of the United States, casting his vote for Henry Clay. During the campaign, when Clay would visit Dayton, he was always the guest of Mr. Steele, and on such occasions the large yard of the Steele dwelling (now numbers 128 to 132 North Main Street), filled as it was with cedar and fruit trees, would be illuminated with lanterns—a very unusual display in those days for Dayton.

Mr. Steele was appointed associate judge by the Legislature of Ohio, serving fourteen years, and in 1834 was chosen to represent Montgomery and Preble counties in the Legislature. He was one of the original stockholders in the Woodland Cemetery Association, was made president when the association organized, and was elected one of the board of trustees. He was one of the earliest trustees of the First Presbyterian Church, was a member of the building committee when the first building was erected in 1817, and chairman of the building committee for the erection of the second church building. He died shortly after its completion in 1841. Judge Steele was a Christian gentleman of the old school, courteous, unassuming, correct in all business transactions.

Robert W. Steele, born in Dayton July 3, 1819, was educated here, prepared for college by E. E. Barney in the Dayton Academy, and graduated at Miami University in 1840. He then entered the law office of Messrs. Crane

& Davies, but his health failing, he engaged largely in out-door pursuits. In 1842 he was appointed by the City Council a member of the first Board of Education, holding this position by repeated elections for thirty years. Twelve years of this time he was president of the board. In 1844 Mr. Steele was one of the incorporators of the Cooper Female Seminary, and served as one of the trustees until the property passed into private hands. In 1847 he was one of the founders of the Dayton Library Association, and for many years director and president. In 1860, when the Library Association was united with the Public School Library, he was appointed by the Board of Education chairman of the Library Committee, and served in that capacity until 1875, when he retired from the Board of Education. He was afterward elected a member of the reorganized Library Board, serving until his death.

In 1852 Mr. Steele was elected a member of the Board of the Ohio State Agricultural Society, and in 1853 had charge of the first State fair held here. In 1853 he was elected secretary of the Woodland Cemetery Association to succeed Robert C. Schenck, on his appointment as Minister to Brazil, and on the death of John W. Van Cleve in 1858 was elected president of the association, filling that office until his death. He united with the Presbyterian Church at an early age, and served as a ruling elder for many years. In 1866 he was appointed by the New School General Assembly a member of a committee to meet a similar committee appointed by the Old School General Assembly to devise measures for the reunion of the two branches of the church. This committee did much of the preparatory work which resulted in the cordial and happy reunion of the divided church.

In 1867 Mr. Steele was appointed by the county commissioners one of the trustees of the Children's Home and served for nine years, during which time the present grounds were purchased and the building now occupied erected. In 1867 Governor Cox appointed him a member of the Board of Ohio State Charities, on which he served for five years.

Mr. Steele was twice married—first to Elizabeth Smith. They had a large family of children, of whom Mary Davies, Sarah S., Agnes C., Egbert T., and William C. are still living. Mr. Steele's second wife was Clara P. Steele, who, with their one daughter Charlotte, is still living in Dayton. Mr. Steele died in 1891.

In 1806 a few important changes occurred in Dayton. D. C. Cooper and John Compton, as partners, put up a two-story brick store building on lot 38, at the northeast corner of First and Main streets, and James Steele also built a two-story brick store building on the opposite corner, thus drawing business somewhat away from the river.

In 1807, the people feeling the need of better schools, the Dayton Academy was incorporated by James Welsh, Daniel C. Cooper, William McClure, George F. Tennery, John Folkerth, and James Hanna. That winter a debating club was organized and spelling-matches held regularly in the academy. In 1807 the roads were opened between Dayton and Piqua, New Lexington, Salem, Greenville, Xenia, Germantown, Lebanon, Franklin, and Miamisburg; but as no care was taken of them, they were soon cut into deep wagon-ruts, being but little better than no roads at all.

As a result of the election held October 21, 1808, Daniel C. Cooper was sent to the Senate, Philip Gunckel and Edmund Munger to the House of Representatives, and Daniel Hoover was elected to fill the place of Edmund Munger, as commissioner.

In 1806 an effort had been made to start a newspaper by a Mr. Crane of Lebanon, but it was not successful, and Mr. Crane, being taken with the chills and fever, returned to Lebanon. On September 18, 1808, the first number of the *Repertory*, published by William McClure and George Smith, was issued. It was to be a weekly newspaper, printed with the old-style type, on a sheet of foolscap, eight by twelve and one-half inches, two columns, and to cost two dollars a year. Advertisements cost a dollar a square for three weeks, and twenty-five cents extra for each additional issue. Some of the advertisements in this and other early papers will be found at the end of this book, together with a few of the representative advertisements of to-day, showing a marked difference in the mercantile aspect for the one hundred years, and raising the question as to what the advertisements will be one hundred years from now. The foreign news in this paper was usually about three months old. On October 21, 1808, the following notice appeared: "The office of the *Repertory* is removed to the south side of Second Street, between Main and Jefferson streets, in consequence of which the publication of the paper will be suspended for a few weeks." The next number, issued February 1, 1809, was a four-column folio, twelve by twenty inches, edited by Henry Disbrow and William McClure.

In 1809 Paul Butler and Henry Disbrow established a regular freight line by water to Lake Erie. They built two keel-boats in the street at the corner of Main and Main Cross (Third) streets, in front of the Court-house, and, when finished, hauled them on rollers to the river, where they were launched. They were poled up the Miami and Laramie to the mouth of Stony Creek, the head of navigation. One of the boats was then hauled across the portage twelve miles to the St. Mary's (or Auglaize) River, and thence down the Maumee to Lake Erie. There was a large warehouse at the Maumee Rapids for the storage and transfer of freight. These two boats, the one on the Miami and the other on the Maumee, did a good business for many years between Dayton and Lake Erie. In 1809 the river was very low between Dayton and Cincinnati, and, on account of a change in the channel at Hamilton, navigation was considered rather dangerous, but on the 23d of May the *Repertory* says: "A flat-bottomed boat owned by Mr. John Compton, of this place, descended the Miami yesterday. She was loaded with pork, flour, bacon, and whisky, and destined for Fort Adams. This boat and several others made the trip in safety, but were three weeks on the way."

At this time there was in Dayton a cabinet-maker (Matthew Patton), a carpenter (John Dodson), and a cooper (David Steele), who, on First Street, near St. Clair, was making flour- and whisky-barrels.

The farmers commenced raising sheep, and after the shearing and washing of the wool, the mother, with two cards like the present horse cards, only larger and a great deal finer, carded and straightened the wool, and by a dextrous movement with the backs of the cards made it into a roll, which was then spun into yarn on the large spinning-wheel. Then, as almost every family had a loom, the weaver would come and weave the yarn into cloth for the winter use. For summer wear and sheets flax yarn was used. Flax, one of the first crops raised, was usually planted on Good Friday and pulled about July 1. It was put through a brake, scutched, and spun on the small wheels seen in so many houses now as relics of the olden times. The large wheels were used only for wool. The woolen cloth was seldom colored, and from this fact comes the saying of the "old gray coat." Mr. Cooper afterwards erected a sawmill on his mill-race near where Sears now crosses Cooper Street, and built a carding-machine and fulling-mill north of the flouring-mill at the head of Mill Street, and advertised that by July 1 he would have his carding-machine in operation. This, the first carding-machine and fulling-mill in Dayton, was run first by James Bennett, and later by Mr. Emley. They carded the wool and made it into rolls about two and a half feet long and a half inch in diameter, which were taken carefully home (usually carried in a sheet to keep them from being mashed), spun into yarn, and, after being woven into cloth and blankets, carried back to the mill to be fulled and stretched. It was always necessary to take a pot of lard to the mill with the wool, to be used in the carding.

Soon after, a weaving establishment was started by James Hanna at the south end of Main Street, and James Beck advertised to dye cotton "a deep blue at seventy-five cents per pound, and linen or wool at sixty-two and a half cents." A nail factory was established in 1809 on the north side of the race, between Sears and Foundry streets, by a Mr. Wilson, and a wrought-iron nail factory on Main Street, opposite Grimes's Tavern, by John Strain & Company. John and Archibald Burns, whitesmiths, made edge tools. David Stutzman also made edge tools and sickles.

Peter Bellaw, who came here in 1810, had been engaged with the Hudson Bay Company and stationed at Detroit for so long a time that he could speak several of the Indian languages. On coming to Dayton he purchased a four-acre lot of D. C. Cooper, west of Brown Street, and south of Green, at that time a wilderness, where he built a log cabin.

THE TOWN OF DAYTON INCORPORATED   141

Here three children were born—William, Henry, and Mary Ann. William was born September 15, 1817, and is still living in Dayton, at present on Springfield Street. He had nine children, of whom eight are living.

Dayton early showed an inclination to become a manufacturing town, owing largely, probably, to the influence of Mr. Cooper, who never sold a piece of ground without reserving the right to carry water through it, at a reasonable remuneration to the owner; and a toast at the Fourth of July celebration in 1810 was, "Manufactories: May our exports exceed our imports." At that time there was a tanyard on lot 229, at the south end of Main Street, the number of mills had so increased that every available mill site was taken, and flour, whisky, pork, and grain were shipped down the river by flatboats. An effort was made to have the channels of the Miami, Mad River, and Stillwater declared public highways, and to prohibit fish-baskets and brush dams, as they interfered with navigation, but it was not successful.

In 1809 the first secret society, the St. John's Lodge of Free and Accepted Masons, was organized in the academy building on St. Clair Street. Business was good, and prices fair. Wheat sold for fifty cents a bushel, and whisky for thirty-seven and a half cents a gallon. At the fall election in the Court-house one hundred and ninety-six votes were cast. On September 6 the first county convention was held at the Court-house in the evening. David Reid was moderator, and Benjamin Van Cleve clerk. The nominees were, for representatives, Joseph H. Crane, of Montgomery County, and David Purviance, of Preble; sheriff, Jerome Holt; coroner, David Squier; commissioner, John Folkerth. Opposition candidates were nominated on the 9th of the same month, but at the election, at which six hundred votes were cast, the above entire ticket was elected.

Until the early part of 1804 Cincinnati was the nearest postoffice. Benjamin Van Cleve was the first postmaster in Dayton. His commission was issued at Washington on December 13, 1803, but did not reach Dayton until January, 1804. After receiving the appointment, Mr. Van Cleve opened the office at his home, on the southeast corner of First and St. Clair streets. Until in 1806 all the settlers north of Dayton, as far as Fort Wayne, had to come here for their mail. When the route from Cincinnati was first opened, the mail was received in Dayton once in two weeks, but after Mr. Van Cleve's appointment it was changed to once a week. This route was up the Little Miami, through Lebanon and Xenia to Urbana, and down through Piqua, Dayton, and Hamilton to Cincinnati. In 1809 a contract was signed with George F. Tennery, of Troy, by William George, William McClure, and Joseph Peirce, "Committee in behalf of the undertakers for carrying the mail from Dayton to Urbana," to the effect that "the said George binds himself, his heirs, etc., to carry the mail from Dayton to Urbana once a week and back to Dayton, . . . allowing the said George two days to perform the trip, the post-rider to be employed by the said George to be approved by the undertakers," for which the committee "agree to furnish the said George with a suitable horse, furnish the person carrying the mail and the horse with sufficient victuals, lodging, and feed, and one dollar for each and every trip, to be paid every three months."

Postage was always collected of those receiving mail, and in some cases the parties were so slow in making payment that the postmaster was obliged to announce through the paper: "Neither letters nor papers will be given out of this office in future until postage is paid. It has become necessary to make this new arrangement, and it is hoped

THE TOWN OF DAYTON INCORPORATED 143

my friends will not wish me to break it." Mr. Van Cleve held the position of postmaster until his death.

On April 6, 1825, the mail arrived from Columbus in a carriage, and two days later was sent to Cincinnati by stage.

In 1829 the *Journal and Advertiser* says, "Mail is now received from Washington and Baltimore in *six* days, from New York in *eight* days, and Boston nine or ten."

The following is a complete list of the postmasters in Dayton: Benjamin Van Cleve from 1803 to 1821, George S. Houston from 1821 to 1831, D. Cathcart from 1831 to 1843, James Brooks six months, Thomas Blair, J. W. McCorckle, Adam Speice, Edward A. King, William F. Comly, Mr. Hubbel, William M. Green, Fielding Loury, A. D. Wilt, W. H. Gillespie, L. J. Judson, E. B. Lyon, and J. C. Ely. In 1816 the rates of postage were graduated from six cents for a distance not exceeding thirty miles, to twenty-five cents for over four hundred miles.

At the spring election in 1809 Isaac Burnett was elected president of the Select Council, and John Folkerth recorder *pro tem*. During the year Council passed an ordinance requiring all men to work two days in each year upon the streets. At this time there were three excellent physicians in Dayton. Dr. William Murphy came in 1805, and died in 1809. Dr. John Elliot, a surgeon in the Revolutionary army, and also in Wayne's army, was mustered out of service with his regiment in 1802, came to Dayton soon after, and was highly esteemed as a physician. He had two daughters—Julia Ann, who married Joseph H. Crane, and Harriet, who married Joseph Peirce. Dr. Elliot died February 26, 1809, and was buried with military honors.

Rev. James Welsh, M.D., who came here in 1804 as pastor of the First Presbyterian Church, was also a practicing physician, and was the first doctor, as well as the first settled minister, in the town. He always kept a supply of medicines, and in 1810 he advertised the following list of medicines on hand for sale: "Yellow bark, oil of vitriol, verdigris, elixir paragorick, flowers of zinc, conserve of roses, Spanish flies, sugar candy, crabs' eyes, Venus turpentine, and polypodium felix, a famous worm medicine purchased by the late king of France." In 1816 Dr. Welsh laid out a rival town across the river (now Dayton View), and offered great inducements to settlers, but the project failed, and in 1821 he applied to the court to vacate his plat. He left Dayton in 1817, and died in Vevay, Indiana, in 1825. Before he left, Dr. Edwards, Dr. Charles Este, and Dr. John Steele were settled here.

On April 1, 1809, Dr. P. Wood opened the first drug-store in Dayton at Reid's Inn, and advertised in the *Centinel*, "that he has opened an assortment of medicine, and that of the first quality, which he will dispose of by the smalls." In this same paper is the following receipt for rheumatism: "Dissolve some mineral alkali in the proportion of about one ounce or a little more in a quart of water and take a wine-glass full of the solution three or four times in twenty-four hours, or as often as the stomach will bear it. This will cure (or kill) in three or four days."

On April 12, 1809, the paper announces, "A flat-bottomed boat arrived here yesterday from the mouth of Honey Creek, and this morning proceeded on her way to New Orleans, loaded principally with walnut and cherry plank"; and, "By a gentleman of respectability, who arrived a few days since from Fort Wayne, we are informed that John Johnston, superintendent of the public store at that place, has been appointed agent of Indian affairs, in the room of William Wells, removed." On November 23, the fol-

FIRST PRESBYTERIAN MEETING-HOUSE IN 1804.

From "Early Dayton," by permission of the U. B. Publishing House.

FIRST PRESBYTERIAN CHURCH IN 1896.

lowing announcement is made: "The Rev. Gideon Blackburn, a missionary appointed by the General Assembly of the Presbyterian Church in the United States to the Cherokee Nation of Indians, will preach at the Court-house in Dayton this evening, at early candle-lighting." When notice of a meeting to be held was given, the people would come from all the country round. In summer the young folks would walk five or six miles, carrying their shoes and stockings in calico bags until within a short distance of the meeting place.

The *Repertory* was discontinued about January 1, 1810, and Dayton was without a newspaper until May 3 of the same year, when the *Ohio Centinel* was started by Isaac G. Burnett. It was a four-column folio, eleven by nineteen inches, to be issued weekly, at two dollars a year in advance, or two dollars and fifty cents at the end of the year. This paper had a circulation extending to Greenville and Detroit, and contained all the legal notices for that entire territory. It was really a valuable paper in those days, but as, during 1812 and 1813, the men were almost all in the army, it had to suspend.

On May 16 of this year an editorial says, "It is a subject of regret that the prospect of a market in New Orleans is very uncertain in the present unsettled and precarious state of our foreign relations," and later on, showing the valiant spirit of the times, tells of a man who, in passing through the woods, "tomahawk in hand, met a large bear," which he caught "by the left leg and soon dispatched," adding that if such is the courage of all the boys, "General Harrison need not despair should he meet the devil in the wilderness."

On February 27, 1812, is the following:

"OBITUARY.

"On Saturday, the 22d inst., Ann Crane, aged eighteen months, daughter of Joseph H. Crane, Esq.

"When at the dread last trumpet's sound
Souls shall to bodies join,
Millions shall wish their lives below
Had been as short as thine."

The next paper was started October 3, 1814,—the *Ohio Republican*, by Isaac G. Burnett and James Lodge, with the motto, "Willing to praise, but not afraid to blame." Mr. Burnett was elected to the Legislature a month after the paper was started, and sold his interest to his partner, who issued it until October 9, 1816, when, the subscribers not paying their dues, he concluded the business was not profitable and closed the office.

The Fourth of July was a day of special celebration. The *Centinel* on July 5, 1810, says: "A number of citizens of this town and neighborhood convened yesterday to celebrate the anniversary of our independence. They met on the bank of the river and formed a procession to the Courthouse, where an ode was sung, an appropriate prayer made by Dr. James Welsh, the Declaration of Independence read by Benjamin Van Cleve, and an eloquent and well-adapted oration delivered by Joseph H. Crane, Esq."

After dinner they drank a number of toasts, to the discharge of cannon, one being, "The State of Ohio, the youngest of the Federal family: May she be the foremost to suppress insurrection and chastise foreign insolence."

In 1811 the Declaration of Independence was read by Joseph H. Crane and the oration delivered by Benjamin

THE TOWN OF DAYTON INCORPORATED

Van Cleve. There were two dinners prepared—one by John Strain, the other by Mr. Graham, to which free cards of admission were generously given. The toasts were drunk amid repeated cheers and the discharge of cannon. In 1816, the fortieth anniversary of independence, it was decided to have a more elaborate celebration than usual, and a meeting to make arrangements was held at Reid's Inn on June 21. The dinner was prepared by Captain J. Rhea. Isaac Spining was president of the day, William George and Dr. Este vice-presidents. Dr. Este read the Declaration of Independence, and Benjamin Van Cleve Washington's Farewell Address. The Revolutionary soldiers were given the post of honor in the parade. At four o'clock the ladies prepared a lunch in the grove, to which all were invited. In the evening there was a ball at Colonel Reid's Inn, and a vocal concert at William Bomberger's, just across the alley.

The census for the county in 1810 showed 7,722 inhabitants, and the tax levy for Dayton Township was $865.78½, and for the entire county $2,414.30. Curwen says: "The income arising from taxation alone now [1850] amounts to more than ninety thousand dollars," to which I will add that in this, our centennial year (1896), for Dayton alone the tax valuation amounts to $41,282,070, and for the county $62,695,810.

The census showed the population of Dayton to be three hundred and eighty-three, and the town was too small to appear on any of the school maps, but so, also, was Cincinnati. In regard to Cincinnati, the *Centinel* has the following:

"September 15, 1810. According to a census which has just been taken, it appears that the town of Cincinnati contains 388 houses and 2,320 inhabitants, 31 looms, 230 spinning-wheels. Within the year past there have been 6,480 yards of cloth of different kinds made there. Few towns in the United States have improved more rapidly than Cincinnati within a few years past."

At the town election this year D. C. Cooper was elected president of the Town Council, and James Steele recorder. The Council passed an ordinance requiring the improvement of sidewalks on Water Street, from Main to Mill streets; on First, from Ludlow to St. Clair, and on Main Street, from Water to Third, by laying the walks "with stone or brick, or to be completely graveled, and a ditch dug along the outer edge of the walks." When this order was not complied with, the fines imposed were to be spent in making street crossings. Teams were especially requested not to drive over the walks except when it could not possibly be avoided.

In September, 1810, the following contribution appeared in the *Centinel:*

"MR. BURNETT. *Sir:* By inserting in your paper the following ticket for the ensuing election and continuing it until that time you will oblige a number of your subscribers.

"Republican nomination: Governor, Return Jonathan Meigs, Jr.; Congress, Samuel Huntington; Senator, David Purviance; State Representatives, Robert Patterson, Alexander McConnell; County Commissioner, John H. Williams.

"The above persons were nominated by a number of Republicans in Dayton, and will be supported by them at the ensuing election."

The tickets in 1811 are again published in the *Centinel,* and among them is the following communication:

"MR. BURNETT: By giving the undernamed ticket a publication in your paper, you will oblige many electors.

"Assembly, Dr. Abraham Edwards, George Newcom; Sheriff, Samuel Archer; Coroner, James Wilson.

"Fellow Citizens: The above ticket we take the liberty of recommending to your liberal patronage at the approaching election, as we believe them good and worthy characters. We have no hesitation in recommending them to you as such. MANY ELECTORS."

THE TOWN OF DAYTON INCORPORATED

In the issue of October 3 there were five tickets. The election returns show that Dr. Edwards and George Newcom were sent to the Legislature, A. Brower was elected commissioner, and James Wilson coroner.

The names of the suburbs of the town at this time were unique, but descriptive. As the buildings south of Third Street were mostly cabins, that part of the town was called "Cabintown." The ground north of Third and east of the canal basin had been fenced in by Mr. Cooper as a pasture for his oxen at night, and was called "Buck Pasture," a name retained for many years. A ravine just west of Wilkinson Street from the river south was called "Rattlesnake." Barnhard Speck was a baker, with his oven on the northeast corner of Third and Wilkinson streets, where Mr. Daniel Keifer now lives. That section of town was called "Specksburg." Mr. Speck used to make gingerbread and carry it around on muster days, selling a section about four by six inches for six and one-quarter cents. Cooper Park was then called the "Common," and extended from Spratt Street to Fifth, and from St. Clair Street on the west to Cooper's Race on the east.

In 1811 all buildings other than dwellings were exempted from taxation, and the revenue for 1811–12 amounted to $1,748.67, while the expenses were $1,968.66. This year a standard half-bushel was ordered by the commissioners, and James Wilson appointed keeper of the measure. He advertised in the *Centinel* that he would be at his home in Dayton "every Saturday to measure and seal half-bushels." During this winter a bridle-path was cut through to Vincennes,—two hundred miles,—and the State "corduroy road" built east and west through town. It was, however, almost worse than no road, the mud-holes being filled with logs that in wet weather would float, letting the horses' feet down between in a way not pleasant to man or beast.

Dr. Este, who was a meteorologist, states in the *Centinel* in April, 1811, that at two o'clock on the 24th the thermometer stood at eighty degrees, on the 25th at eighty-two degrees, and on the 26th at eighty-one degrees. He says that by "noon" is not meant twelve o'clock, but the warmest part of the day.

Many strange things happened during the year of 1811, well calculated to make the superstitious think the world was coming to an end. In September a comet was seen passing from north to south. On the 17th of the month a total eclipse of the sun occurred, lasting from 12:30 to 3:30. The chickens all went to roost and the cattle returned from the fields. Well might the people declare: "These are indeed times of wonder,—comets, eclipses, tornadoes, earthquakes. In an age of superstition these would be held to be portentous signs. Powers of the physical world, are ye not satisfied?"

In October a man by the name of Hughes, who had been in prison in West Virginia, pretended to have had a revelation "foretelling the destruction of mankind" on the 4th of June, 1812. This story was published, finding a ready sale all through the West and Southwest. To make it seemingly more plausible, in addition to the phenomena that occurred in September, on the 16th and 17th of December earthquake shocks were felt in and around Dayton, the first and most severe between two and three Monday morning. The *Centinel* says: "Some left their homes in affright, and all were terrified by the unusual phenomenon. The horses and cattle were equally alarmed, and fowls left their roosts in great consternation. It was not preceded by the usual token of a rumbling noise." More than forty shocks were felt between the 16th and 21st. A surveyor attempted to do some work on a road he was surveying on both Monday and Tuesday, but could not get his needle to settle. This earthquake was general. The following description is taken from a letter written December 20, by a gentleman on his way down the Mississippi to New Orleans, and published in the *Centinel:*

"On the night of the 15th we came to anchor on a sand-bar about ten miles above the Little Prairie. Half past two o'clock in the morning of the 16th we were aroused from our slumbers by a violent shaking of the boat. . . . We weighed anchor early in the morning and in a few minutes after we had started there came on in quick succession two other shocks more violent than the former. It was then daylight, and we could plainly perceive the effect it had on shore. The bank of the river gave way in all directions and came tumbling into the water. The trees were more agitated than I ever before saw them in the severest storms, and many of them from the shock broke off near the ground, as well as many more torn up by the roots. . . . One circumstance occurred which, if I had not seen with my own eyes, I could hardly have believed, which is the rising of the trees in the bed of the river. I believe that every tree that has been deposited in the bed of the river since Noah's flood now stands erect out of the water. Some of these I saw myself, during one of the shocks, rise up eight or ten feet out of water. . . . Immediately after the first shock, and those which took place after daylight, the whole atmosphere was impregnated with a sulphurous smell."

On Thursday morning, January 23, 1812, another severe shock was felt, and on Friday morning, February 7, the third. The *Centinel* says it was by far the most awful of any, and "left impressions upon the mind which time will scarcely erase. . . . Many of the inhabitants left their houses, the fowls their roosts, and, we are told, the brutal herd manifested the same consciousness of danger." On June 27, 1812, a violent tornado passed over the county, about eight miles north of town, which greatly alarmed the people, but did not do much damage except to the forests. The timber was so torn and splintered that it was utterly useless, and the path, about half a mile wide, could be plainly seen for many years.

David Lindsley, a shoemaker, with Charity, his wife, and Ephraim, their son, came to Dayton in 1811, and lived in a frame house on Main Street, the present site of the Steele High School building. Ephraim, born in New Vernon, New Jersey, January 28, 1803, attended school in Dayton, and studied civil engineering, but his health failed, and he went to Morristown, New Jersey, where he learned the trade of printing. He was employed in the publishing house of Harper & Brothers in New York for about two years, but returned to Dayton, devoting himself to his trade for the balance of his life. In 1835, his first wife having died, he married Tryphena Crane Bradford, who came to Dayton with her parents, Abraham Crane and wife, in 1822 or 1823, and taught school in this neighborhood until her marriage to David Bradford, of Beavertown. After Mr. Bradford's death she again taught school until her marriage with Mr. Lindsley. She died March 10, 1872. Mr. Lindsley died February 5, 1873.

John Perrine was of Huguenot ancestry. The family, leaving their home near Nantes, France, after the revocation of the Edict of Nantes, went to Holland, and came to America about 1686. They settled first on Staten Island, afterwards moving to New Jersey. Mr. Perrine

THE TOWN OF DAYTON INCORPORATED 153

was born in Middlesex County, New Jersey, in 1774, and came to Dayton with his family in 1812. He lived on what is now the southeast corner of Monument Avenue and Wilkinson Street, then almost an unbroken forest. His wife died in 1814 and was the first person buried in what was afterward known as the "old graveyard," on Fifth Street. He was a quiet, unassuming Christian, with a high regard for right and wrong, one whose place was never vacant at the weekly or Sabbath-day service until unable, by the infirmities of age, to attend. He was a lover of flowers, making them a study, and on making his home with his son James had almost if not the first private greenhouse in Dayton at a time when there were no public ones. He lived to see his children all honored citizens in the communities where they lived, noted for their honesty and high integrity. James, Johnson, and Henry were successful merchants, living and dying in Dayton, and Garret, a farmer, lived in Clark County. Mr. Perrine died in the ninety-fourth year of his age, having few of the infirmities and none of the querulousness of age, leaving behind only pleasant memories.

James Perrine, when quite young, commenced clerking for H. G. Phillips, becoming at once the trusted clerk, and in a few years a partner, under the firm name of Phillips & Perrine. They were life-long friends. Later he entered into partnership with his brother as J. J. V. Perrine & Company. After this partnership was dissolved, James continued the business himself, in the store still standing at the northeast corner of Jefferson and Second streets. Mr. Perrine was a positive character, noted for his high integrity, truthfulness, and honesty. He was to many what the savings-banks are to-day. Always foremost in everything for the good of the city, he took great interest in Woodland Cemetery, and was one of its directors until his death. He was president of the Dayton Bank, director of the Second National Bank (now the Third), and one of the directors and originators of the Dayton Insurance Company. In 1830 Mr. Perrine married Julia Darst, taking her to the home he had prepared, where they always lived and the family still reside, on Second Street. It was a home of generous hospitality. Mr. Perrine died in January, 1863, after a few days' illness, mourned not only by his family, but many friends. The closing of all places of business showed the respect in which he was held.

In 1799 Stephen Johnston, with his wife and six children, emigrated from Ireland to Philadelphia, where the father soon died. The youngest son, John, with the aid of a Catholic priest, who had been tutor in the Johnston family in Ireland, and had been sent as a missionary to America, procured a position in the War Department in Philadelphia, under Mr. Bird. After serving for several years in this capacity, John was sent to Fort Wayne, Indiana, as United States factor to distribute Government supplies to the Indians, and having received some instruction in surgery, he frequently assisted Dr. Elliot in his department. The mother, with the remainder of the children, emigrated to Piqua, Ohio. In 1811 Mr. Johnston was made Indian agent, with Piqua as headquarters, but during the War of 1812 he lived in Dayton.

Colonel Johnston was a Whig, and when General Jackson was elected President was removed from office, but on the election of General Harrison in 1841 was reappointed. During the interval, the Indians could not understand why he did not furnish their supplies as usual, so he voluntarily gave them from his own resources, and shortly before his death presented his bill to Congress for twenty-one thousand dollars. His claim passed both houses, but was not signed by the President. Colonel Johnston spent the last years of his life at the home of his daughter, Mrs. J. J. Patterson, on the Rubicon Farm, but died in Washington just at the breaking out of the Rebellion. Of his fourteen children, Mrs. Patterson is the only one living.

CHAPTER VI.

THE WAR OF 1812.

As EARLY as 1808 "all free, able-bodied citizens between the ages of eighteen and forty-five were enrolled in the militia by company commandants," with the exception of preachers, judges of courts, jail-keepers, customs and post officers, stage drivers, and ferrymen on mail routes. They were required to have a good musket, fusee or rifle, a bayonet, belt and knapsack, two spare flints, a pouch for twenty-four cartridges, or a powder horn, and twenty-four balls. Officers also wore a sword or hanger. In active service the militia were subject to the rules and regulations of the United States Army. Training days and the Fourth of July were the big days for the people. When Colonel Jerome Holt on Saturday, September 18, 1810, called the Fifth Regiment to Dayton for "training purposes," business was suspended, and everybody—men, women, and children—came to see the parade, eat ginger-cake, and drink cider.

When James Madison was inaugurated President in 1809, he first turned his attention to the troubles with England, and in 1812 war, commonly called the War of 1812, was declared. "Benjamin Franklin once heard a person speaking of the Revolution as the 'war of independence,' and reproved him, saying: 'Sir, you mean the Revolution; the war of independence is yet to come. It was a war *for* independence, but not *of* independence.'"

As early as April, the Indians on the frontier being

troublesome, the President issued a call for "one thousand two hundred Ohio militiamen for one year's service." Immediately upon receiving the President's call for the militia of Ohio, Governor Return Jonathan Meigs ordered the major-generals of the Western and Middle divisions to report, with their respective quotas of men, at Dayton on the 29th day of April. Major David Reid ordered the First Regiment, Fifth Brigade, First Division of the Ohio militia to meet at Dayton on the usual parade ground by ten o'clock, on the second Tuesday of April, the 14th, armed and equipped as the law required for battalion muster. At this muster the volunteer bill passed by Congress February 20, 1812, and the President's order calling for volunteers, were read, the officers expecting a sufficient number would volunteer to form a company, but only twenty responded. General Munger, who had been ordered to raise a company out of this brigade to march to Detroit, then ordered the battalion to assemble on the 16th, at Adams's prairie, at the bend of the river near Alexandersville, and Major Adams was also ordered to report with his battalion at the same time and place. General Munger raised a company of United States Rangers from these two battalions, and gave the command to Captain Perry, who, on the 23d, received marching orders, and left immediately for Laramie.

General Munger, who had emigrated to Marietta from Vermont in 1797, was a typical pioneer general, well loved by his men. At one time, when no one could be found to properly shoe the horses and oxen required to transport the army stores, he had his own tools and leather apron sent in from his farm and shod them himself.

Early in April of this year Governor Meigs issued an order making Dayton the headquarters of the Western

Army, and appointed April 30 as a day of fasting and prayer, on which day religious services were held in the Court-house. On the 14th one thousand four hundred troops were camped here, principally volunteers, under General Gano and Colonel Lewis Cass. On May 1 the first companies began to arrive, and bivouacked on the town common (now Cooper Park), but received what might be called a rather chilly welcome, as no preparations had been made, either by the Government or the citizens, for the comfort of the men. There were no tents, and many were without blankets. By the 18th twenty companies were assembled. Governor Meigs arrived here on the 6th, and was received with a military salute of eighteen guns. On the 7th he reviewed the troops. Soon after his arrival the Governor ordered General Munger to organize troops for the defense of the frontier, and the public stores at Piqua, amounting to upwards of forty thousand dollars, were removed to Dayton.

On May 25 General Hull took command. On the 26th he marched his force of three regiments across and up Mad River about three miles, where "Camp Meigs" was established, and the American standard raised. As the flag unfurled, the troops, forming in a hollow square around it, "expressed their determination not to surrender it but with their lives."

Although war was really not declared until in July, General Hull commenced his march for Detroit on the 1st of June. These being the first soldiers to leave for the seat of war, Governor Meigs and staff, and many people from Kentucky and Cincinnati, as well as almost the entire population of the county, followed to bid good-by to friends. The first word of Hull's surrender, August 15, 1812, was brought to Dayton by one of the teamsters from this town, who, seeing what was being done, took his best horse, made his escape, and hurried to Dayton with the news. When he reached here at noon on August 22, the indignation of the people was great, and there was but little sleep on that Saturday night. By seven o'clock on Sunday morning a complete company of seventy men was enrolled, organized, equipped, and marching under Captain James Steele to the frontier. The only list of names that can be found of those seventy brave men is the pay-roll while the company was at St. Mary's, and that contains but fifty-two names, just eighteen short of the full number.

On the 26th Governor Meigs ordered Captain William Van Cleve's company of Dayton Rifles to march to the frontier west of the Miami, under the direction of Colonel Jerome Holt.

In December great exertions were made to provision the army. Colonel Patterson, forage-master, advertised for fifty ox-sleds and fifty horse-sleds, to be used in transporting supplies, and it was from volunteering, as Curwen says, to drive a team with provisions for the army, when many shrank from the danger, "that our great orator [Tom Corwin], then a lad, afterwards acquired the sobriquet of the 'Wagon Boy of Ohio.'" In response to a card, dated September 29, 1812, wherein "General Harrison presents his compliments to the ladies of Dayton and its vicinity," the ladies in ten days made about one thousand eight hundred shirts for the army, using the calico furnished by the Indian Department, annuities withheld from the tribes that had taken up arms against the Americans.

The women at home were no less heroic than the husbands, devoting their time while the men were in the army to making the living for the families, which in those days meant, as a rule, much hard work in the fields, as well as in the house. On the day that General Hull moved his troops Lieutenant Gwynne, of the United States Army, opened the first recruiting office in Dayton. The soldiers coming and going made a stir, and brought new life, and this was indeed a busy little town.

Peace was declared with England on February 15, 1815, and the Governor of Ohio appointed March 31 as a day of thanksgiving.

Many of the soldiers who had been through this valley for the first time during the war were so impressed with its rich and beautiful country that they came back to settle. The population increased, new stores were opened, and more houses had to be built. Prices for grain and stock steadily advanced, and the following items from a ledger page in October, 1814, will show some of the current prices in domestic goods:

"Dan'l C. Cooper.

"1.	For ½ lb. Pepper............	.37½
	1 oz. Mace	1.00
"10.	1 lb. Y. H. Tea..........	3.00
	12 lights Glass...........	1.50
"25.	1 pr Morocco slippers....	2.75
	1 " Stockings............	1.75
	6 lb. Bees wax...........	1.50."

During the war a great deal of money had been made in Dayton, new houses erected, and land platted as far as the Staunton road (the new Troy pike). A ferry was established at the head of Ludlow Street in December, 1814, by Charles Tull, but to cross on it the farmers had to leave their horses and wagons on the north side, and carry their produce. During this year a family by the name of Fairchild came to Dayton. They had one son, Eddy, born in February, 1810, who is still living in Dayton. In 1839

MR. TIMOTHY SQUIER.

MRS. TIMOTHY SQUIER.

THE HENDERSON & ELLIOTT SHOP, NORTHWEST CORNER OF MAIN AND FOURTH STREETS.

he built the house in which he is now living on Walnut Street, then a forest.

On February 23, 1813, Henderson & Elliott bought of D. C. Cooper the south half of lot 186 (where the Kuhns Building now stands), fifty feet, for fifty dollars, on which they built a one-story frame shop for their business as cabinetmakers. Mr. Henderson lived on Fourth Street near the shop. He afterwards sold his interest to Mr. Elliott and moved to Lafayette, Indiana. Mr. Elliott was a bachelor, and continued to keep the shop until his death. The last few years he did but little work, excepting to turn rolling-pins, on an old foot-lathe in the corner of the shop, as wedding presents for his bachelor friends. The one he gave me, made out of cherry, is still in use. That shop was a great place for the boys of forty or more years to congregate at early candle-lighting to discuss politics and play practical jokes on each other. The sketch on the opposite page is from an original drawing of the old shop as it was when Henderson & Elliott occupied it. In 1862 it was partitioned into four small storerooms, and the wooden awning added. When this change was made, and the bunk occupied by James Elliott removed, it was found that quite an impression had been worn in the boards against which his head had rested for so many years. In 1882 the shop was taken down to make room for the present Kuhns Building.

CHAPTER VII.

DAYTON TO 1840.

JOHN ENSEY, born in Frederick County, Maryland, came to Dayton from Baltimore in 1806. In 1810 he married Sarah Thompson, who was but two years old when brought to Dayton by her mother, Catharine Thompson, on the pirogue. They had ten children, seven of whom were sons, and all lived to honorable and successful manhood. Dennis Ensey, now living on Tecumseh Street, was one of the original contractors on the Southern Ohio Lunatic Asylum. He has two daughters living in Dayton—Mrs. Thomas De Armon and Miss Jennie Ensey. John B. Ensey, one of his sons, was a noted surgeon in the Civil War, and Isaac Van Cleve Ensey was a lieutenant in the Army of the Potomac. Dr. William Webster Ensey, of this city, is his son.

Mr. Ensey taught school for a number of years, and lived to a good old age with his faculties unimpaired. To the last he took an unswerving interest in education. His grandchildren never escaped the catch-words in spelling, and stood in awe of the hare-and-hound problems, which were always in the end explained. He was kind-hearted and tender to the little ones, and I well remember, when about seven years old, being carefully covered and allowed to take a nap on the recitation bench during school hours. His wife, familiarly called "Aunt Sallie," was a devout Christian, and never allowed anything to interfere with her attendance at the regular church services. She is remembered with love and reverence by all of her descendants.

Alexander and Rebecca McConnell, in 1806, came to Dayton, and entered a section of land lying just east of the National Soldiers' Home, which they cleared. They had five children, all but two of whom moved farther west. Thomas Jefferson McConnell, in 1826, married Sarah Tyler, daughter of William and Judah Tyler, and in 1855 moved to Madison, Wisconsin. They had eleven children. Their eldest, Alexander, married Mary Johnston Bradford in 1855, and now lives on a farm south of Dayton, near Beavertown.

Benjamin Kiser, born on the south branch of the Potomac, Virginia, December 22, 1779, on May 15, 1806, married Mary Fryback, coming to Dayton the same year. They had twelve children. In 1810 Mr. Kiser was appointed ensign of a militia company, and his descendants still have his commission, signed by the Governor of Ohio, Samuel Huntington. During the War of 1812 his wagons and teams were appraised, "in obedience to an order from the quartermaster." They were valued at $866.50. Benjamin Kiser was also "pressed into service to transport General Winchester's baggage," for which he was "to find himself and team, and to receive four dollars per day." In 1823 he was commissioned by Governor Morrow as lieutenant of the Third Company of the First Regiment, and on this commission is the following affidavit:

"I accept the resignation of Benjamin Kiser, Esq., a lieutenant of the 3d Company, 1st Regiment, 2d Brigade, 5th D. P. M., he having served as a commissioned officer for more than five years in this regiment.
"WARREN MUNGER,
"L. Col. Comd't 1 R. 2 B. 5 D. P. M.
"DAYTON, August 17, 1825."

After the close of the War of 1812 Mr. Kiser devoted himself to teaming, and during the years 1828 to 1832 worked the Edgar stone quarry near the Shakertown pike.

He then devoted himself to agricultural pursuits, until his death, which occurred near Lafayette, Indiana, November 1, 1835. His wife died in 1855, at the age of seventy years.

Daniel Kiser, the son of Benjamin and Mary Kiser, was born April 2, 1807, and at the age of fourteen went to live with his uncle, Daniel Kiser, who had charge of the county infirmary. In 1835 they removed to the Kiser farm (now North Dayton), where they devoted their lives to agricultural pursuits. On October 28, 1832, Mr. Kiser married Eliza Varner, who was born September 19, 1812, near Frederick, Maryland. They had seven children. Mrs. Kiser died January 15, 1853, and on March 17, 1857, Mr. Kiser married Hannah Cox, of Franklin, Ohio. They had three children, all of whom are living. Mr. Kiser was an enterprising, industrious farmer, and acquired a large and valuable property. He stood high in the community, and served as county commissioner, and director of the infirmary. He died October 17, 1869.

Henry Diehl, born in Hagerstown, Maryland, came to Dayton in 1806. He first learned the coppersmith trade, but being dissatisfied with that, turned his attention to making chairs, having an extensive shop on Main Street, next to H. Best & Son's present store, where he also made spinning-wheels and reels. He married Susanna Johnson. They had four daughters. Martha Jane married John Rouzer.

John Rouzer, who came with his father to Dayton in 1822, learned the trade of carpentering and started a shop, which has developed into the large business of the John Rouzer Company, on Wyandotte Street. In 1853 he married Martha Jane Diehl. They had seven children. The oldest daughter, Kate, married L. Flotron, and their son, John Flotron, was adopted by his grandparents. Mattie married Horace Justice.

John Compton, one of the early merchants of Dayton, in 1806 formed a partnership with Mr. Cooper, and they had a store on the northeast corner of Main and First streets. Mr. Cooper sold out, and Mr. Compton moved the business to the southwest corner, where the Dayton Club House now stands. He owned a large farm on the Cincinnati turnpike, south of Calvary Cemetery, on which he had a distillery. He also built a house on South Jefferson Street, on the ground now occupied by the Pony House, where he resided until his death. His son Charles studied law, and married late in life. Lenox Compton was a farmer and resided on the Compton farm south of town.

Thomas and Priscilla Cottom left their home at Snow Hill, Worcester County, Maryland, for Paris, Kentucky, in 1804. In 1807 they moved to this vicinity, living for the first two years on the Hamer farm, and afterwards on the Findlay farm, near where the Dayton Manufacturing Company is now located. In 1812 they moved into town.

Leven Cottom, their son, born at Snow Hill, Maryland, March 3, 1793, in 1812, when nineteen years of age, commenced working for a physician here who was making castor oil, but had great difficulty in clarifying it. One day a man who had heard of his trouble called on him and offered to sell the secret for ten dollars, first showing that it could be done. The money was paid and the information given, when, lo! *water* alone was needed. Leven next worked for David Hawthorn, a brickmason and plasterer, making mortar and carrying the hod for sixty-two and a half cents a day, working from sunrise to sunset. He next farmed outlots. While thus engaged, H. G. Phillips, seeing that he was a worthy boy, gave him iron on credit with which to build a wagon, so that he could do hauling to and from Cincinnati. When the roads were good, sixteen barrels of flour or twelve barrels of whisky were a load for four horses. In 1828 he was engaged with the engineers on the canal at twelve dollars a month, and continued at that work until the officers, in a spirit of economy, reduced the wages to nine dollars, when he quit. He next worked for Messrs. Swain & Demorest, who had a commission house and wholesale grocery on East First Street. In 1832 he married Priscilla, daughter of William and Judah Tyler, and built a cabin on the farm which Mrs. Cottom inherited from her father, now owned by their sons, David and James. It is located on Salem Avenue, Dayton View, a short distance north of the terminus of the electric road. Leven Cottom died March 8, 1884. His wife died March 30, 1885.

William Tyler and Judah, his wife, came to Dayton after the War of 1812. They bought land in Harrison Township, which they farmed, and which was inherited by their daughter Priscilla. Their daughter Sarah married Thomas J. McConnell. William Tyler was a second cousin of John Tyler, who was elected Vice-President with General Harrison in 1840. Judah, William Tyler's wife, died in 1856. Mr. Tyler died in 1861.

In 1805 James Grimes, his mother, and five sisters left Rockbridge County, Virginia, for Ohio, traveling in a wagon drawn by four horses. They crossed the Ohio River at Cincinnati, and in 1809 Mr. Grimes purchased Section 20 in Madriver Township, part of which he afterwards sold to William C. Davis. In 1811 Mr. Grimes loaded two flatboats on the Ohio River with produce for New Orleans, but on reaching that place was not able to sell to advantage, so went on to Cuba, where he disposed of his entire stock at a handsome profit and returned to Dayton in 1812, having been over a year making the trip. He married Edith Williamson, and had eight children. In

1816 he sold one hundred and sixty acres of Section 20 to David Duncan, and in 1852 the remainder of his farm to John Harries, and moved to Greenville, where he died in 1853.

Of the five sisters who came to Dayton with him in 1809, Betsy married Edward Newcom; Peggie, Mr. Campbell; Polly, Mr. Crawford; Annie, Mr. McConnaughey; Martha, Mr. Fulton.

William Huffman was born in Monmouth County, New Jersey, May 24, 1767, and on June 14, 1801, married Lydia Knott, who was also born in Monmouth County, January 19, 1779. They came to Dayton in 1812, and purchased a two-story stone house on the northwest corner of Jefferson and Third streets, where the Beckel House now stands. Mr. Huffman opened a general store, which he left largely in the care of his wife, while he devoted himself to looking after outside interests. They were active Baptists, and many of the first meetings of the Baptist Church in Dayton were held on the porch of their home. Mrs. Huffman died March 21, 1865, and Mr. Huffman January 23, 1866. They had four daughters: Mary Ann, who married the Rev. David Winters; Catharine (Mrs. Morris Seeley), Eliza J. (Mrs. Alexander Simms), and Lydia A., who married William Merriam, and had one son—William H. After Mr. Merriam's death she married John Harries.

William P. Huffman, the only son, was born in Dayton October 18, 1813, receiving his education here. After leaving school he read law in the office of Warren Munger, Sr., for the purpose of better fitting himself for a business career. In the spring of 1837 he moved out to the Huffman Prairie, in Greene County, about six miles east of Dayton, and on October 18 married Anna M. Tate, daughter of Samuel Tate. In the spring of 1848 they returned to

Dayton, and bought a home at the northeast corner of Jefferson and First streets, where they lived for many years, Mr. Huffman devoting himself to the real-estate business, banking, etc. He was much interested in public improvements, particularly in the Dayton and Springfield turnpike and the Cooper Hydraulic, and was one of the incorporators of the Second National Bank, and its president for many years. Mr. Huffman was for a long time before his death an active member of the Baptist Church, contributing generously to all calls for help. He was also a member of the board of trustees of Denison University, and chairman of the finance committee. In 1861 he erected a handsome residence on Huffman Hill, where he died July 2, 1888. Mrs. Huffman is still occupying the homestead. They had ten children.

Samuel Shoup, with his wife and family, came down the Ohio River on a flatboat, *en route* for Dayton, in 1810. While near Blennerhassett's Island a little boy was born, and named by the mother Joel Ohio. There were six children in all—Daniel, Samuel, Emanuel, George, Joel Ohio, and Sophia, the only daughter, who married Warren Munger, Sr.

Joel Ohio Shoup was married twice—first, to Margaret Worley. They had three children, all deceased. His second wife was Isabella Tate, and their family consisted of seven children—five girls and two boys. Three, the two oldest and the youngest, are dead.

Samuel Tate, Sr., was born near Milton, Pennsylvania, in 1796, and came to Ohio in 1818. He married in Pennsylvania Martha McCurdy, and they crossed the mountains on horseback. After reaching Dayton he rented Jonathan Harshman's distillery, which he ran nine years. He had to sell the whisky in Cincinnati, and the only way to get it there was by wagon. He afterwards purchased the Hamer farm, better known as Tate's Hill, where he erected a distillery and resided until 1846, when his wife died, and he removed into Dayton. He had six children, of whom Mrs. William P. Huffman, Mrs. Belle Shoup, and Samuel Tate, Jr., are now living.

Mary A. Darst, daughter of Jacob Darst, was born near Shakertown, October 19, 1811. On May 10, 1829, she married Lorenzo Dow Cotterel, a farmer and grocer of Greene County, who died November 13, 1875. They had thirteen children, of whom six—three boys and three girls—are still living. Mrs. Cotterel's husband and five sons were in the War of the Rebellion at the same time. One boy, Abraham, at Fort Donaldson, when not nineteen years old, scraped the snow away to sleep on the ground beside a fallen tree. The next day a rebel boy, a prisoner, said to him, "I shot at you all day and could not hit you, so you take this gun and keep it." Abraham died from the effects of this exposure. Mrs. Cotterel, in her eighty-sixth year, is still living in Dayton, and is now engaged in making log-cabin quilts.

Before the War of 1812 one blacksmith could easily attend to all the work of shoeing the horses, repairing wagons, agricultural implements, etc., but at this time (1815) with increased work came increased competition, and Dayton boasted four blacksmiths—Obadiah Conover, Jacob Kuhns, James Davis, and John Burns.

Obadiah Burlow Conover was born April 12, 1788, on a farm in Monmouth County, New Jersey, adjacent to what is now known as "the Old Brick Church," near Middlepoint. He learned the trade of blacksmithing, and determined to emigrate to the West. In 1812 he located in Dayton, where he carried on his trade, manufacturing wagons, plows, and other farm implements. After the fire at Cooper's Mills in 1820, he was very much overheated, and jumping into the river for a bath, took cold, from which he never entirely recovered. He gave up his shop and opened a general store at the corner of Main and Third streets, after a time forming a partnership with R. D. Kincaid.

It was customary in Dayton for all merchants not only to sell domestic wine and whisky, but to keep a bottle standing on their counters where all could help themselves. In 1827 and 1828 the temperance question was agitated for the first time in this community, and being intimate with Mr. Conover's oldest son, Burlow, I was much about the store and heard many discussions between Mr. Conover and his friends. The question with him was, what to do with the liquor he had in his cellar. It seemed like a waste to let it run into the ground, but he felt he could no longer either sell it or give it away, so the bungs were drawn, settling once and for all the liquor question in that store.

The church records, unfortunately, prior to 1814 were not kept, but it is certain that Mr. Conover joined the First Presbyterian Church soon after coming to Dayton, and was elected an elder in June, 1823. On April 13, 1814, he married Sarah Miller, daughter of John Miller, an elder in the church. She was born in Kentucky October 20, 1794, came to Dayton in 1799, and died January 12, 1872. Mr. Conover died January 6, 1835. They had eight children, two of whom died young. Burlow, the oldest, studied at South Hanover, Indiana, expecting to be a missionary in China, but died about the time of his graduating.

Harvey Conover, also a graduate of South Hanover, was a merchant for many years in Dayton, and also manufactured linseed oil in partnership with Daniel Keifer. He died in 1893, leaving six children.

Wilbur Conover, born May 10, 1821, graduated at Miami University in 1840, entered the office of Odlin & Schenck, and was admitted to the bar in 1842. In 1844 he and Robert C. Schenck formed a partnership, which was dissolved, and he entered into partnership with Samuel Craighead. On September 11, 1849, he married Elizabeth W. Dickson, who died September 27, 1868. Mr. Conover died October 3, 1881. They had five children, of whom Frank, an attorney in Dayton, is the only one living.

Obadiah M. Conover, a graduate of Princeton, was for many years professor in the college at Madison, Wisconsin, and during the last years of his life was law reporter for that State. He died in London, England, on the 29th of April, 1884, leaving three children.

Harriet Conover married, on September 28, 1852, Hiram Strong, who was born October 28, 1825, at Centerville, Ohio, graduated at Miami University in 1846, and was admitted to the bar in 1849. He was first in partnership with William W. Bartlett; afterwards with Hon. Lewis B. Gunckel. This firm was recognized as one of the leading law firms of Dayton. When war with the South proved inevitable, Mr. Strong was one of the first to give up business and offer his services, and in August, 1862, he was made lieutenant-colonel of the Ninety-third Ohio Volunteer Infantry. He was wounded at the battle of Chickamauga, and carried by his men on a litter down the mountain to the hospital at Nashville. He died there October 7, 1863, leaving a wife and four young children, all of whom are living. As said most truthfully in an obituary published at the time of his death, "of the many noble men who have lost their lives in this war, there was no better or nobler than Colonel Strong."

Martha Conover married Collins Wight November 7, 1843. Mr. Wight was born in Barnard, Vermont, May 1, 1817, his father, Benoni Wight, having come to this country from the Isle of Wight. Collins was educated at the Norwich Military Academy, now West Point, and could have entered the United States Army had he so desired. When twenty-one he started west, walking the entire distance, giving lectures on astronomy and chemistry, and carrying his apparatus and instruments in a small, hand-made wooden trunk. He stopped in Dayton to lecture, and wandered into the academy building, where examinations were in progress for a successor to Mr. Barney. Being taken for an applicant, questions were asked and answered, and to his surprise the position was offered him. Mr. Wight accepted and spent the remainder of his life in Dayton, taking great interest in its progress and loving the home of his adoption. Martha Conover Wight died March 8, 1884. Mr. Wight died October 16, 1890, leaving three children. At the time of his death Collins Wight was engaged in the lumber business, in which his oldest son, Harry, succeeded him. Harry Wight married Hattie Campbell, and died December 23, 1894, leaving his wife and two little children—Barbara and Collins.

On November 11, 1813, the Dayton Manufacturing Company, the first bank in Dayton, was organized, and articles of incorporation prepared, by H. G. Phillips, J. H. Crane, William M. Smith, Henry Brown, Isaac Spining, John Ewing, J. G. Burns, Philip Gunckel, and Joseph Peirce. A meeting for the election of directors was held December 23, 1813, but nothing was done until 1814, when the board was elected as follows: H. G. Phillips, Joseph Peirce, John Compton, David Reid, William Eaker, Maddox Fisher, Charles Russell Greene, Isaac G. Burnett, Joseph H. Crane, D. C. Lindsay, John Ewing, David Griffin, and John H. Williams, and on July 4 John N. C. Schenck, George

Groves, Fielding Gosney, and Benjamin Van Cleve were added to the directory. The board organized with H. G. Phillips president and George S. Houston cashier. A lot was purchased on the east side of North Main Street for two hundred dollars, and a stone house erected (now owned and occupied as a residence by Joseph Bimm) at a total cost of $2,600. Here the bank, with a capital stock of $61,055, opened its doors for business on August 18, 1814. Banking hours were from 10 A.M. to 1 P.M. The president was to receive a salary of one hundred and fifty dollars and the cashier four hundred dollars per annum. The vignette was an old-fashioned loom. The first loan recorded is "$11,120, to J. Dillon, Department Quartermaster-General, for the public service." During the winter of 1814 the one- and two-dollar bills issued by the bank were raised, the ones to one hundred dollars and the twos to twenty dollars—the first fraudulent money known in Dayton. In 1816, small coin being scarce, the bank issued notes for fifty, twenty-five, twelve and a half, and six and a quarter cents, called change tickets.

Mr. Phillips resigned as president on November 10, 1814, when Joseph Peirce was elected, who served until his death, in September, 1821. Benjamin Van Cleve was then elected president, but lived only two months and was succeeded by Colonel George Newcom. James Steele was made president February 14, 1823. On his death in August, 1841, James Perrine was elected to fill that office, which he held until the bank closed its business in 1843. The cashier, George S. Houston, died in May, 1831, and was succeeded by Charles R. Greene. In that year the bank changed its name and took a new charter as "The Dayton Bank." This charter expired January 1, 1843, and as that was before the law granting renewal of charters went into effect the bank gave notice that it would not make any further collections, and asked depositors to withdraw all deposits. On January 3 the directors were made trustees, and Alexander Grimes agent to close up the business. In 1848 he made his final report, showing not a dollar to have been lost to note-holder or depositor. On February 25, 1843, the banking house was sold at auction to H. G. Phillips for $1,350.

On May 21, 1845, the Dayton Branch of the State Bank of Ohio was organized with a capital stock of three hundred thousand dollars, the directors being Peter Odlin, Alexander Grimes, C. G. Swain, Robert W. Steele, J. D. Phillips, Samuel Shoup, Warren Estabrook, David Stout, and Herman Gebhart. Peter Odlin was elected president, and David Z. Peirce cashier. This bank continued to do business for twenty years, when it was reorganized as the Dayton National Bank. The first election of directors for the Dayton National Bank, at which nine directors were elected, was held February 7, 1865. The board was as follows: Peter Odlin, president; J. H. Achey, Horace Pease, G. W. Rogers, Harvey Conover, Herman Gebhart, Joel Estabrook, Dr. H. Jewett, and T. A. Phillips. C. G. Swain was appointed cashier. This bank received an extension of its charter in 1885.

On March 15, 1813, the mechanics of Dayton met at Hugh McCullum's tavern and formed the first workingmen's association. In the *Ohio Republican* of April 10 there was a call for the ladies who were disposed to aid in the establishment of a Bible society to meet at Mrs. Brown's on Wednesday afternoon, and on that day the Dayton Female Charitable and Bible Society was organized. The object was to distribute Bibles, and material comforts to the poor and sick. Each lady was to give a dollar a year for buying Bibles, and twenty-five cents quarterly for the charity fund.

Mrs. Robert Patterson was elected president; Mrs. Thomas Cottom, vice-president; Mrs. Dr. Welsh, corresponding secretary; Mrs. Joseph H. Crane, recording secretary; Mrs. Joseph Peirce, treasurer. The Rev. Dr. J. L. Wilson, pastor of the First Presbyterian Church of Cincinnati, a noted man in his day, preached a sermon for the benefit of the society in the Methodist meeting-house on Sunday, the 25th of June.

In 1814 the rivers again became very high, and Dayton had the second flood of note. John W. Van Cleve several years later gave the following description: "The water was deep enough to swim a horse where the warehouses now stand at the head of the basin (First Street), and a ferry was kept there several days. The water also at that time passed through with a considerable current from the head of Jefferson Street to the east end of Market Street (East Second) through the hollow in the western part of the town, and the plain through which the feeder passes, east of the mill-race, was nearly all under water."

On July 24, 1814, Dr. A. Coleman, of Troy, as secretary, in the *Ohio Centinel* calls a meeting of the Seventh District Medical Society at Major Reid's tavern on the first Monday in September. In the *Republican* of October 16, 1815, Dr. John Steele, secretary of the Board of Censors of the Seventh Medical District of Ohio, called a meeting of all "emigrant physicians who have commenced the practice of medicine within the limits of the district since 1812, to attend for examination." On July 3, 1816, the first medical society of Dayton was formed, to meet on the first Mondays of April, July, and November, of which Dr. Steele was secretary.

In 1814 and 1815 the revenue of the county had increased to $3,280.51, and in 1815 there were over one hundred houses in the town. More room was needed for county offices, and the commissioners contracted with James Wilson for a brick building to be erected on the site of the present new Court-house, to cost $1,249. This building, standing three feet above the sidewalk, two stories, forty-six feet front, and twenty feet deep, was completed and occupied in the spring of 1817. The first floor was paved with brick. In August, 1818, the *Watchman* rented the second story "at fifty dollars a year and free publication of the annual report of the treasurer and election notices." Later the county offices occupied the entire building.

At the age of nineteen the town began to put on airs, and concluded to have some fun as well as work. On February 13 there was a display of "wax works and figures," and the next year a play was advertised to be given at the dwelling of William Huffman, on Jefferson Street, on April 22, called "Matrimony; or, The Prisoners." The tickets were fifty cents, and gentlemen were respectfully requested not to smoke in the theater.

The first societies of a social nature were formed during this year. In July the Dayton Bachelors' Society was organized, with George S. Houston president and Joseph John secretary. The meetings were usually held in "Strain's bar-room," and the calls for meetings made through the *Ohio Republican*. This society was not long-lived, as the members gradually joined the ranks of the benedicts. On September 24 the president married Mary Foreman, and soon after the secretary, Joseph John, married Jane Waugh. John Steele was then made president and Alexander Grimes secretary. George S. Houston was also secretary of the Moral Society, organized at the Methodist meeting-house on July 22, with James Hanna president and William King, Henry Robinson, Matthew Patton, John Patterson, and Aaron Baker managers. The object of this society was "the suppression of vice and immorality, Sabbath breaking and swearing; to assist magistrates in the faithful discharge of their duties; but not to exercise a censorious authority over individuals." Quarterly meetings were to be held on the first Saturday of October, January, April, and July.

In 1815 the first structure for market purposes was built in the middle of East Second Street (called Market Street), about one hundred feet east of Main. It consisted of two rows of posts, with counters running lengthwise, covered with a roof, the eaves extending out for some distance beyond the posts. The counters in the middle were for the use of the butchers, and those under the eaves for the farmers and gardeners. Extending from the market to Main Street were two long horse-racks. There was a well and a pump in the middle of the street about fifty feet east of Main. This market was opened for business on the 4th of July, 1815, and market hours were on Wednesdays and Saturdays, from four to ten o'clock A.M. An ordinance, forbidding the sale of market products within the market space except during the regular hours, with a few exceptions, took effect April 1, 1816. After it was found necessary to have more market space, there was a struggle between the old location and Cabintown for the market-house, resulting in a victory for Cabintown. The first intention was to erect the building in the middle of Main Street, south of Third; but many were so dissatisfied with this plan that nothing was done until July 27, 1829, when it was decided to place the building in its present location. The additional property necessary to widen the alley was purchased for $1,196.20, and the Main Street end built first, the space toward Jefferson Street being reserved for market wagons. In 1836 the building was extended to Jefferson Street, and in 1845 a second story was added to the west half, to be used by Council, and for City Hall and Library. The building was used until 1876, when the present city buildings were contracted for. The old market on East Second Street was taken down in 1830. In 1838 an effort was made to hold market on Tuesday, Thursday, and Saturday in the early morning, and on Monday, Wednesday, and Friday afternoons, but it was not a success. For the morning market a bell would ring at four o'clock, and all who desired a choice cut of meat, and especially fresh vegetables, would hurry to the market on the tap of the bell. In 1830 William Clark was appointed by Council as clerk and marshal, on a salary of seventy-five dollars a year. At this time flour was five dollars a barrel, wheat seventy-five cents a bushel, a pair of venison hams fifty cents, butter twelve and a half cents, eggs eight cents. In January, 1817, wheat had gone up to a dollar a bushel, and flour to six dollars a barrel.

About 1815 Moses Stout, with his wife and son, David, settled in Dayton, and in 1817 David went into the saddlery business on Main Street, north of Second. A few years later he opened a dry-goods store on Main Street, between Second and Third. He then erected a building on the ground where Engle, Kramer & Company have their hardware store, and opened the first stove store in Dayton. Mr. Stout was a strong Baptist, and assisted in organizing the First Baptist Church. He was a member of the Town Council, was town and city treasurer for over twenty years, and also treasurer of the School Board. He was a stockholder of the Woodland Cemetery Association, his oldest son, Elias R., succeeding him as a voter. David Stout was one of the originators of Crutchett's Gas Light Company, of which he was treasurer, and afterwards was one of the principal promoters of the Dayton Gas Light and Coke Company, of which he was also treasurer for many years. He mortgaged his private property for the use of the company at one time when it was greatly in need of money. Mr. Stout was also active in organizing the Cooper Cottonmill and the carpet factory. Where the Atlas Hotel now stands Mr. Stout built one of the early brick houses in Dayton, then in Cabintown, which he occupied as his home until 1839. This house remained unaltered until 1892. In 1839 he moved to a new home on the corner of Second and Perry streets, where in 1840 he entertained as his guests one hundred and eight visitors to the great Harrison Convention. Mr. Stout died April 13, 1858. He had eight children, three of whom are living and residents of Dayton —Elias R., Atlas L., and David Orion.

Moses Simpson, born in New Jersey September 5, 1793, emigrated to Dayton, and in 1814 married Eliza Baker, daughter of Aaron and Hannah Maxwell Baker. They had four children: Elizabeth (Mrs. Robert Allen); Jane Maria (Mrs. George Morris); Electra Emeline, who married Seth Crowell and had six children, three of whom—Moses, Silas, and Anna F., wife of William Marietta—are still living; and Silas M. B. Simpson, who was born October 27, 1826, on the northeast corner of First and St. Clair streets, and died there April 27, 1887, having lived all his life on the one lot. On October 27, 1853, he married Henrietta Sophia Dover, daughter of Samuel B. Dover. They had three children. Mrs. Simpson and one son, William A. Simpson, live in this city.

In 1814 Robert Strain erected a two-story brick building on the northeast corner of Fourth and Main streets, and in 1815 opened the "Traveler's Inn." After his death, his two daughters, Mary and Martha, sold the property to the United Brethren Publishing House, and moved to a home on West Third Street, where they died when very old. Many thought Mary had passed her hundredth birthday, but she retained her faculties and eyesight to the last. The sisters were for many years members of the First Presbyterian Church, and Mary, at her death, in 1871, left her property to the church to be used towards a parsonage.

Daniel Stutsman, born in 1790, came to Dayton in 1814, from Hagerstown, Maryland, and married Margaret, daughter of Peter and Katharine Ella Lehman. Mr. Stutsman was a whitesmith, or sickle-maker, and a man of benevolent disposition, and when the cholera broke out in 1832-33 devoted his entire time and energy to nursing the sick. Among those he nursed and prepared for burial was my brother, Robert Andrew Edgar. Mr. Stutsman was the last one stricken with the cholera, on September 5, 1833, and died a most happy Christian death the next day. His last words were, "This is the happiest day of my life, for I shall see my Saviour." He was one of the founders of the first Methodist church of this city. He left a wife and six children.

John Grove Stutsman was in his sixteenth year when his father died, and at once determined to be the protector of the family. He was highly esteemed as a man of more than ordinary ability, and was ever interested in all public affairs of the day. He was elected one of the first members of the Board of Education, and served a number of terms. He was also a member of Council, was instrumental in having the levee built, and superintended the planting of trees along the levees, in the public-school yards, and in the park, the latter at his own expense, soon after it was deeded to the city. He learned the gunsmith trade with William H.

Brown, and was the first in Dayton to do gas-fitting. He advocated the stone-arch bridges across the canal, and superintended the building of the first one. He died in 1869.

Jonathan Stutsman, born in 1786, came to Dayton with his brother Daniel in 1814, and married Katharine, daughter of Peter and Katharine Ella Lehman. Soon after his arrival, he established himself as a coppersmith on the present site of the Phillips House. "For his two days' tax on the road he cut logs to fill in the pond at the corner of Main and Third streets." His oldest daughter, Mrs. Susan Eaton, is still living, in her eightieth year.

Robert McReynolds was born in east Virginia on February 7, 1772, and in 1815 came to this county. He first purchased land of Robinson, who was building a flour-mill at Harries' Station, then Snapptown, and hauled one hundred perch of stone as part payment for the land. He died on the farm in 1843. His son Joseph, born in Louden County, Virginia, in 1797, married Barbara Butt in 1819. They lived on the Gillespie farm and then moved to the Leatherman place, where Joseph started probably the first dairy in Dayton. He afterwards bought a tract of land on Lodwick Alley, now Fifth Street, and continued the dairy business. His son John has lately written me: "When he [the father] lived on the Leatherman place, I was born, August 18, 1822. The old log cabin is still standing. It must be near eighty years old, and is in a good state of preservation. My father used to haul grain to Cincinnati with an ox team and on the return trip would bring various articles of groceries. He also worked on the Miami and Erie Canal when it was built through Dayton." In speaking of his grandfather, Henry Butt, Mr. McReynolds writes: "He often told me that he assisted in clearing Main Street from the Court-house north to the river. In front of the old Court-house there was a large pond of water. They filled it by cutting down trees and hauling and rolling them in, then carrying the brush and placing it on the logs, then hauled ground and by that means made the road." A few years since, when a trench was dug in Third Street, I think for the sewer, the old logs, of black walnut, were found as sound as ever. I brought a piece of the wood home, thinking to make a souvenir, but it was so hard I could not work it.

Thomas Morrison, a carpenter, came here at an early day, married, and had several children. He was a prominent contractor and builder and an energetic business man. In 1834, having no job on hand, he concluded to seek a market elsewhere. He made up an assortment of doors and window-sash, built a flatboat, added to his cargo flour and whisky, and started down the river. For his crew he took Gorton Arnold, Thomas G. Carpenter, David Davis, and Henry Diehl, his apprentices. Henry Diehl only went to the mouth of the Miami River. On reaching the mouth of the Forkadeen River, the party went up to Jackson, Tennessee; but the venture was not a success. They were thirty-one days poling the boat from the Mississippi to Jackson. After a ten months' trip, when returning home on foot, tired out, they stopped at a farmhouse to ask for a night's rest, but were refused. As they turned from the door, Mr. Morrison picked up an ax, and, passing a pond near by, where the frogs were merrily singing, threw the ax into the pond. On reaching home, he wrote the man, telling him where to find the ax, and giving some advice on hospitality. Although their trip had not been successful, what Spanish milled silver they had, divided as usual into halves, quarters, eighths, and sixteenths, became very burdensome, and they exchanged it for shinplasters of the Vincennes Bank, of Indiana, which, on reaching home, they found to be worthless. Mr. Arnold, however, preserved some of them, and I am indebted to James O. Arnold for the piece from which the accompanying cut is made. With the exception of David Davis, all the party were living to enjoy the fifty-sixth anniversary dinner, hale and hearty old men.

David H. Morrison, son of Thomas and Sarah Morrison, was born December 19, 1817, on the lot where the homestead, now occupied by the Garfield Club, stands. On November 11, 1840, he married Harriet J. Skinner, daughter of Robert J. and Mary M. Skinner, of Wapakoneta, Ohio. At the suggestion of his teacher, the late E. E. Barney, he became a civil engineer, and took his first lessons on the construction of the Miami and Erie Canal in 1836 and 1837. Among his early associates in the survey were E. J. Barney, Jeremiah Peirce, Alexander Conover, Beck Schenck, and William Bomberger. He was for some time the city engineer, in which office he gave the highest satisfaction, being noted as an exact man, of strict integrity and the very highest sense of honor. He was looked upon as one of the best designing and constructive engineers in the State, and was frequently consulted on knotty points by engineers, both in Dayton and elsewhere, all of whom spoke in the highest terms of his remarkable abilities in his profession. Mr. Morrison, in 1851, built the first iron bridge west of the Alleghany Mountains. He died July 21, 1882.

Thomas G. Carpenter was born in Harrisburg, Pennsylvania, May 27, 1803, came here in 1815, and learned his trade of house carpenter with Thomas Morrison. In 1828 Mr. Carpenter married Hannah Heitman. They had seven children, one of whom, Mary Jane, married Joseph Clemens, who was wounded in the late war, and died at the Soldiers' Home. Henrietta Peirce married Colonel W. H. Martin, Eliza married Walter Hantchett, Hettie married Elam Wike, and Samuel married Laura Shartle. Mr. Carpenter was paralyzed and confined to the house for many years before his death.

Silas Broadwell, who was married in Morristown, New Jersey, to Sarah Byram, came to Dayton in 1816. He had an old red warehouse at the head of Wilkinson Street for storing produce until the river was high enough to float the boats to the Ohio. This warehouse was carried away by one of the floods. Mr. Broadwell owned considerable land west of Perry Street and north of Second, and probably lived near the corner of Bridge Street and Franklin Avenue. He had a large family of children, of whom all are dead except one daughter, Anna, who married George Josselyn, and is now living in Cedar Rapids, Iowa.

Ephraim Broadwell married Jane Ross Gardner, and came to Dayton at an early date. He was town marshal, I believe, in 1832 and 1833. In the winter of 1832 there was a great deal of snow, and several of the boys got jumpers, cow-bells, and boat horns, and went out for a sleigh-ride. Mr. Broadwell as marshal started out to stop the noise. They would quiet down when he would be near them, and then when nearly out of sight begin again, keeping the poor old man on the chase a good part of the night. In 1833 his son, William, bought out Henry Herrman's dry-goods store on Second Street.

David Heck moved here on September 29, 1818, and settled in Jefferson Township. He was the father of six children, of whom David L. (eighty years old), Elizabeth, Susan (Mrs. Wallace), and Polly still survive.

Henry Stoddard, born in Woodbury, Connecticut, March

18, 1788, received a common-school education, and at the age of sixteen commenced earning his living as a clerk. He then read law, was admitted to the bar in 1812, and in 1816, in company with George B. Holt, started west on horseback. Dayton then was a place of about six hundred. The successful lawyer had to ride the circuit through an unbroken wilderness, and for many years Mr. Stoddard made the circuit on horseback, through mud and rain, at night often sleeping in the woods. He was one of the most successful lawyers in Dayton, and in 1833 was appointed the attorney of the Dayton Manufacturing Company, at a salary of fifty dollars a year. For four years prior to 1844 Mr. Stoddard was in partnership with Judge Haynes, and in 1844 retired from active practice of law. Mr. Stoddard was an active member of the First Presbyterian Church, and from 1846 until his death a ruling elder. He was twice married; first to Harriet L. Patterson, who died October 1, 1822, leaving one son, Asa Patterson Stoddard, now living in St. Louis, Missouri. Mr. Stoddard's second wife was Susan Williams, daughter of John H. Williams, one of Dayton's pioneers. Mrs. Stoddard was a woman of great beauty and brilliant intellect, and was noted in Dayton for her charity. During the last cholera epidemic, she not only gave freely of her means for nurses and delicacies for the poor, but, when nurses could not be procured, she would often take that place herself. Mrs. Stoddard died April 4, 1861. Mr. Stoddard died November 1, 1869, having been an invalid for some time before his death. They had four children — Henry, Eliza (Mrs. Colonel S. B. Smith), John W., and Fowler, of whom three are living.

George B. Holt, who came west with Henry Stoddard, was born in Norfolk, Litchfield County, Connecticut. When very young he entered the law school of Judges Reeve and

Gould in Litchfield, and in 1812, when but twenty-two, was admitted to the bar. Mr. Holt decided to seek a home in Ohio, the far West, and arrived in the little village of Dayton in 1819. The next year he commenced the practice of law, and in 1821 married Mary, the second daughter of Dr. William Blodget. The lawyers on the circuit, after forcing their horses to swim the streams, often swollen by spring freshets, would have to ride miles through the woods before coming to a "house of entertainment," or the hospitable log cabin, for rest and refreshment. Elected to the Legislature in 1824, Mr. Holt participated in the discussion of many important laws, among them the *ad valorem* system of taxation and the canal bill, and was a member of the committee on bill for the common-school system. In 1828 he was elected to the Senate. During the last session of the Legislature of which he was a member he was made president judge of the Circuit Court, and in 1842-43 was reëlected to the same office. He also served as prosecuting attorney, and devoted part of his time to agriculture and stock raising. He was president of the Board of Health during the cholera epidemic. Elected to the constitutional convention, he was chairman of the committee on jurisprudence and was active in forming the constitution of the State. Although a Congregationalist, he was a member of the Presbyterian Church in Dayton. Judge Holt was president of the Montgomery Pioneer Association from its formation until his death on the evening of October 30, 1871, in his eighty-second year. He had three daughters—Eliza, Martha, and Mrs. Belle H. Burrowes.

Dr. William Blodget, of English and French extraction, one of his ancestors being a descendant of a French Protestant refugee, was born at Stafford, Connecticut, March 26, 1776. After his marriage he emigrated to Dayton, where he established himself in the practice of medicine with good success. He died October 26, 1838, at the home of his son-in-law, Judge Holt, his wife having preceded him, and was buried in the old graveyard on Fifth Street.

Dr. Job Haines, born in New Jersey October 28, 1791, graduated at Princeton, studied medicine at Morristown and Philadelphia, and in January, 1817, came to Dayton, bringing with him in his saddle-bags the first water-cress ever grown here. Dr. Haines "informs his friends and the public that he is ready at all times to attend to the business of his profession." He was the first secretary, and at one time one of the trustees, of the Montgomery and Clark County Medical Society, organized in Dayton at Reid's Inn on May 25, 1824, and was appointed one of the first fire-wardens in 1827. Dr. Haines was Mayor of the town in 1833, and, owing to the cholera that year, from which there were thirty-three deaths between June and September, appointed July 23 as a fast day. The population at that time was about four thousand. Dr. Haines was a devoted member of the First Presbyterian Church, and often, when without a pastor, he would read a sermon to the congregation. He died on July 23, 1860, being universally mourned.

Samuel Forrer was born in Dauphin County, Pennsylvania, January 6, 1793, of Swiss descent, and in 1817 or 1818 came to Dayton, which continued his home until his death, March 25, 1874. In 1818 he was appointed deputy surveyor of Hamilton County, also deputy surveyor under Colonel Richard C. Anderson, and in 1818 and 1819 surveyed the military lands north of Greenville. In 1820 he examined the summit between the Scioto and Sandusky rivers, at the expense of William Steele, of Cincinnati, to ascertain the feasibility of uniting Lake Erie and the Ohio River by a navigable canal. From 1822 to 1825, in the employ of the State, he made surveys for the canal, and, after work was begun, was resident engineer on the Miami and Erie Canal, and continued in the service of the State until 1831. In 1832 Mr. Forrer was appointed a member of the Board of Canal Commissioners, and when it was abolished and a Board of Public Works created, was made a member of that board. In 1838 he was appointed consulting engineer of Indiana, together with Sylvester Welch, chief engineer of Kentucky, and in 1849 was engaged in locating the Ohio Central Railroad from Zanesville to Wheeling, and in the surveys of many of the railroads and turnpikes leading from Dayton. He was a contractor on the Wabash Canal in Indiana, on the Pacific Railroad in Missouri, and was consulted by engineers and capitalists from all over Ohio and adjoining States. Our Woodland Cemetery owes much of its beauty to his skill in locating driveways, he having been employed by Mr. Van Cleve to lay it out. On February 8, 1826, Samuel Forrer married Sarah Hastings Howard. Mrs. Forrer was born in Belmont County, near St. Clairsville, December 27, 1807, and died in Dayton, December 11, 1887. They had six children: Elizabeth H. Forrer, who married the late Jeremiah H. Peirce, and died January 16, 1874; Edward Forrer, who died December 28, 1838; Augusta Forrer, who married the late Luther B. Bruen; Ann Forrer, who died January 11, 1837; Mary Forrer, who married the late Jeremiah H. Peirce October 5, 1882; Howard Forrer, who was born November 11, 1841, and killed at Decatur, Georgia, July 22, 1864, while performing his duties as adjutant of the Sixty-third Regiment, Ohio Volunteer Infantry. Mr. Forrer had three brothers and four sisters. One brother, Christian Forrer, kept the Montgomery House in Dayton for some years.

James H. Mitchell came to Dayton, after graduating at Yale, in 1820, to take charge of the academy, and married Miss Skinner of Lebanon. As surveyor he assisted in laying out new plats for the Cooper estate and others, and in laying out Woodland Cemetery, and was one of the surveyors of the Miami and Erie Canal.

John Bimm, a native of Hesse-Cassel, on the Rhine, Germany, came to this country when but nineteen years old. He married Christina Dansenbaker, who was born near Deerfield, New Jersey, and in 1818 came to Dayton. Mr. Cooper offered him the lot on which the county jail now stands for five days' work, but as it was then a pond, Mr. Bimm thought that too much to pay for it. Mr. Bimm lived for a while on the farm of Robert Edgar, on the Shakertown road, and afterwards on the farm of H. G. Phillips. While living there he bought about thirty acres of land of Dr. John Steele, on the Valley Pike, where he erected a two-story frame house, in which he died in 1847. Mrs. Bimm died in 1845. They had ten children, of whom only three—Elizabeth, Isaac, and Ezra—are still living.

Robert J. Skinner came to Dayton in 1816, and at once made preparations to publish the *Ohio Watchman* by purchasing the "good will" and materials of the *Republican.* The first number was issued on November 27, with the motto "Truth, equality, and literary knowledge, the three great pillars of republican liberty." On April 5, 1818, Mr. Skinner enlarged his paper and changed the motto to "A free press is the palladium of liberty." On November 7, 1818, he married Mary Hollis, of Philadelphia, their bridal trip to Dayton, on horseback, taking six weeks. When Market Street was opened, Mr. Skinner gave to the town the ground for the street and one-half of the Main Street front on which the market-house now stands. He also built a large three-story building on Market Street, known for many years as "Skinner's New Building." Thomas Buchanan Read, artist and poet, took the lady's part in a play given in the large hall of this building by the Thespian Society.

In December, 1820, Mr. Skinner took into partnership George S. Houston, and the name of the paper was changed to the *Dayton Watchman and Farmers' and Mechanics' Journal.* On August 6, 1822, Mr. Skinner sold his interest in the paper to A. T. Hays, and it was published by George S. Houston & Company. On January 15, 1826, Mr. Houston sold his interest to A. T. Hays and Ephraim Lindslay, but they only published the paper until November 21 of the same year, when it was discontinued.

In 1830 Mr. Skinner was appointed by General Jackson receiver of the United States land office at Piqua. He, in company with Joseph Barnett, Peter Aughenbaugh, and a Mr. Wiles, had purchased the land and laid out the town of Wapakoneta, and the land office being removed to that place he, as receiver, removed his family there, and continued to serve as receiver until the office was moved to Lima. During this period the celebrated specie circular was issued and many two-horse wagon loads of gold and silver coin were hauled to "the settlements," Dayton and Cincinnati.

On January 27, 1816, a meeting was held at Grimes's Tavern to make an effort to erect a bridge across Mad River at the Staunton road, then the most important road north, but for want of money the project fell through. The next year the county commissioners built a bridge at a cost of $1,400, a single arch span. Previous to this all the rivers had to be forded or crossed by ferries. Dr. Welsh established a ferry at the west end of First Street, for the purpose of going to his farm, now Dayton View, and to Rench's Mills at Salem. William King established one at the west end of Fourth Street, for the purpose of going to his farm, now Miami City, and to the Gunckel Mills at Germantown. These ferries were large flat-bottomed boats, on which a two-horse team could drive, and were poled across the river by two men.

In 1818 a company was incorporated by Robert Patterson, Joseph Peirce, David Reid, H. G. Phillips, James Steele, George S. Houston, William George, and William King, and on April 18 the contract for a toll bridge to cross the Miami at Bridge Street was given to Nathan S. Hunt, of Hamilton. In January, 1819, the bridge was opened to the public, and in 1852 it was washed away by high water. The toll-house stood at the northwest end of the bridge, and the rates of toll, taken from receipts given at the time, were as follows: "Loaded wagon and team, two horses, $12\frac{1}{2}$ cents; empty wagon and team, two horses, $6\frac{1}{4}$ cents; two-wheeled carriage, $6\frac{1}{4}$ cents; man and horse, 3 cents; person on foot, 2 cents."

In 1835 the county commissioners appropriated six hundred dollars to build a covered wooden bridge over the Miami at Main Street, the balance to be raised by subscription. In 1836 the bridge was opened for travel, and in the flood of 1867 was washed away by high water.

The Third Street Bridge Company was incorporated in 1838 by Jacob D. Lowe, Peter Aughenbaugh, H. Van Tuyl, Jacob Wonderlich, and Valentine Winters. The bridge was commenced the same year, and completed in 1839, by Peter Stoneberger. The original covered bridge, at one time a toll bridge, is still standing.

In May, 1818, the first stage line was started between Dayton and Cincinnati by Mr. Lyon, who made weekly trips during the summer. On June 2 John H. Piatt, of Cincinnati, and D. C. Cooper, of Dayton, started a line, and announced in the *Watchman* that the stage left Cincinnati every Tuesday at 5 o'clock A.M., and arrived at Dayton Wednesday evening. It would leave Dayton on Friday at 5 A.M. and reach Cincinnati on Saturday evening. The fare was eight cents a mile, and fourteen pounds of baggage were allowed each passenger. One hundred pounds were equal to one passenger.

In 1820 two colored men, John Crowder and Jacob Musgrove, started a stage with four horses, carrying twelve passengers.

In 1822 Messrs. Worden & Huffman had a line to Columbus, and Timothy Squier one between Dayton and Cincinnati, which he continued in 1825 to Columbus. In May, 1827, the Cincinnati, Dayton, Columbus & Portland Company, of which H. G. Phillips and Timothy Squier were the Dayton proprietors, began running triweekly stages from Cincinnati through Dayton to Columbus, making the trip in four days. The fare from Cincinnati to Dayton was three dollars, and to Columbus six dollars.

On August 11, 1828, the following announcement was made:

"The public are informed that during the watering season the daily line of mail coaches from Cincinnati by way of Hamilton and Dayton to Springfield will pass by the Yellow Springs. Traveling ladies and gentlemen wishing to visit the Springs shall be sure of a seat, as the subscribers keep a hack in readiness should the coach be full.

"T. SQUIER & Co."

The first show to visit Dayton was in 1819—an African lion, exhibited at Reid's Inn. The next year the first elephant ever seen here was exhibited in the log barn of the same inn, and on September 22 and 23, 1823, there was a "Grand Exhibition of Living Animals," with "good music on the ancient Jewish cymbal, and other instruments." On April 26, 1824, a "large and learned elephant" was advertised at Reid's Inn for two days. In July, 1825, the first circus visited Dayton.

In 1820-21 Elisha Brabham, a millwright, assisted in building the old red mill on the corner of Water and Mill streets, on the foundation of the mill that burned June 20, 1820. He was the first miller, assisted by Alexander Swaynie, and afterwards by Henry Franz. For many years the farmer would take his wheat or corn to the mill to be ground, the toll, a certain measure full, being taken out of the hopper before the grist was ground, as payment for the grinding. It was said that the miller would make a mistake sometimes and toll twice. Subsequently millers exchanged flour by the pound for wheat by the bushel, and finally they commenced paying cash for wheat. Elisha Brabham was the first man in Dayton to deal in wheat.

In 1822 the sheriff received a salary of $50 per annum, the clerk $50, and the auditor $150, in addition to certain fees to which they were entitled. At this time the money used was Spanish silver, and to make change a dollar would be divided into four quarters, and the quarters into four pieces, worth six and a quarter cents each. This was called "cut money." In 1830, when the dimes and half dimes first reached here, it was quite the fashion to have a set of vest buttons made of the half dimes.

In 1820 Henry Stoddard, as the representative from this county, was asked by the master mechanics of Dayton to petition the House to pass a bill giving them a first lien on buildings they erected until their wages should be paid, and the bill which he succeeded in having passed is still in force.

Farmers generally made their own summer hats out of rye straw. They would first soften the straw by soaking it, then on rainy days and in the evenings plait it, and sew the plaits into shape. Sometimes they would take a straight buckeye limb, four to six inches in diameter, fifteen to eighteen inches long, and plane off fine shavings. They would then drive five or six pins through a board about an eighth of an inch apart, the points coming about a quarter of an inch above the surface of the board, and the shavings by being drawn over the pins would be divided into the proper width for plaiting. A hat made in this way would wear for a long time.

Lewis Hamblin Brown built the levee from Wilkinson Street south as far as Washington Street, where he was stopped by injunction. Mr. Brown married Maria Ashmore Jones at Hamilton before coming to Dayton. They had four children—Mrs. Susan J. Kiddy of Dayton, Mrs. A. E. Minnick of St. Louis, Missouri, Lewis H. Brown of St. Louis, and Mrs. Sarah M. Clingman, wife of John Clingman, of Dayton. On August 20, 1822, the *Watchman* announced that a public meeting would be held in the Presbyterian meeting-house on Wednesday at 2 P.M., to form a Bible Society for Montgomery County. The organization was completed September 14, when Dr. Job Haines was elected president. In 1823 the Rev. Thomas Winters of Germantown requested, and obtained, the privilege of starting a branch society in that town.

After the burning of Cooper's Mills, on June 20, 1820, the first fire of importance, the Select Council at once provided ladders to be kept hanging in the market-house, and ordered every householder to procure two buckets made of harness leather, with leather bales, have his name painted on them, and keep them in a convenient place, and this constituted the entire fire department at that time. In the spring of 1825 Council gave $226 to one of the merchants going east to buy a fire-engine in Philadelphia. It was shipped by sea to New Orleans, up the Mississippi and Ohio to Cincinnati, and then brought by wagon to Dayton, not reaching here until in the fall of 1825. It was a box about four by six feet, twenty inches deep, with a force pump and crank. It had to be filled with buckets, and the water was thrown on the fire through a short piece of hose, by turning the crank. Two lines would be formed from the engine to the pump, one to pass the full buckets, the other to return them empty. Relays of men were at the pump to keep it constantly going. In 1827-28 eighty-eight leather buckets were purchased by Council at a cost of $112.50, one-half of them to be kept on the engine, and the other half at the homes of the men ready for use. For twenty years these buckets were inspected every April by the fire-wardens. The first fire-wardens, appointed by Council in March, 1827, were Dr. Job Haines, Matthew Patton, Alexander Grimes, James Steele, and Abraham Darst, with John W. Van Cleve as chief engineer of the Fire Department. In 1833 a new engine was purchased, the "Safety," with suction hose and gallery, and five hundred feet of new hose. This year cisterns were dug in the street intersections on prominent corners, and a well sunk at the curb, from which the cistern was to be kept filled.

After the purchase of the "Safety," the Safety Fire Engine and Hose Company No. 1 was organized, with James Perrine foreman, Valentine Winters assistant foreman, J. D. Loomis secretary, T. R. Clark treasurer; leader of the hose detachment, Thomas Brown; assistant leader, Henry Diehl; directors, William P. Huffman, Jacob Wilt, Peter Baer, Henry Deichler, and Abraham Overleas. The next engine purchased was the "Independent"; after it the "Oregon." These three, although great improvements over the first, were not satisfactory, and in 1852 four new engines were purchased — the "Neptune," the "Vigilance," the "Deluge," and the "Pacific." This volunteer fire equipment served Dayton until the paid department was organized in 1863, and the first steam-engine purchased. The burning of the *Journal* office, in July, 1863, was the last large fire at which the volunteer companies officiated.

On August 29, 1822, the first number of the *Gridiron* appeared, with the motto,

" . . . . Burn, roast meat, burn;
Boil o'er, ye pots; ye spits, forget to turn."

The paper was published weekly, at a cost of one dollar a year, by John Anderson, who endeavored by "roasting" people to correct manners and customs which he thought defective; but the paper was not a success, and in eighteen months was discontinued. On November 21 it announced that the Thespian Society would present the farce, "Of Age To-morrow," on the following Saturday, for the benefit of the Dayton Library.

CHAPTER VIII.

DAYTON TO 1840—CONTINUED.

IN 1824 there was considerable talk about improving the channel of the Miami River, so that steamboats could run between the Ohio River and Dayton, and a communication in the paper says, "It is pleasing to anticipate the time when we shall have boats at our doors ready to carry us to the *gulph* of Mexico, or the city of New York, and when we shall have stages passing on the National Road through Dayton from the remote State of Maine to Missouri." Unfortunately the scheme did not prove practicable. In March, 1825, thirty boats were tied up here on account of low water. On the 23d rain began to fall and the *Watchman* says, "On Saturday all was the busy hum of the seaport; wagons were conveying flour, pork, whisky, etc., to the different boats strung along the river. Several arrived during the day from the north. On Sunday morning others came down, the water began to fall, and the boats, carrying about forty thousand dollars' worth of the produce of the country, got under way." The boatmen always preferred to start on a falling river, as it was easier to keep in the channel. The last boat left for New Orleans by the Miami River in February, 1829. All freight after that was shipped by the canal.

A meeting of Dayton citizens was called at Colonel Reid's Inn on June 29, 1821, to appoint a committee to work with those of other places to raise money for surveying a route for a canal from Mad River to the Ohio.

The act providing for the improvement of the State of Ohio by navigable canals, making Dayton a point, was passed in 1825, and the population at once began to increase.

There was a great difference of opinion as to the location of the canal through town, the *Watchman* suggesting it should be down the middle of Main Street, the channel to be not more than forty feet wide, and the sidewalks reduced to twelve, leaving a wagon road of thirty-four feet in width on each side, and making Main Street the finest street in Ohio. The citizens, fearing it might be a mile from the Court-house, employed Micajah T. Williams, a school-teacher and engineer, to locate the route through town, the State engineers agreeing to his plan, placing the basin between First and Sixth streets. On May 17, 1825, the Canal Commissioners met in Dayton and opened six hundred bids for construction contracts.

On Monday, September 3, 1825, excavation was commenced in Dayton on the basin, and the event was celebrated that evening by an artillery salute. Opposition to the canal was based on the theory that it could not be made to hold water, and for a while it seemed as if this might prove true. On Friday, September 26, 1828, water from the sawmill tail-race, near the corner of Fifth and Wyandot streets, was let into the canal by the contractors, and a great portion of it leaked away. Those who had doubted said, "I told you so," but others went to work and by using great quantities of straw, brush, and clay, which were thrown in the bed, and oxen driven up and down to make a mortar, the bottom finally puddled, and there was no further trouble.

When the first canal-boat built in Dayton, the *Alpha*, was completed, a temporary dam was built at the bluffs. and on August 16, 1828, the boat was launched near Sixth

Street. On January 1, 1829, the canal was opened to within four miles of Cincinnati, and the Dayton Guards, a military company of boys, George Bomberger captain, made one of the first through trips. From the very first Governor Brown had been a strong advocate of the canal, and in January the *Advertiser* announces, "On Sunday, January 25, at daybreak, came the boats *Governor Brown*, the *Forrer*, the *General Marion*, and during the night the *General Pike*." The *Governor Brown* was fitted exclusively for passengers. Twenty to twenty-four hours from Cincinnati to Dayton, sixty-six miles, was considered very good time.

On February 5, the *Governor Brown* being frozen up here, Captain Archibald gave a supper, "which rivaled that in the best hotels." The captains of the other boats in the basin served supper at Squier's Hotel, where toasts were drunk, one of them being, "The ladies of Dayton — the only produce of the country which we do not wish to see exported." On April 21 the paper announced the arrival of the first steam-packet, the *Enterprise*, and on May 26 the *Miami Herald* states that the *Experiment* "made her trip to this place on Saturday last." This boat had an observation sitting-room, where passengers could enjoy "all the air passing and an uninterrupted view of surrounding country." During April it was estimated that seventy-one boats arrived and seventy-seven left Dayton; that the number of passengers for Dayton was nearly a thousand, and that the toll collected here during 1829 amounted to $6,738.31. Merchandise was brought by water from New York in *twenty* days by way of the Erie Canal to Buffalo, Lake Erie to Cleveland, down the Ohio Canal to the Ohio River at Portsmouth, then down the river to the Miami Canal and up the canal to Dayton, a distance of one thousand one hundred and fifty-two miles. Dayton was then at the head of navigation, and supplies of every kind were forwarded from here, wagon trains from Miami, Clark, Champaign, Greene, and other counties at times completely blocking First Street from Madison to St. Clair. Work on the aqueducts over Mad River and the Miami, north, was commenced in 1833, but not pushed, the canal not being opened to Piqua until 1837, and to Toledo until 1845. The first boat reached Dayton from Toledo in June of that year. The canal between Dayton and Cincinnati cost $567,000. Since its completion from Toledo south it has been known as the Miami and Erie Canal.

In 1825, by actual count, there were just one thousand one hundred and thirty-four people in Dayton—five less than at the taking of the census in 1820; but as the building of the canal was then a certainty, business began to pick up and all the houses and cabins were occupied. Improvements generally were seen, and the decennial census of 1830 showed two thousand nine hundred and thirty-four people in Dayton, the population having doubled during the five years. There were then two newspapers—the *Miami Republican and Dayton Advertiser*, edited by George B. Holt, and the *Dayton Watchman*. In April, 1826, William Campbell purchased both papers, and on November 25 combined them as the *Ohio National Journal and Montgomery and Dayton Advertiser*, with the motto, "Principles and not men, where principles demand the sacrifice." In December he sold the paper to Jephthah Regans. On December 4, 1827, Mr. Regans sold a half-interest to Peter P. Lowe, and the name was changed to the *Dayton Journal and Advertiser*. In 1828 John W. Van Cleve purchased Mr. Lowe's interest, and the paper was then published by Regans & Van Cleve until the death of Mr. Regans. On January

From a photograph by Elizabeth B. Edgar.   CANAL-BOAT OPPOSITE THE FAIR GROUNDS.

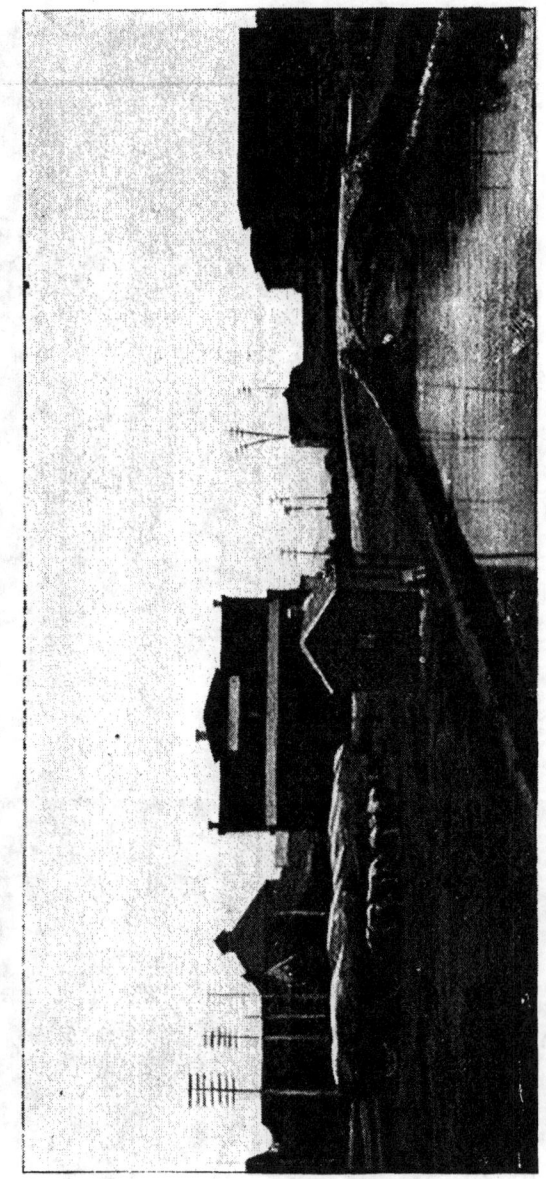

From a photograph by Elizabeth B. Edgar.

THE OLD HAY MARKET, EAST OF COOPER PARK, LOOKING NORTH FROM THIRD STREET.

27, 1829, the editor announced: "Foreign News. We have none to lay before our readers for this good reason: there is not an item of foreign news in any of the papers received since the first of the present month."

After the death of Mr. Regans, Richard N. Comly bought his interest, and in July, 1834, Mr. Van Cleve sold out to William F. Comly. This firm, R. N. & W. F. Comly, in 1835 removed the office to the third story of the brick building number 132 North Main Street, and afterwards to the frame building on South Main Street which was burned by the mob. They also enlarged the paper to a seven-column folio, and in December, 1840, issued a daily paper for a short time, and then a triweekly paper until May 6, 1847. Then the first number of the first volume of the *Daily Journal* appeared, and it has been published continuously ever since.

In 1857 R. N. Comly transferred his interest to John P. Comly, and in April, 1862, after William F. Comly was appointed postmaster by President Lincoln, the paper was sold to Lewis Marot and William H. Rouzer, who owned it at the time the office was burned on the night of May 5, 1863. The next afternoon, without the intermission of a single day, the *Journal* was published in a small three-column folio.

After the fire Major W. D. Bickham took the *Journal*, and continued editor and proprietor until his death, March 28, 1894. William F. Comly's connection with the *Journal* covered a period of sixty years, excepting when he was postmaster, being placed on the regular office force soon after his term of office expired, and relieved from duty only a few months before the death of Major Bickham.

During the Harrison Presidential campaign in 1840 the Comlys published the *Log Cabin*, stating in their prospectus on April 18 that they expected to issue thirteen numbers for fifty cents, payable in advance. John W. Van Cleve wrote many of the songs and engraved most of the illustrations for this paper. A short series of seven numbers was issued from the 26th of June, for twenty-five cents.

The *Watchman*, in the spring of 1824, suggests that the streets be drained and turnpiked "instead of making canals of them," and that some means be provided for weighing hay. Up to January, 1825, all hay was sold by the load, but on the 11th of that month Thomas Morrison erected hay scales on Fourth Street, east of Ludlow, charging thirty-seven and a half cents a ton.

In January, 1828, the three rivers of Dayton were all higher than usual. The Third Street race bridge was carried away and all the southern part of the town submerged, and the State dam just built was much damaged.

In April the New Lights and others interested published "by subscription a book, entitled 'A Christian Hymn-Book,' to contain two hundred and fifty hymns," the cost to subscribers being seventy-five cents, and those subscribing for twelve copies received one extra free. As it was not possible to get better terms than those offered by Mr. Burnett, it was published at the *Centinel* office—the first book published in Dayton.

In 1826 James Perrine was appointed agent for the Protection Fire Insurance Company, of Hartford, Connecticut, probably the first insurance agent in Dayton, and George S. Houston the same year advertised as a real-estate agent. S. T. Harker came here in 1828, built a large warehouse, and carried on a wholesale business of groceries, packing pork and beef, and making soap and candles. John Dodson, a carpenter, was appointed flour inspector when the canal opened to Cincinnati. He had a long, hollow auger, like the letter U, with a screw bit at the end, which he would run through the barrel and draw out full of flour, then holding it over a bucket, said to hold about twenty-five pounds, would sift the flour through his hand, to see if it was free from specks. If it was, the barrel would be branded superfine; if not, fine. The superfine usually sold for about fifty cents more a barrel. The report was that some days his bucket would be filled twice a day.

Augustus George was whisky inspector at the same time. In 1829 the Dayton Temperance Society was formed, with William King moderator and Dr. Job Haines secretary. Aaron Baker, Daniel Ashton, David Winters, David L. Burnett, John Steele, Job Haines, Henry Jewett, William M. Smith, and Henry Bacon were appointed a committee to prepare a constitution and an address to the public.

The following extracts from a letter written by John W. Van Cleve to Samuel Bacon in June, 1829, will give some idea as to society and business affairs in Dayton. He says: "Marrying goes on very slow in Dayton. The only match that seems certain is Davies and Mary Peirce. They have settled the matter between them, and will not hold off long. Peter Lowe is going ahead after Ann Bomberger, who has got to be a very beautiful girl. Jephthah Regans and Ann Williams love one another very hard, and I don't believe they can keep apart very long. If you were to be dropped down in Dayton you would hardly know it. Great improvement is going on. The streets are all busy, drays running, hammer and trowel sounding, canal-boat horns blowing, stages flying—everybody doing something. The corporation has graveled nearly all of the streets in town, and are now about erecting a new market-house in Main Street, opposite Obadiah B. Conover's and Skinner's. The first idea was to build the market-house in the middle of

Main Street. I didn't like that so well. I am sorry to see Main Street have anything in it which will obstruct the view. Property is selling very high. You probably noticed in the paper the sale of some lots at the head of the basin, about a third of an acre [about where Pinneo & Daniels' shops are now], for $2,920. On Saturday last a public sale was made of an outlot that belonged to Ezra Smith, near old Mrs. Hess's, being the corner lot nearest the sawmill, containing about three acres [the corner of Fifth and Brown streets]. The lot was divided into twenty-seven building lots, and streets, and sold for $2,200. The three lots behind the Presbyterian meeting-house [the property now owned by Simon Gebhart, Lewis B. Gunckel, Miss Martha Perrine, and C. E. Pease] sold for $1,800. Harshman gave Compton $3,200 for the brick corner opposite Dodson's, where Seely kept store [the present location of the Dayton National Bank]. The executors of D. C. Cooper's estate have leased a water-power to be taken out of the sawmill race opposite Lawyer Smith's and let into the head of the basin, and a cotton-factory is to be built to run one thousand spindles and looms to weave the yarn made. The head of the basin is becoming entirely surrounded by warehouses."

About the year 1820 Lovel Bebee, a school-teacher, came here, and married a daughter of Samuel Thompson, of the pirogue party. He furnished Dayton with its first great sensation by his mysterious disappearance in December, 1826. He had been assisting a family in butchering, near the present junction of Brown and Warren streets, and at supper call started for a bucket of water from a spring at the foot of the hill in front of the present Deaconess Hospital. He was never seen or heard of afterwards, although hunting parties scoured the country for fifty miles in every direction.

Harriet Bebee, his daughter, was born in September, 1821. She married Emson Brown, who came to Dayton in 1832. Mr. Brown was connected first with the old carpet factory, the present Kratochwill mill building, where was made the first flowered ingrain carpet ever made west of the Alleghany Mountains. Mr. Brown was afterwards connected with the Curtis Woolen Factory. He was a prominent member of the "Underground Railway," organized the first colored Sunday school in Dayton, and was for a time at the head of the old volunteer fire-company "Oregon." In 1860 Mr. Brown removed to Piqua, where he died in 1867. Mrs. Brown is still living in Piqua.

James F. Thompson, born January 1, 1811, emigrated to Montgomery County in 1819, coming down the Ohio River in a flatboat to Cincinnati. In 1837 he married Mary A. Riley. They had five children,— Elihu, Levi H., Franklin, Wilbur R., and Eliza Jane,— all of whom, with the sixteen grandchildren, are living. He was elected to the Legislature in 1875.

Gorton Arnold was born in Chenango County, New York, in 1804, and at the age of sixteen joined an emigrant party for Ohio. They had three teams with "Ohio" painted on their wagons, and reached Dayton after being on the road six weeks. Gorton apprenticed himself to Thomas Morrison to learn the carpenter trade. Subsequently Mr. Morrison took him into partnership, and they became well-known contractors and builders, continuing in partnership until 1847. Thomas Brown, contemporary with them, did the brick work, and they the wood work on the same buildings, the principal contractors here. In 1837 Mr. Arnold married Ritta Ann Oliver, the daughter of James Bracy Oliver, born February 27, 1815. In 1839 he purchased the farm on which he resided until his death. The homestead, built in 1832, is now occupied by his son, James Oliver Arnold. After leaving the East, Mr. Arnold lost sight of his sister Frances, who was two years younger, and heard nothing of her for fifty-two years, when, through Marcus Eells, he obtained the clew which resulted in their reunion at Norwich, Connecticut. Mrs. Arnold died September 21, 1888. Mr. Arnold died in 1889, at the age of eighty-five years.

John W. Dryden, born March 17, 1799, married Elizabeth Hammacher in 1822, and came to this county. They lived for a number of years on Fourth Street, next east of Grace Methodist Episcopal Church. Of the ten children, four are still living: Daniel H., who married Jane Smith of St. Mary's, Ohio, and was auditor of the county from 1854 to 1860, and treasurer from 1868 to 1873; Fannie, who married A. A. Butterfield; Minta I., for twenty years librarian of our Public Library; and Chauncy K., who married Martha Smith. John W. Dryden died in 1870. His wife died in 1879.

Andrew Wiggim, a farmer, born in Tyrone County, Ireland, married Elizabeth Little, and in 1817 emigrated to this country. They were fourteen weeks crossing the ocean in a sail-boat. In 1822 they came to Dayton. Mr. Wiggim died August 10, 1859. His wife died November 18, 1864. Their son John, born in Tyrone County, October 30, 1810, a miller by trade, was a member of Council for two terms, and superintendent of the Work House in 1875. He died March 8, 1882. Huey, also born in Ireland, October 4, 1814, carried on extensive cooper shops, one where the Callahan Foundry now is and another in Union City, Indiana. He was paralyzed for eight years before his death on August 31, 1884. Samuel is a farmer in Madriver Township.

James Dodds, born in 1799, emigrated to this county,

married Mary Yeazel in 1822, and settled on land near Carrollton. There was an old fortification on it, from the earth of which he made brick, many of the old houses in Carrollton being built of this brick. His daughter, Mrs. Belle Pease, is living in this city.

John Engle, a saddler by trade, was born in Washington, Pennsylvania, April 21, 1800, and came to Dayton on July 1, 1822. With the exception of eighteen months spent in Xenia, Dayton continued his home until his death, August 21, 1892. On April 20, 1825, he married Susanna Hivling, of Xenia. They had five children: one son, David W. Engle, who is in the hardware business in Dayton; Mrs. C. C. Keifer, of Urbana; Mrs. Emily J. Endslow, of Chicago; Misses Julia H. and Martha T. Engle, of Dayton.

The Rev. Thomas Winters, father of David and Valentine Winters, was born in Harbaugh's Valley, Maryland, December 23, 1778. He became a minister in the Reformed Church in 1800, and settled in Germantown in 1815. He died at the home of his son, John P. Winters, West Alexandria, October 2, 1863.

David Winters, his oldest son, was born in Martinsburg, Virginia, December 24, 1801. In the fall of 1824 he came to Dayton, and on January 11, 1826, married Mary Ann Huffman, daughter of William and Lydia Huffman. Mr. Winters was for many years the pastor of four churches, the First Reformed Church of this city, which he organized, being one, besides doing much missionary work through the county. As the result of his labors in the field he traveled over, at the time of his death there had been over thirteen churches built with which he was in some way connected. He had preached eight thousand sermons, confirmed two thousand four hundred, baptized three thousand, married five thousand and ninety couples, and attended one thousand three hundred funerals. It was a common thing for him to travel from two to three thousand miles a year on horseback. He died May 9, 1885.

Valentine Winters, born in Clearfield County, Pennsylvania, July 8, 1807, was two years old when brought to Ohio in 1809. He commenced supporting himself when a boy of seventeen by working in Robertson's brickyard at Germantown for ten cents a day, but his brother David procured a position for him in the dry-goods store of Andrew Irwin, father of A. Barr Irwin, at a salary of fifty dollars a year and board, the contract to be for two years. At the close of his two years' engagement he secured a situation with Harshman & Rench, at two hundred dollars a year and board. While in Mr. Irwin's employ, one Sunday he, with Edwin Smith, Samuel Bacon, and Jephthah Regans, attended the Shaker meeting at Shakertown, and met Jonathan Harshman and his sister Catharine for the first time. Edwin Smith made a bet of one dollar that Valentine Winters could not obtain the privilege of taking Catharine Harshman home. The bet was taken, however, and won, and later also the lady, for on January 1, 1829, they were married by his brother David. The next year Mr. Winters became a partner in the firm of Harshman & Rench, under the name of Harshman, Rench & Company. In 1840 Mr. Harshman withdrew from the firm, and the business was continued by Rench & Winters. In the fall of 1843 Rench and Winters dissolved partnership, Mr. Rench taking the warehouses and canal-boats and Mr. Winters the store on the corner of Main and Third streets.

In 1845 Mr. Winters was largely instrumental in organizing the Dayton Bank, under the independent law of Ohio, and was elected cashier, Jonathan Harshman being president. In 1851 or 1852 Jonathan Harshman, Jr., Valentine Winters, James R. Young, and Robert Dickey formed the private banking house of Harshman, Winters & Company, and opened their bank on the northeast corner of Main and Third streets. In about two years Messrs. Dickey and Young sold their interest, and the bank name was changed to Harshman & Winters. In 1857 Mr. Harshman retired. Mr. Winters then sold his dry-goods store to his nephew, D. W. Winters, and devoted his time entirely to the bank, taking into partnership his son, Jonathan H. Winters, under the firm name of V. Winters & Son. In 1882 this private bank was sold to the Winters National Bank. Valentine Winters was from 1857 to 1866 a member of the Board of Control of the State Bank of Ohio, and president of the Preble County branch of the State Bank from 1857 to 1866, the close of its charter. He was one of the organizers of the Ohio Valley Bank in Cincinnati, and continued a director until it closed its business. Mr. Winters was active in the organization of the Mad River & Lake Erie Railroad, also of the Dayton & Western Railroad, and built and equipped the first railroad in Minnesota, from St. Anthony to St. Paul. He also assisted in the organization of the Firemen's Insurance Company in 1835, and was one of the directors and treasurer of the company until his death.

During the summer of 1851 Mr. and Mrs. Winters withdrew from the Reformed Church, and on September 6 of that year united with the Third Street Presbyterian Church. On April 4, 1882, Mrs. Winters died after a prolonged illness. Mr. Winters lived for many years after, and died December 20, 1890. They had a large family of children, of whom Mrs. N. B. Darst, Mrs. Robert Dickey, Mrs. Lewis B. Gunckel, Mrs. James C. Reber, and John H. Winters are still living in Dayton.

Thomas Clegg, with his four little boys, James B., John, Joseph, and Samuel, left England for this country in 1818. In 1824 he came to Dayton and started the Washington Cotton Factory on the Cooper race just above Foundry Street, and in 1833 he changed the location to south of Third Street. In 1828 Mr. Clegg and Mr. McElwee established an iron foundry between Cooper Street and Monument Avenue, where the first iron was melted in Dayton, and started the first brass foundry near the east end of the Steele High School building. He associated with himself in many business ventures his son, Joseph Clegg, under the firm name of Thomas Clegg & Son. Being familiar with the manufacture of gas in England, in 1830 Mr. Clegg made an exhibition on a small scale at the old National Hotel on Third Street. In 1832 he erected the first freestone front building in Dayton on the northwest corner of Jefferson and First streets, and in 1835 erected a sawmill between Wyandot and Wayne streets. In 1850 he made an overland trip to California, where he stayed about ten years, but returned to Dayton and died here in 1879 at the age of eighty-nine.

William Westerman was brought to Dayton by his parents in 1824, and in 1828 apprenticed himself to Clegg & McElwee to learn the molding trade. On becoming of age he went into partnership with Joseph Clegg, and subsequently with Atlas L. Stout, in a foundry and machine shop, which was the predecessor of the Globe Iron Works. After some years Mr. Westerman sold his interest, and devoted himself to buying real estate. Mrs. Westerman and their one daughter, Mrs. M. L. Edgar, of New York, are still living.

Peter Perlee Lowe, son of Jacob D. and Martha Perlee Lowe, born in Warren County, Ohio, June 11, 1801, was educated in the schools of that early day and studied classics under Mr. Kemper, of Cincinnati, Ohio. He studied law in the office of the Hon. Thomas Corwin, of Lebanon, Ohio, was admitted to the bar in 1825, and immediately came to Dayton to form a partnership with Henry Bacon. For many years, like the other pioneer lawyers, he rode the circuit on horseback. The prominent lawyers at that time on the circuit were Henry Bacon, Joseph H. Crane, Edward W. Davies, Peter Odlin, Robert C. Schenck, Charles Anderson, Henry Stoddard, Judge Holt, of Montgomery County; Walter E. Thomas, L. S. Smith, Ralph Hart, Charles Morris, of Miami; Ben Stanton, of Logan; Goode, of Shelby; Conklin & Young, of Champaign; Generals Mason and Anthony, of Clark; Ellsworth, of Greene; Corwin, Dunlevy, Probasco, and Smith, of Warren, and Woods, Bell, and Millikin, of Butler. Mr. Lowe was admitted to practice in the United States courts in 1832, and was elected prosecuting attorney for this county in that year. In 1837 he was elected to the Legislature, and served as chairman of the judiciary committee. In 1860 he was delegate to the convention that nominated Abraham Lincoln for President. During the war of 1861-65, being beyond the years for army service, he sent a man as his representative in the field. For many years he was a member of the First Presbyterian Church, and served as treasurer and trustee, and was one of the trustees of Miami University for eighteen years. Mr. Lowe married Ann Bomberger, who died in 1877. They had four children: Jacob D., his law partner (who died at the age of twenty-five); William B., a captain in the United States Army; Sarah Perlee, who died in 1880, and Annie L., who married Joseph H. Rieman, of Baltimore, Maryland, in 1861. Mr. Lowe died in 1886.

Edward W. Davies was born in New York City, January

16, 1802, and when but four years old his parents emigrated to Cincinnati. Mr. Davies came to Dayton in 1826, and commenced the practice of law, first in partnership with Judge Crane, and later with Colonel John G. Lowe. In 1832 he was clerk of the Common Pleas Court, was attorney for the Cincinnati, Hamilton & Dayton Railroad Company for some years, and in 1858-59 successfully conducted the suit when the will of David Zeigler Cooper was contested. Mr. Davies was instrumental in securing the passage of the bill creating the Board of Police Commissioners for Dayton, and for many years was president of the board. Together he and Alexander Grimes, as trustees of the David Zeigler Cooper estate, changed the bed of Mad River. In 1829 Mr. Davies married Mary Ann Peirce. She died in September, 1881. Mr. Davies died December 11, 1873. They had seven children, of whom four are still living—Samuel W. Davies, Joseph Peirce Davies, Mrs. Julia Davies Schenck, and Mrs. Eliza Davies Dart.

Andrew Gump came to Dayton in March, 1825, and commenced clerking for William Eaker. In October, 1829, he married Ruth Crampton and opened a store at Little York, but soon returned to Dayton. In 1839 he built the family residence on West Second Streeet, and in 1857 erected a three-story store building on East Second Street, and later other business blocks. He died some years ago. His wife, two sons, and a daughter are still living here.

About 1750 Edward Weakley, with four brothers, came to Cumberland County, Pennsylvania, from England, and all became Revolutionary soldiers. Thomas Weakley, Edward's son, emigrated to Montgomery County, Ohio, in 1826, with his wife, Ann, three daughters, afterwards Mrs. H. S. Williams, Mrs. Augustus Newell, and Mrs. John Hays, and a son, Edward. Edward Weakley married Catharine Gunckel, of Germantown, Ohio. They had eight children, three of whom are living in Dayton. Captain T. J. Weakley and George Willis Weakley are prominent business men, and Herbert H. Weakley is the editor and principal owner of the *Evening Herald*. He organized the present Dayton Board of Trade, and for the first two years of its existence was president and active manager.

Henry Herrman was born in the Duchy of Baden, Germany, on May 22, 1797, and in 1826 emigrated to the United States, reaching Dayton in September of that year. In 1828 he married Ann Bimm, who was born in New Jersey, October 26, 1811. Mr. Herrman was a good business man, quick to arrive at conclusions and expert in figures. About 1852 he took T. S. Babbitt, who had married his daughter Catharine, into partnership in a dry-goods store on Main Street. Mrs. Herrman, the mother of eight children, was for many years a devoted member of the Disciples Church. She died March 7, 1874. Mr. Herrman died January 22, 1877.

Charles Soule was born in Freeport, Maine, September 2, 1809. In 1826, when seventeen years old, he came to Dayton, and worked at carriage painting for Mr. Dolley, on the present jail lot. His first portrait was that of Mr. Dolley, who advised him to give his entire attention to that work, and his success from the first was encouraging. One of his best-known portraits in Dayton is that of Judge Crane, which has a prominent place on the walls of the Law Library. He married Elizabeth M. Mead, daughter of Benjamin and Abigail Mead. Mr. Soule died in Dayton March 31, 1869. Mrs. Soule died on November 5, 1891.

Benjamin Wicks Mead married Abigail Webb Thatcher Hall, in Boston, and came to Dayton in 1829. The trip was made in wagons, taking three months, three weeks, and three days. Mr. Mead was very ingenious, and made a large clock, casting the parts in brass. The clock is now in the possession of Mrs. N. B. Darst. He was the first to discover and put in a state for use Epsom salts, and "British oil," now our coal oil. He also invented a dredge for cleaning rivers, which was sunk during a freshet in the Mississippi River, and in April of this year (1896) raised at Burlington, Iowa. Mr. Mead died in St. Louis in 1849.

Peter Light, a cabinet-maker, located on a farm near Dayton in 1826, and the stone used in adjacent locks of the canal was taken from his quarry. In 1827 he married Charlotte Love. He died March 30, 1878, nearly eighty-one years of age. Mrs. Light died May 19, 1880. They had five children, of whom Peter B. and Samuel B. are still living in Dayton. The homestead is owned by Samuel B. Light.

Peter Light had two sisters and three brothers, who came to Dayton at a later date. One brother, Joseph, was a carpenter, and his nephew writes me: "A church was built on the corner of Second and Ludlow streets—I think the first Presbyterian church in the city. The tower, a marvelous affair for those early times, was so high that the workmen refused to do anything more on account of the great danger at so great a height. Being a carpenter, Joseph engaged to, and did, complete the steeple *alone*, on the stipulation that he be paid five dollars per day for his services."

David Stone, of Walpole, New Hampshire, came here during 1826. He was at one time identified with the American Fur Company, trading with the Indians and trappers for furs and ginseng root. About the year 1830 Mr. Stone took his son William B. into business with him, and for quite a while they engaged in the produce and packing trade, located on the corner of Fifth and St. Clair streets. They did business in Vicksburg, Natchez, and New Orleans, and while under twenty-one years of age William loaded a flatboat at Cincinnati and started down the Ohio and Mississippi on a trading expedition, stopping at all the stations on the way, as far as New Orleans, making a successful trip.

A story was told of David Stone, and verified, that during his business career in Dayton he conceived the idea of getting a corner on anvils. They were plentiful and cheap, and he went quietly about and bought up all he could find for sale, depending upon the difficulty of transportation and the long time it would take to get a new stock for sales at a high profit. It was not long until others found they were short on anvils and Stone was long, and he made considerable money out of the deal. This transaction was regarded as and called a "Yankee" trick.

After David Stone's death at Dayton, in November, 1839, William B. Stone engaged in the grocery business with David Peirce, and also turned his attention largely to fine stock. He was very fond of sport, and was said to possess the best hunting outfit in the West. He died in Dayton November 28, 1850, leaving a wife and two children. The only one of his immediate family living is a son, Charles A. Stone, now residing in Chicago. He has beeh for nearly a generation actively engaged in the shipping business there.

John L. Belville, of French Huguenot descent, was born in New Castle, Delaware, December 21, 1800, and after completing his course at Princeton Theological Seminary was licensed to preach by the Presbytery of New Castle in 1827. As a missionary he was stationed by the Board of Domestic Missions at Dayton, and reached here about June 1, after a journey on horseback and alone. He immediately commenced holding meetings in the town and country, at private houses, in school-houses, and in the woods, frequently riding miles over bad roads, or no roads, to keep an appointment. In May, 1828, he married, in Bucks County, Pennsylvania, Elizabeth Mann Long, and, returning to Ohio, became stated supply, and soon pastor, of Washington Church, this county, in the organization of which he had assisted. The territory embraced by his congregation included Centerville, Miamisburg, Carrollton, Alexandersville, and Woodbourne. By his efforts a church building was erected in 1829, which is still standing, and is noted as being the only country church in the county of the denomination wherein services have been continuously maintained for so long a period. In 1840 he accepted a call as pastor of the church at Bellefontaine. When failing health compelled him to relinquish active work he retired to his farm near his old church, preaching as health permitted until 1870, when he removed to this place. He was for a few years in charge of an academy at Centerville. He died September 21, 1880, being at that time the oldest member of Dayton Presbytery. Mr. Belville was present and assisted at the organization of the Synod of Cincinnati, now merged into the Synod of Ohio, and was several times elected moderator of that body, as well as also of his presbytery. Three times he was chosen a commissioner to the General Assembly, and took an active part in its deliberations.

Dr. Hibbard Jewett came to Dayton in 1828. He was in partnership with Dr. Steele for a time, and in 1842 formed a partnership with his brother, Dr. Adams Jewett, which lasted until 1860. He was a strong abolitionist, and took an active part in the underground railroad. He died October 26, 1870.

John W. Harries, born in 1783 in Gelledewyll, Cannarthenshire, South Wales, Great Britain, emigrated with his family to New York in 1822, having at that time five children. His wife (Mary Williams) died and he married Mary E. Conklin, of Huntington, Long Island. They had two children born in New York, and in 1829 started west, arriving in Dayton on the canal-boat *Experiment* on July 5. After reaching Dayton three children were born—Mary, Rosetta, and Emma. Mr. Harries for many years had an ale brewery on North Jefferson Street. Mrs. Harries died at the age of sixty-five years. Mr. Harries died February 22, 1873, at the age of ninety years. The oldest son, Thomas, a Presbyterian minister, preached many times in Dayton. John married Mrs. Lydia Merriam, a widow (daughter of William Hoffman); William married Mary Huston; David married Lottie Smith, of New York; Ann married Mark Reed; Charles married Elizabeth Regans, daughter of Jephthah Regans; Caroline married William Young, of Piqua; Mary died when quite young; Rosetta married Jonathan Harshman Gorman, and Emma married William Henry Simms.

Daniel Altick, born in Franklin County, Virginia, August 6, 1802, came to Dayton in the spring of 1828, and in 1829 married Rachel Wolf. He was employed for two years with Peasley & Mead, noted for their artistic skill in working metal and wood. Mr. Altick died July 25, 1875, in his seventy-fourth year. His wife died September 11, 1889. The only surviving children are William Altick and Mrs. Melissa A. Herst, of Dayton, and Mrs. Martha J. Stoneberger, of Osborn.

In 1828 Gideon Beall came to Dayton with his wife, Ann, her sister Lucy, and brother, Washington Weston, and Francis Waring. Francis Waring and Washington Weston clerked for George W. Smith, but Waring soon moved to Greenville. At this time there were five boys clerking "at the head of the basin"—Washington Weston, William C. Davis, Joseph Clegg, William Harker, and the writer; not bad boys, but full of fun, of whom four are still living—William C. Davis, of Huntsville, Alabama; Joseph Clegg, William Harker, and myself. Washington Weston left Dayton in 1835, but later returned, and from 1856 to 1863 controlled the Dayton Paper Mills, after which he removed to Greenville, where he died.

About 1833 Joseph Weston joined the family in Dayton. He wrote for a while in the clerk's office at Hamilton, and afterwards obtained the same position in this county. Later he formed a partnership with Daniel E. Mead in the paper-mill. Mr. Weston married Sarah Demarest, but she did not live long, and his sisters, both widowed the second time, Mrs. Ann Hasselman and Mrs. Lucy Green, made their home with him on the corner of Second and Ludlow streets. In 1882 or 1883 Mrs. Hasselman died, Mrs. Green died in May, 1888, and Mr. Weston died in California, whither he had gone to spend the winter, in January, 1894. Mrs. Green's son, John W. Green, with his family, now resides in the old home.

Frederick Boyer, born in Harrisburg, Pennsylvania, in 1790, came to Dayton in 1829. He died in 1860 at the age of seventy years. Of his nine children three are living—Mrs. Wollaston, J. F. Boyer, and Sarah Boyer.

Thomas J. S. Smith was born in Cumberland, Maryland, December 10, 1806, graduated at Jefferson College, Pennsylvania, and came to Dayton in 1830. He taught school in the old stone bank building, number 224 North Main Street, studied law, and was admitted to the bar in 1832. On May 28, 1833, he married Jane Bacon, daughter of Henry Bacon, one of the pioneer attorneys here, and moved to Troy, Ohio.

In 1844 he returned to Dayton, became interested in railroad projects, and was president of the Dayton & Michigan Railroad at one time. In 1856-57 he represented this county in the Legislature. Mr. Smith was for many years a prominent member of the First Presbyterian Church. The two sons, General S. B. Smith and J. McLain Smith, are still residents of Dayton.

At the age of twenty John Bidleman left his father's farm in Cumberland County, Pennsylvania, and tramped his way westward, riding on wagons when opportunity offered, until he reached Cincinnati. He arrived in Dayton in 1830, and opened a shoeshop at the head of the basin on First Street. He enlarged his business from time to time, subsequently bought a tanyard, and sold his make of leather in all parts of the United States. On October 2, 1836, he married Evaline Phelps, sister of Winslow S. Phelps, for many years cashier of the Dayton National Bank. They had eight children—Winslow R., Emma P., John H., Eva S., Jacob G., Charles D., Carrie L., and Mary J. Mr. Bidleman died in July, 1895, at the age of eighty-five, having outlived his wife six years.

The following extract from an obituary of Thomas Brown, written by Judge Dustin, and published in the *Journal*, were given me by his daughters as a fitting account of his life, so many years of which were spent in Dayton:

"Thomas Brown was born April 10, 1800, in the village of Manahawkin, Monmouth (now Ocean) County, New Jersey, where he spent most of his childhood days. After learning the trade of builder, he, in company with a friend, walked from Philadelphia to Lebanon, Ohio, where his two brothers then resided, and in 1828 moved to Dayton.

"Mr. Brown was a member of the first School Board, a member of the General Assembly for two years, a director of the State Prison from 1848 to 1851, and one of the lessees of public works under the law of 1861. Prior to 1851 he was a contractor and builder, and erected many public and private buildings in this and other counties of the State. Thereafter he was engaged in various enterprises, and finally purchased an interest in the firm of S. N. Brown & Company, of which his son was the leading partner, and when the firm became incorporated, was elected president, and continued in that position until he died.

"Mr. Brown voted at eighteen Presidential elections, and was fully up with the times, the first man in Dayton to use natural gas, and always ready to adopt new methods. In 1824 he married Sarah Groome Brown, widow of his brother John, by whom he had four children—Ellen, Samuel N., Charles R., and Caroline. Mr. Brown died at the age of ninety-four years."

James Findlay Schenck, on May 4, 1822, when but fifteen years old, started for West Point, on horseback, was admitted as a cadet, and remained two years. In March, 1825, on receiving the appointment of midshipman in the United States Navy, he traveled first to Washington, District of Columbia, and then to Norfolk, Virginia, on horseback, where he was ordered on duty on the sloop of war *Hornet*. In 1864 he was promoted to the rank of commodore, given command of the *Powhatan*, at Hampton Roads, and assigned to the Third Division of Admiral Porter's fleet. On September 23, 1868, he was promoted to the rank of rear-admiral, and in 1869, at the age of sixty-two years, was placed on the retired list.

In 1829, while on short leave of absence, Admiral Schenck married Dolly Smith, of Smithtown, Long Island, and in 1836 bought a home in Dayton, at the corner of First and Wilkinson streets, where his family afterwards resided, and there he died December 21, 1882. His wife died September 7, 1876. They had four children: Sarah, the widow of Captain Crane; Jane Findley, who married Hon. A. Barr Irwin, of Kuttawa, Kentucky; Casper, pay inspector in the United States Navy; and Woodhull, an officer in the Imperial Maritime Customs of China, who died in California on his way home on furlough in 1880.

Robert C. Schenck graduated in 1827 at Miami University and in 1830 received the degree of Master of Arts. He then entered the law office of Hon. Thomas Corwin, of Lebanon, Ohio, was admitted to the bar the following year, and came to Dayton. He formed a partnership with Judge Joseph H. Crane, then with Peter Odlin, and from 1844 to 1850 with Wilbur Conover, under the firm name of Schenck & Conover. In 1840 Mr. Schenck represented this county in the State Legislature, and in 1843 was elected to Congress, holding his seat until 1850, when he declined renomination. In 1851 he was appointed by President Fillmore United States Minister to Brazil.

When the Civil War broke out he was first commissioned brigadier-general, and later major-general. In the second battle of Bull Run he received a wound, permanently injuring his right arm and hand. On the 5th of December, 1863, General Schenck retired from the army to again represent the Third Congressional District in Congress, and was made chairman of the military committee. In 1871 he was appointed United States Minister to Great Britain, serving until 1876, when he retired from public life, and made his home in Washington, District of Columbia.

General Schenck married Rennelche Smith. They had six daughters, of whom three are still living in Washington.

Dr. John Boyd Craighead, second son of Thomas and Rebecca Weakley Craighead, was born April 22, 1800, near

Carlisle, Cumberland County, Pennsylvania. On November 25, 1829, he married Mary Wallace Purdy, of Mansfield, Ohio, and in 1830 moved to Dayton, where, until his death, he occupied a foremost position in his profession. His wife died December 29, 1839, leaving two young sons— John P. Craighead, now of New York City, and William Craighead, of this city. In May, 1841, Dr. Craighead married Rebecca Dodds, of this city. Joseph Boyd Craighead, of Richmond, Indiana, and Mrs. Mary E. Soper, of Chicago, Illinois, are the surviving children of this marriage. Dr. Craighead was a devoted member of the First Presbyterian Church of Dayton. He died December 8, 1868, and Mrs. Craighead, who survived him, died August 28, 1884.

Daniel W. Iddings, a clerk in Robert A. Edgar's store in 1833, graduated at Oxford, Ohio, in 1842, and was admitted to the bar in 1846. He was Mayor of the city from 1856 to 1858, president of the Council for ten years, and registrar of bankruptcy from 1867 until the law was repealed. Mr. Iddings married Maria Atkins, daughter of William Atkins. They had two sons, who, with Mrs. Iddings, are still living in Dayton. Mr. Iddings died in 1883.

Joseph Barnett, born in West Hanover Township, Dauphin County, Pennsylvania, in 1779, on April 8, 1813, married Elizabeth Allen, daughter of Colonel William Allen. They moved to Dayton in 1832, and on July 31 purchased of William King one hundred acres of land at thirty dollars per acre. The present boundaries of this purchase would be not far from Third Street on the north, Germantown Street on the south, Broadway on the east, and Euclid Avenue on the west. Mr. Barnett erected a brick house near the center of his land (now the northeast corner of Home Avenue and Summit Street), and after the Eaton pike was built (Third Street) made a road to it, which is now Summit Street. Mrs. Barnett died October 16, 1837, and on April 9, 1839, Mr. Barnett married Jane Carr Rogers, daughter of Robert Rogers, of Springfield, Ohio.

Mr. Barnett took an active part in the Presidential campaign of General William H. Harrison in 1840, and was one of the marshals to escort Harrison's party into town from the Harshman residence, where they had passed the night. At that time Mr. Barnett literally kept open house. The table was loaded with provisions, china, and silver; the house, barn, and corncrib were left open for any to enter and help themselves, while the family came to town to take part in the general festivities of the day. Mr. Barnett said that, to his knowledge, nothing was lost, stolen, or destroyed.

Mr. Barnett was greatly interested in all public improvements, particularly the turnpikes and later the railroads, was a member of the Ohio Senate from this district for two terms, and a member of the constitutional convention in 1849. He and his wife were devoted members of the First Presbyterian Church, and enthusiastic members of the colony that organized what is now Park Presbyterian Church. Mr. Barnett headed the subscription list for the first building on East Second Street with six thousand dollars. When it was decided to change the location to west of the canal, he purchased the site of the present church edifice of Horatio G. Phillips for four thousand dollars cash, had the deed made to the trustees of the church, and to provide against debt on the new building left the church two thousand five hundred dollars in his will. Mr. Barnett died January 2, 1858. His wife survived him, making her home with her sister, Mrs. Effie A. Edgar, where she died November 4, 1871.

Hezekiah Loomis was born in Tolland County, Connecticut, May 21, 1779. In 1808 he joined the navy, and was on board the *Vixen* with Commodore James Decatur at the battle of Tripoli. On his return home, he named his son, born in Dauphin County, Pennsylvania, in 1807, James Decatur. After retiring from the navy, Mr. Loomis came to Dayton to make his home with his sons, and died here on August 18, 1862. James Decatur Loomis came to Dayton with Joseph Barnett in 1832, was first in partnership with Mr. Barnett, and later with William Barnett and William Pritz. On November 13, 1834, he married Isabella McQuead. Mr. Loomis died April 15, 1879. Mrs. Loomis died December 21, 1893, in her eightieth year, leaving three daughters—Misses Hannah and Annie, who reside in the family homestead, and Mrs. Warren Munger.

Peter Post Conover, in 1832, when thirteen years of age, came to Dayton from New Brunswick, New Jersey, learned the carriage trade in Samuel Dolley's shop, and continued to do business at the same place until he retired, in 1875. He married one of Mr. Dolley's daughters, and bought a lot on the corner of Maple and Perry streets for seventy-five dollars, where he built his home, still in the possession of his children. Mr. Conover's two sons, Samuel Dolley and Adams Jewett, are in business in the city.

Peter Odlin came here in 1832, and was first in partnership with Hon. Robert C. Schenck, and afterwards with John G. Lowe. In 1861 he was elected a member of the Legislature, was chairman of the Finance Committee until the close of the Rebellion, and in 1869 was elected Senator. He was a delegate to the Philadelphia Convention which nominated General Taylor, and also on the electoral ticket for Fremont. He was president of the Dayton branch of the State Bank from 1845, and after its organization as the Dayton National Bank, until his death. While in the Legislature Mr. Odlin was the author of several bills which became laws, among them the one allowing soldiers on the field to vote, and the law prohibiting the sale of liquor in Dayton on election days. In 1821 Mr. Odlin married Anna M. Ross. She died in 1872. Mr. Odlin continued the practice of his profession up to the time of his death, October 21, 1877, in his eightieth year, having made a strong and able speech in court but a month before.

Eliam E. Barney came to Dayton in 1834 as principal of the academy, and on October 10, 1834, married Julia Smith, of Galway, New York. In 1840, owing to poor health, he gave up teaching, and bought a sawmill from Ebenezer Thresher, on the corner of Wayne Street and the canal. When the Cooper Female Seminary was completed, at the request of the trustees he took charge of it. In the summer of 1849 Ebenezer Thresher and Mr. Barney started the Car Works. In 1854 Mr. Thresher sold his interest to Caleb Parker, who had recently moved to Dayton from Boston, and the business was continued under the name of Barney, Parker & Company until 1864, when Mr. Parker sold his interest to Preserved Smith, and the firm name was changed to Barney, Smith & Company. The business was conducted by this firm until 1867, when a joint stock company was formed as the Barney & Smith Manufacturing Company, of which Mr. Barney was president until his death. Mr. Barney was also vice-president of the Second National Bank, director of the Wisconsin Central Railroad, and president of the Cooper Hydraulic Company. He was a prominent member of the First Baptist Church, and assisted largely in placing it on a firm basis. Mr. Barney died December 17, 1880. His wife survived him many years. They had six children, of whom five are still living—Eugene

J. Barney, Mrs. Agnes Barney Platt, Mrs. Mary Barney Platt, Albert Barney, and Edward E. Barney.

Augustin King married Mary Webb in Troy, New York, in 1811. In 1834 he located in Dayton, and, with Colonel James Greer, organized the manufacturing firm of Greer & King, so well known in Dayton for over fifty years. His wife, Mary King, died in 1843. He died in 1856. Their children were Caroline (Mrs. James Greer), Edward A., and Rufus J., who alone survives.

Colonel Edward A. King, born in Cambridge, New York, in 1814, was appointed postmaster of Dayton by President Pierce, in which position he was retained by President Buchanan. He served in the war for Texan independence, in the Mexican War, and in the Rebellion, and was killed while in command of a brigade at the battle of Chickamauga.

James Greer, born in Westmoreland County, Pennsylvania, on December 21, 1807, came west and first settled in Columbus, Ohio, where, on August 7, 1828, he married Caroline E. King. In 1834 he came to Dayton and engaged in stove manufacturing with Augustin King, and for many years prior to his death, which occurred very suddenly on February 13, 1873, was associated in the same business with his brother-in-law, Rufus J. King. He was a public-spirited citizen, a liberal-minded man, prominent in business circles and society. An enthusiastic geologist, he collected a fine museum, which is now a part of the permanent exhibit in the Public Library building. He was a member of the Academy of Natural Sciences at Philadelphia, and wrote many papers for geological and archæological societies. He was an original member of the Third Street Presbyterian Church of this city. Colonel Greer had three children: Admiral James A. Greer, who, at the time of his retirement, was senior officer of the United States Navy; Mrs. Thomas J. Wood, of this city; and Horace Greer, who died in 1872.

Christopher Thompson came to Dayton, with his family, from Manchester, England, and in 1836 started a foundry on the Cooper Hydraulic, and afterwards formed a partnership with McGregor & Callahan. It was always said that no man could make a casting equal to Mr. Thompson. His son, Ralph Langton Thompson, in 1848 married Mary Jane Davis, the daughter of Owen Davis, and granddaughter of Thomas Davis, one of the original nineteen settlers. In 1853 they moved to Terre Haute, where Mr. Thompson went into the milling business. He died in 1881, and Mrs. Thompson and her daughter, now Mrs. Fred Beaver, returned to Dayton. Mrs. Thompson died here in 1891.

Frederick Gebhart in 1838 came to Dayton from Pennsylvania, with his wife and children, and purchased a lot on Third Street, just east of Main, from John W. Van Cleve for five thousand dollars. Here he erected a three-story brick building, which he occupied for many years as a dry-goods store. He had nine children, the two youngest of whom were born in Dayton,—Alexander, John, Josiah, Mrs. Joseph Newcomer, Mrs. Isaac Haas, Mrs. H. L. Pope, Mrs. Cahill, Walter, and Annie. All are living except John and Mrs. Cahill.

Hiram Wyatt, a baker by trade, came to Dayton in April, 1834, and opened a bakery on East Third Street. On January 22, 1835, he married Elizabeth Elder. They had two children—a son and a daughter. His wife died in 1838, and on February 21, 1839, he married Mary C. Davis, of Zanesville. Mr. Wyatt died in December, 1893. They had five children, three of whom are still living. There are few as well known in Dayton as Mrs. Wyatt.

John H. Achey, born in Lebanon, Pennsylvania, September 2, 1802, came to Dayton in 1838, and in 1843, in partnership with James H. Brooks, started the first lumber yard in Dayton. Their pine lumber was brought down the Ohio River on rafts from Pittsburg, then up the canal, and was thoroughly water-soaked, but after the water evaporated there was no further trouble. In 1849 he was a director of the Dayton branch of the State Bank, a member of the State Board of Control, and in 1865 assisted in organizing the Dayton National Bank, being until his death its president. He was a leading member of the Methodist Church, and a Knight Templar for over twenty years. In October, 1829, he married Mary Rife, of Middletown, Dauphin County, Pennsylvania, and had three children, of whom only one, Mrs. Juana Neal, of California, is still living.

David Laymon, born in Lancaster County, Pennsylvania, January 13, 1807, in the autumn of 1838 came to Dayton in a one-horse wagon, with his wife, two children, and all the household goods. In 1843 Mr. Laymon united with the First Lutheran Church, then located on the corner of Fourth and Jefferson streets. In 1856 he removed his family to Liberty, Indiana, where he resided at the time of his wife's death, January 1, 1881, when he returned to Dayton and made his home jointly with his two daughters, Mrs. William Altick and Mrs. Charles H. Jarrell, who, with an only son, David Laymon, survive him.

William Hoff, who settled in Miamisburg in 1838, was well known among Dayton merchants, with whom he did a large business, and was respected throughout the community for his honesty and integrity. He died in February, 1872, leaving two daughters—Mrs. Hoover, of Miamisburg, and Mrs. George A. Black, of Dayton.

Francis Ohmer was born in Lorain, France, in 1796, married Margaret Floquet in 1822, and in November, 1831, sailed, with his family, for the United States, reaching New York City in January, 1832, and in 1837 came to Dayton, where Mr. Ohmer worked at his trade as a tailor. They had eight children, of whom five sons, Nicholas, Michael, Peter, Augustus, and George, and one daughter, Mrs. Stewart, still live in Dayton. One daughter, Mrs. Sage died, and another daughter, Mrs. Kemper, lives in Philadelphia.

William Dickey was born August 10, 1805, near Middletown, Ohio. His mother, a native of Pennsylvania, was a second cousin of George Washington. In 1839 Mr. Dickey came to Dayton and engaged in the manufacture of brick, contracting on the Miami and Erie Canal, and, associated with his brother, Robert R., quarried limestone. They also owned a line of packets between Cincinnati and Toledo, and Toledo and Terre Haute, Indiana. In 1850 Mr. Dickey, in connection with Joseph Clegg and Daniel Beckel, started a private bank. He was one of the organizers of the Miami County Bank, one of the incorporators of the Dayton Gas Light and Coke Company, and president for many years. Mr. Dickey was influential in organizing the Ohio Insurance Company in 1865, and was president of that company until his death. He died July 15, 1880. His only son, Samuel, died the following year, on August 9. Mrs. Dickey and their two daughters, Mrs. H. C. Graves, of Dayton, and Mrs. Charles B. Oglesby, of Middletown, Ohio, are still living.

Horace Pease was born in Suffield, Connecticut, February 14, 1791, and in 1827 settled in Carrollton, going into partnership with his brother Perry in a small distillery to make wine from apples and peaches. In 1839 they built a flour-mill on East Third Street, now occupied by Joseph

R. Gebhart & Son, and Horace moved to Dayton to take charge of it. In 1852 the partnership was dissolved, Horace taking the Dayton property. Mr. Pease was sent to the State Legislature in 1834, and was one of the board of county commissioners when the old Court-house was built. In 1821 he married Ann Stiltz, of Baltimore, Maryland. She died in 1829, leaving four children, and in 1832 Mr. Pease married Sarah Belville, of New Castle, Delaware. They had seven children. In 1849 Mr. Pease started the Buckeye Iron and Brass Works, of which his son, Charles E. Pease, is now president, it having been incorporated in 1875. Walter Pease was an officer during the Civil War, and Webster Pease invented a machine for cutting chewing tobacco. Mrs. James Stockstill, Mrs. Horace Phillips, and C. E. Pease are the only children living. Mrs. Pease died in 1862, and Mr. Pease died July 29, 1875.

William Clark, born in Dedham, Massachusetts, January 18, 1805, at the age of sixteen learned the millwright and machinist's trade, and located in Dayton in 1839. Here he engaged in the manufacture of paper for thirty or more years, and was successively in partnership with Amos Stephens, B. F. Ells, L. F. Claflin, and C. L. Hawes. I believe he was the first to manufacture the heavy strawboard now generally used for boxes, book backs, etc. Mr. Clark left two daughters, who are still living.

Beniah Tharp, among the first to make brick here, had his brickyard on Brown Street. He first married a cousin of John W. Van Cleve, and after her death married the sister of Jacob Sturr, on the Brandt pike. Mrs. Tharp and her sister, Mrs. Conrad, are still living in Dayton.

Jacob Sturr came here in 1830, and bought a farm about six miles north of town on the Brandt pike, where he lived until his death in 1853.

DAYTON TO 1840—CONTINUED

Thomas Mathison came to Dayton in 1839, and bought a half acre of land on West Third Street, with a cabin, which is still standing, on it. Mr. Mathison died some years ago. Mrs. Mathison is still living in the old house.

Miss Maria Boyd came to Dayton from Philadelphia, and established a milliner store in the old Colonel Reid building, on Main Street, in 1839. She was the fashionable milliner of that time. Being a sincere Christian, a member of the First Presbyterian Church, and believing Revelation 14:13, she devoted her days to ministering to the sick, the poor, and the needy. Her good deeds and Christian character should long be remembered by the people of Dayton. She died April 2, 1879. Psalm 37:37.

In the winter of 1828-29 the charter of the town was amended so the Mayor was to be elected, instead of being chosen by the Select Council.

In 1828 seventy new buildings were erected, and in 1829 ninety-nine, and the town divided into five wards.

In 1830 a looking-glass factory and a horn-comb factory were started, and on August 7, 1832, the comb factory advertised that they would pay cash for "horns and cattle tails." Jesse Boogher has a pocket comb made by his brother Gideon and himself on Main Street in 1832.

In 1830 Council, at a special meeting, granted a free license, and the Methodists gave their meeting-house, around the interior of which a track was laid, for the exhibition of "a locomotive engine and railway," and for a small fee those who wished might ride. In July, 1831, a second locomotive, or "steam carriage," was exhibited at Machir & Hardcastle's warehouse near the basin.

In 1830 Morris Seely purchased a large quantity of land, commencing at Third Street, running south, and began, where the Peirce & Coleman planing-mill now stands, to dig a canal parallel with Wayne Avenue to Fifth Street, east on Fifth to P. E. Gilbert's planing-mill, thence south and west, making many elbows and turns for basins, until it crossed the junction of Brown and Warren streets, then west to the main canal. As the money gave out, the canal project failed, and lots on Fifth and Wayne streets sold at public sale for from five to thirty dollars. A. M. Peasley established a pleasure garden on the west side of Warren Street, thinking parties would come down the canal for pleasure and refreshments; but it was not a success, and was finally abandoned.

Philip Keifer, a carpenter, still living in Dayton at the age of ninety-five years, wrote me the following:

"In a still search and long hunt to gather up some of the history and happenings of Dayton: The first three-story block of business rooms built in Dayton was in 1832, on the ground where the Eaker Block now stands, the corner room occupied by Billy Eaker as a dry-goods store, the room on the north, front on Main Street, occupied by Luther Bruen as a store. In 1842 a three-story block was built by J. Harshman on the ground now occupied by the Callahan Bank Building. The brick work was done by Thomas Brown and John Weber, and the carpenter work was done by P. Keifer & Shepperd. The old Court-house was built between 1847 and 1849. The contract was awarded to a man by the name of Cary at his bid of sixty thousand dollars, but in the course of its erection many changes were made, which destroyed the contract. The commissioners refused to pay his bill, and he sued the county. The case was tried in court at Troy, Miami County, and he got a judgment of nearly double the amount. About the year 1837 a stone dealer named Gillmore built a wooden railroad from the west end of his stone quarry down a ravine a little west of Cox's old tavern, gaining the Xenia turnpike where the Pan-Handle Railroad bridge crosses the pike, and along said pike to Third Street; there by a turntable it was turned at near a right angle onto another track, a bee line to his depot, located on the ground now occupied by the Stoddard manufactory. His depot was built up with rocks, more with regard to quantity than elegance. In 1841 he built the Montgomery House, and soon after the flat at the lower end of Ludlow Street, known as the 'Seven Smokes.' In 1844, at the time of the Millerite excitement, they had set the day for the consummation of all terrestrial things. In the latter part of the night of the same day the Lowry still-house burned down. It happened during a heavy snow storm, and each flake of snow reflected the light, that lit up the skies as bright as the full moon would on a clear night. Some of the more timid were badly frightened."

On the opening of the canal Alexander Swaynie established a tavern and wagon-yard on the ground now occupied by the Pinneo & Daniels shops. The wagon-yard was full of teams almost every night, and the frame house crowded, the men thinking themselves fortunate when, having brought their own blankets, they could find a space on the floor. Mr. Swaynie made money rapidly, and in 1838 or 1839 erected a three-story brick building on the site of his first frame. It was fitted throughout with carpets of Dayton manufacture, and was always a first-class hotel.

The National Hotel, on Third Street, the leading hotel of the town, was opened in 1828 by Timothy Squier. In 1848 the name was changed to the Voorhees House, and ten years later to the Phœnix Hotel. The original entrance is now the Third Street entrance to the Beckel House.

In 1837 Calvin Francisco came here and started a pottery in the old still-house of Abram Darst. His son John, a fence maker, is still living in Dayton.

Cholera was first brought to Dayton in 1832 by German emigrants on the canal, of whom a number and the two nurses employed by the town died. In 1833 there were thirty-three fatal cases, and in 1849 there were over two hundred deaths. A board of health was appointed by Council in 1832, but it was not until 1835 that an ordinance was passed requiring malignant diseases to be reported to the Mayor, and in 1849 the cholera hospital was first established.

In February, 1832, during high water, the middle pier of the Bridge Street bridge was washed out and Steele's Dam injured. The suffering in Cincinnati was so great that the citizens of Dayton subscribed $202 "to aid in relieving the distressed people of that city."

In 1836 David Zeigler Cooper executed a deed to the city releasing his reversionary interest in lots 94, 95, and 96, with the understanding that they should be leased and the income used in improving the common, enclosing it, and keeping it as "a walk" for the "citizens of Dayton and its visitors." In April Council desired to negotiate a loan of from one to ten thousand dollars, with which to extend the market-house to Jefferson Street, grade streets, improve the common, etc., and although some objected that the improvements were more for ornament than use, and the taxes would be increased, the loan was authorized and Council recommended to use one-tenth of the money expended in filling Seely's ditch.

Wild-cat currency at this time was the only money, and small coin being scarce, any one having credit could issue their promise to pay, on demand, shinplasters in sums of from six and one-quarter to fifty cents. Thomas Morrison, who issued a great number of these shinplasters, stated in the *Journal*, in 1838, that he had to leave town to complete a contract, much to his regret, as the law prohibiting the circulation of shinplasters was soon to take effect, but that on his return he would pay all, which he did. The cuts are from two of his shinplasters. The Dayton Bank at this time was the only bank in the country that redeemed its notes with specie.

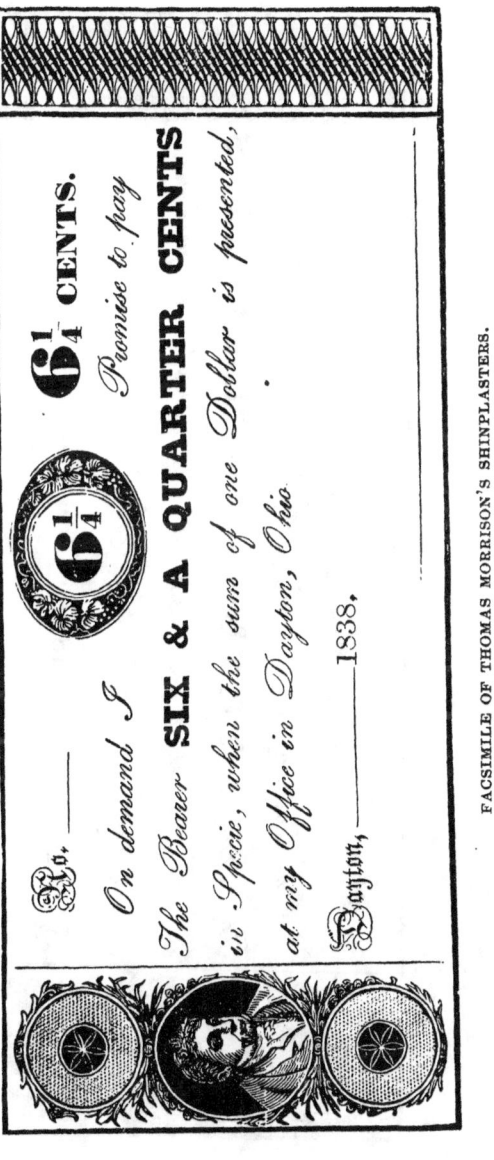

FACSIMILE OF THOMAS MORRISON'S SHINPLASTERS.

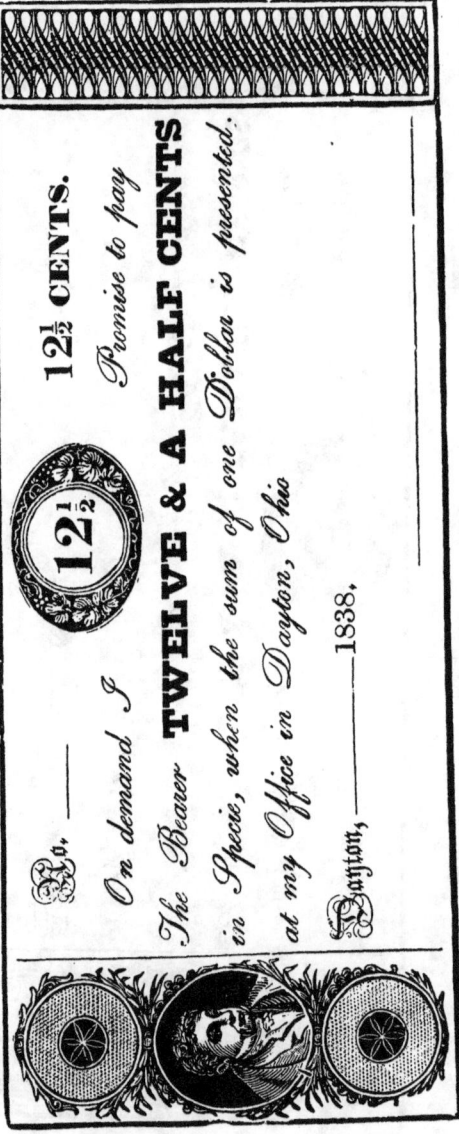

FACSIMILE OF THOMAS MORRISON'S SHINPLASTERS.

DAYTON TO 1840—CONTINUED

In the spring of 1836 the Dayton Philharmonic Society was organized, with Stephen Fry teacher, and C. Hayden secretary, to study sacred music, and on September 11, 1838, the Montgomery County Agricultural Society was organized. The first fair was held in Dayton in October, 1839, at Swaynie's Hotel.

The first colored person in Dayton was Mrs. Daniel C. Cooper's maid. The next, that I remember, was Pompey, the sexton of the First Presbyterian Church; then Joe Crowder; Joe Piner and his wife, Auntie Nett; Tom Jeff and his wife, Eliza; Joseph Wheeler, Catharine Sills, and Madison Penn. Madison Penn lived on my father's farm, and worked for him, I think, as early as 1828. He afterwards came to town and became a whitewasher, an important trade in those days. At one time he was a director of the workhouse.

Joseph Wheeler, born in Halifax County, Virginia, in January, 1800, came to Dayton in 1824, and in June, 1830, married Catharine Sills, then only fourteen years old. They had eight sons and four daughters, of whom five are still living. Mr. Wheeler died February 17, 1871. After his death Catharine, who was born in Frederick County, Maryland, in 1816, married Madison Penn. She is now the oldest colored resident of Dayton, having come here in 1820.

In 1841 a young girl, so light in color that many thought her white, came to make her home with her people, in the vicinity of Wayne, Fifth, and Eagle streets. A mob formed among the lower classes, and in February, when the thermometer was below zero, drove the colored people out of their cabins, pulling down and burning many of the houses. The owner of one of the cabins stabbed the leader of the mob, Nat McCleary, and killed him. There was great suffering from the exposure. Many died and others left town.

When the National Road was surveyed from Cumberland, Maryland, to St. Louis, the straight line took the road about eight miles north of here. Great efforts were made to have it built through town, and Joseph Barnett and Morris Seely were sent to Washington to see if the route could not be changed. The principal objection raised by the Springfield delegation, that the road would not then be a *straight line*, carried weight, and their effort was not successful. The citizens of Dayton, and those on the road between Dayton and Springfield, then formed the Dayton and Springfield Turnpike Company, and subscribed sufficient money to build a turnpike from Dayton to tap the National Road just this side of the corporation of Springfield. Jonathan Harshman, Joseph Barnett, John Kniesly, Charles Hagenbaugh, Valentine Winters, and Peter Aughenbaugh were the board of directors, Mr. Harshman president, Joseph Barnett secretary, Valentine Winters treasurer, and John F. Edgar collector. The books were opened for subscriptions on January 19, 1838, and the contract let May 12. This road was subsequently connected with the National Road at Richmond, by the Dayton and Western Turnpike Company.

The Legislature on March 24, 1836, passed an act authorizing a loan of credit by the State of Ohio to the capital stock of railroad, turnpike, canal, and slack-water companies. Dayton at once availed itself of the provisions of this act, and had five turnpikes well under way, in all about a hundred and forty miles, before the law was repealed in 1840.

In 1838 Alexander Grimes and Edward W. Davies, trustees of David Zeigler Cooper's estate, built a dam just west of the aqueduct, crossing Mad River, and diverted the water into a bayou running north of the old bed from that point to the Miami. When they and the city built the levee, it made a permanent embankment on the south side, and all the land north of First Street, including Bimm's ice park and the Car Shops, down to the present mouth of Mad River, was reclaimed and made available for city lots. The trustees also extended the basin to join the main canal east of the Car Works property, thus making it the main canal. While the soldiers were encamped here in 1812, Mr. Cooper employed some of them to dig the sawmill race, which started from the old race at the north end of Foundry Street. In 1838 this race was abandoned, and Messrs. Grimes and Davies built the Cooper Hydraulic—seven hundred feet long and fifty feet wide, with a fall of twelve feet into the canal. It was fed from the main canal, now the feeder, just north of the lock at Fifth Street, and was to furnish power to all the mills, factories, and shops from Third to Fifth, including the Buckeye Iron and Brass Works, the Pease Flour Mill (Joseph R. Gebhart & Son), and Pritz's Agricultural Works (Sachs & Pruden Brewery). The water-power for the Curtis Woolen Factory (Durst Mills), the Gun-barrel Factory (Osceola Mill), Cooper Cotton Factory, and the old carpet factory (Kratochwill Mill) was taken from the feeder above the lock on the opposite side, and conveyed under Fifth Street, and emptied into the main canal over the wheels of these mills between Fifth and Sixth streets. Joel Holden had a clock factory at the foot of Ludlow Street, where he manufactured twenty-five hundred clocks annually. The factory was run by power from the canal.

Samuel Steele in 1830 built a dam across the Miami south of Stillwater (now known as Steele's Dam), and cut a race through Riverdale to the Miami at Forest Avenue (now the Dayton View Hydraulic). It furnishes power to

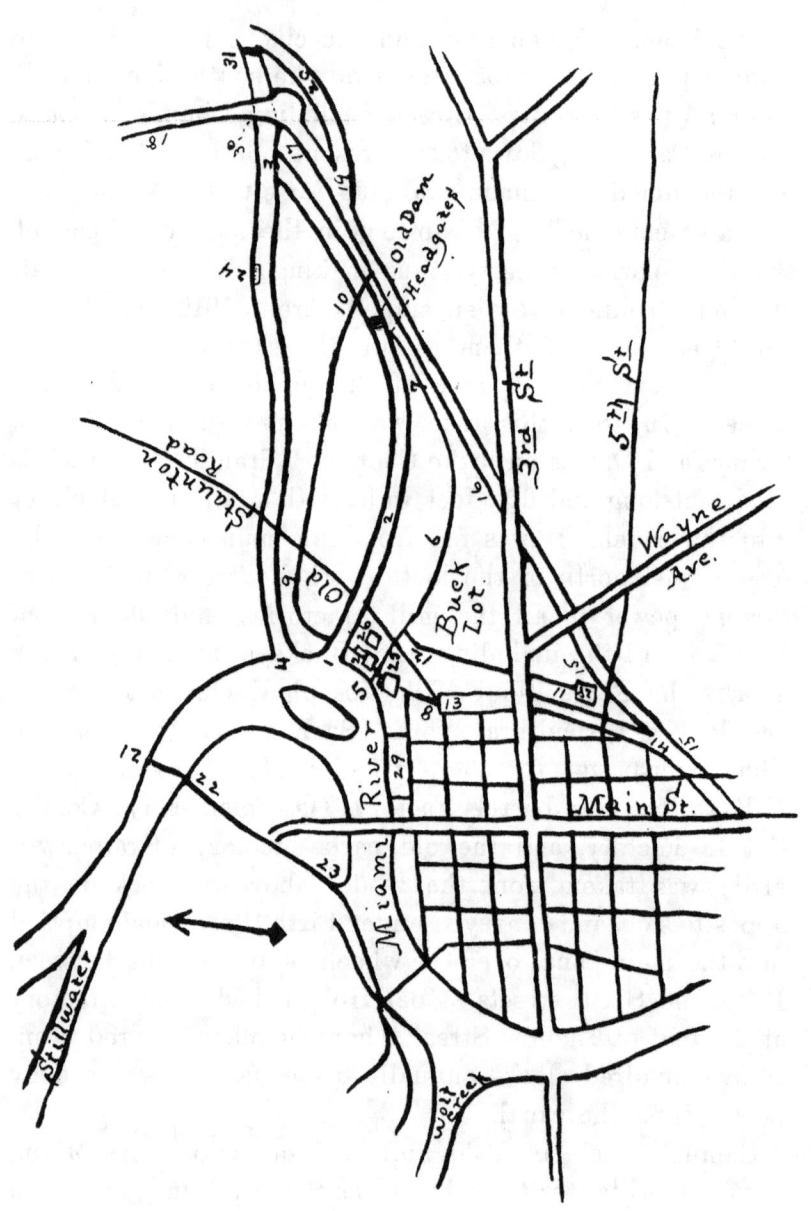

the Stilwell-Bierce Manufacturing Company, A. A. Simonds' edge-tool works, and the Electric Light Company.

The accompanying map shows the old bed of Mad River, 1, 2, and 3; the new bed, 4 and 3; the old race, 5, 6, and 7; the extension of the canal basin, 8, 9, and 10; the race dug during 1812, 11 and 12; the basin from First to Sixth streets, 13 and 14; the old main canal, 15, 16, 17, and 18; old feeder, 19 and 20; Steele's Dam, 21; Dayton View Hydraulic, 22 and 23; Edgar cabin in 1798, 24; fulling-mill, 26; grist-mill and sawmill that burned in 1820, 25 and 27; sawmill built in 1813, 28; Van Cleve Park, 29; aqueduct, 30; State dam, 31.

There are three locks within the territory shown on the map, one at the aqueduct, one at the Car Works, and one at Fifth Street, with a total fall of about twenty-four feet.

On January 5, 1832, the Ohio Legislature passed an act incorporating the Mad River & Lake Erie Railroad Company, authorizing the construction of a road from Dayton, through Springfield, to Sandusky. Books were opened and a large subscription made, but in some way the books were lost or destroyed. A road was then built from Xenia to Cincinnati, and afterwards extended to Springfield, which gave a line by rail from Lake Erie to the Ohio River. Dayton felt this blow for many years. Subsequently the Legislature passed other acts favoring the Mad River & Lake Erie Road, and on February 6, 1847, authorized Springfield to subscribe twenty thousand dollars to the stock of the company, to be applied on the line between Dayton and Springfield. The citizens of Dayton and people living on the route to the first crossing of Mad River, with one man in Springfield, subscribed one hundred and fifty thousand dollars. The contract for the construction of the road-bed was let in the winter of 1848-49 to Andrew DeGraff, and for laying the rails to Harris & Nichols, the first "T" rails laid here. I was employed to superintend that work, and as agent to open an office in Dayton under Superintendent E. F. Osborn. The last rail was laid January 25, 1851. Two days later an excursion passed over the road from Springfield to Dayton, and the next day (January 25) trains began running on regular schedule. During this time the Cincinnati, Hamilton & Dayton Road, the Greenville & Miami, and the Dayton & Western were being constructed. The board of directors of the Mad River & Lake Erie Road having received a grant of seven acres from the David Zeigler Cooper estate lying between Cooper Street and Monument Avenue and east of the canal for depots, authorized me to offer the Cincinnati, Hamilton & Dayton Road thirty thousand dollars to run their road up the west and north bank of the Great Miami River, build their bridge at the junction of Mill and Water streets, and have the union passenger depot at Main Street, where any quantity of ground could be purchased cheap, using the seven acres for freight business. This arrangement would have accommodated the Dayton & Western and the Greenville & Miami, as can be seen by a map of this county, but influence in the southern part of the town secured the depot at Ludlow and Sixth streets.

The first locomotive in Dayton was the "Seneca," belonging to the Mad River & Lake Erie Company. It was run from Sandusky City to Xenia, there taken apart by John Hays and wagoned to Dayton, and set up on the track at the crossing of Webster Street. Boys carried water from neighboring pumps to fill the boiler, the engineer, John Hays, fired up and raised steam, and the writer pulled the cord and blew the first locomotive whistle ever heard in Dayton. How the boys did run, thinking the boiler had exploded. The *Journal* of June 5, 1896, reports that John Hays, the engineer of the "Seneca," was killed during the recent storm at St. Louis.

The growth of Dayton was first materially affected by the construction of the canal, then the turnpikes and the railroads. On April 1, 1796, the census showed in Dayton eight men, three women, four girls, and one baby boy (Dayton Hamer) — in all, sixteen; 1896, seventy-nine thousand three hundred and thirty-one.

When I look back and remember how it used to be in my boyhood days, when the time made by canal-boats and stages was considered *fast*, our only light the tallow dip and lard oil, and stop to realize the life of to-day, with steam and electricity; when I think of the first daguerreotypes taken in Dayton in 1848, and then read in the papers of the wonderful X-ray photography, — all these changes and discoveries, and many more, within the span of one short life, — the power of astonishment is almost exhausted. It is impossible for the present generation to conceive of the wonder and amazement created by the sight of the first locomotive, and the feeling of awe on receiving the first telegram.

CHAPTER IX.

CHURCHES, SCHOOLS, AND LIBRARIES.

IN the spring of 1798 John Patterson, a brother of Colonel Robert Patterson, from Kentucky, settled on Beaver Creek on the southeast quarter of Section 14, Van Buren Township, where he built a cabin and raised a crop of corn, and the next spring brought his family to their new home. Afterwards John Huston, a single man (brother of Judge David Huston, of Greene County), John Buchanan, with his family, James and Peggy Milligan, and William and Sally Stewart, all Kentucky Presbyterians, settled in the Beaver Creek neighborhood and organized a church, calling it Beulah. About 1800 a log cabin was built by the Presbyterians and New Lights in common, near the Ewery graveyard, and the Rev. William Robinson preached there frequently. In June, 1803, a camp-meeting was held in the woods around the meeting-house, under the direction of Robert Marshall, Richard McNamer, and John Thompson, of Kentucky, and James Kemper, of Cincinnati, all Presbyterian ministers. A discussion arose which resulted in the withdrawal of Mr. Kemper and a part of the Presbyterians, some of whom, among them Judge David Huston, came to worship with the Dayton church. Part of those who remained formed the New Light church at Beavertown, and John and Phœbe Patterson, John Huston, Peggy Buchanan, William and Sally Stewart, James and Betsy Milligan, Katy Stewart (John Patterson's sister), and John Southard formed the society of Shakers. John Stewart was elected the first elder. In March, 1806, two elders came to Dayton from the Lebanon, Ohio, village of Shakers and completed the organization, naming this society "Watervliet." At first they did not own property in common and some of the people lived in Dayton. They were frequently ordered through the papers to leave. In May, 1811, they were mobbed, and on August 27 a deed is recorded by John and Phœbe Patterson, witnessed by Benjamin Van Cleve, conveying their farm of one hundred and sixty acres to the Shakers. They now own a valuable farm of over three hundred acres. Within the last few years many of the members have died, and there being few, if any, additions from the outside world, they are now cared for by members sent from a society in New York State.

As the settlers of Dayton were religiously disposed and well-educated people, mostly Presbyterians and Methodists, the churches and schools from the outset occupied an important place in their minds. At that time there was no Home Missionary Society, and the early churches in Dayton were self-sustaining from the first.

The Presbyterians, who had the first organization, held their services for the first three years of the settlement in the cabins of Presbyterian families, and in the fall and winter of 1799 held occasional services in the blockhouse. During the winter of 1799 Mr. Cooper gave them lots 133 and 134, at the northeast corner of Main and Third streets, where they built the first meeting-house in Dayton, eighteen by twenty feet, seven logs high, the floor being two feet from the ground, the roof held down by weight poles, with no windows, no way of heating the room, and for seats slabs from sawlogs. In the spring of 1804 James Welsh, who was also a physician, became the first pastor, and in October the earliest records of the church show that John Miller, Robert Edgar, David Reid, John McCabe, and John Ewing were elected the first board of trustees. During the fall $390 was raised by subscription to make the cabin more comfortable, but the congregation afterward decided to sell it for twenty-two dollars and loan the money ($412) to the county commissioners to be used in building a court-house, with the understanding that they could use the court-room for services. Until the Court-house was completed in 1806 they worshiped in the rooms rented by the county. On May 3, 1806, John McKaig, John Ritchie, and James Hanna were elected the first elders, and in 1807 John Miller and Robert Parks were elected. The church was incorporated in 1812, and the congregation legally organized on April 12 and elected D. C. Cooper, John Ewing, Andrew Hood, J. H. Williams, John Miller, James Hanna, and William King trustees, William McClure treasurer, David Reid clerk, and Matthew Patton collector. On June 15 the board resolved to raise funds to pay the preacher. As the lots donated by Mr. Cooper were found not suitable for a graveyard, Mr. Cooper donated four other lots—two to the Presbyterians, one to the Methodists, and one for general use—on Fifth Street, where all burials were made after 1805. In 1812 the congregation appointed a committee to see to clearing and improving the two Presbyterian lots, and to "call upon the leading characters of the different churches, and learn whether they would join in fencing the burying-ground." In October the committee reported "that the leading characters of the Methodist Church would join in fencing all the lot intended for the burying-ground, but there being no leading characters of the Baptist congregation, they had no report as to them."

With the consent of Mr. Cooper, the lots on the corner of Main and Third streets were subdivided, 133 into five lots facing on Main Street, and 134 into two lots facing on Third Street, with an eleven-foot alley between the two original lots. These lots were sold by auction to the highest bidder—number 1 to Charles Tull for five hundred dollars; numbers 2, 3, and 4 to Joseph Peirce for one thousand dollars; number 5 to Francis Patterson for one thousand dollars; number 6 to Benjamin Van Cleve for four hundred and sixty-five dollars, and number 7 to James Slaght for two hundred dollars. In 1813 a lot for the church was purchased of Mr. Cooper on the northwest corner of Second and Wilkinson streets for two hundred and fifty dollars, but, as some felt this was too far out of town, it was exchanged for the lot on the northwest corner of Second and Ludlow streets for two hundred and fifty dollars additional. In 1816 the money loaned the county was refunded, and in 1817 the first brick meeting-house was erected. During the winter of 1817-18 the first Sunday school was organized, with Mrs. Sarah Bomberger superintendent, which office she held for twelve years. In 1837 a new building, fifty by seventy feet, with basement, was erected. In 1838, before the completion of the building, Peter Odlin and Dr. John Steele, elders, with seventy-three of the members, withdrew and organized the New School, now the Third Street Presbyterian Church. In 1852 a colony of twenty-three organized what is now Park Presbyterian Church, and in 1856 another colony organized the Fourth Presbyterian Church, on Summit Street.

During all this time, however, the First Church continued to grow, and in 1867, during the pastorate of Rev. Dr. Thomas, the present stone edifice was erected, from a design which he prepared.

To the Methodist Church belonged the first minister in Dayton,—William Hamer,—who held services at his home as opportunity offered. On August 12, 1798, the Rev. John Kobler preached in Dayton and organized a class of eight members, William Hamer leader. After his last visit, on April 2, 1799, there is no record of services, except class-meetings, until September 22, 1811, when Bishop Asbury preached from the front of the Court-house to over a thousand people. The Rev. John Collins, who, in 1811, was appointed on the circuit, proposed to the society of twenty-four members that they build a meeting-house, and on December 26, Andrew Read, Thomas Smith, Henry Opdyche, William Cottingham, Thomas Cottom, and Aaron Baker were appointed trustees. When $457.55 was subscribed, Aaron Baker was appointed to make the collections. The church was incorporated in the winter of 1813-14, and Mr. Cooper gave the congregation lot 155, on the south side of East Third Street, near Main, now owned by Daniel Keifer. Their first building, a one-story frame, painted red, was erected in 1814. Before this their meetings had been held in the open air, the log cabin of the Presbyterians, and the Court-house. In 1818 two classes were formed, with Thomas Sullivan and Thomas Cottom leaders, and the Sunday school organized. The first camp-meeting was held in 1819, at the foot of Ludlow Street, where there was a large spring. In 1827 Lorenzo Dow, a noted man at that time, preached from one of the east windows of the church to a large crowd on the open common extending east as far as Jefferson Street. In 1828 a new meeting-house was erected, and in 1848 a brick church was erected on the same site, in the tower of which was placed the first town clock. The church was damaged in 1854 by the falling of the wall of a new building next west of it, but was repaired, rededicated, and used until the present Grace Methodist Episcopal

From "Early Dayton," by permission of the U. B. Publishing House.

GRACE METHODIST EPISCOPAL CHURCH.

FIRST COLORED M. E. CHURCH IN 1840.

CHURCHES, SCHOOLS, AND LIBRARIES   247

Church, on the corner of Fourth and Ludlow streets, was completed.

As early as 1806 a county record shows that an application was made and granted for the southeast corner of Third and Main streets for the "Baptist Union Congregation of Dayton," but there are no further records in regard to it and the property reverted to Mr. Cooper. The first council for the organization of the Baptist Church was held on May 29, 1824, on the porch of William Huffman's residence, and the church organized with nine members. The first Sunday after its organization Mrs. Lydia Huffman was baptized in the Miami River, at Main Street, the first baptism known to have occurred in Dayton. The first pastor was Rev. D. S. Burnett, who, in 1829, became excited over the doctrines of Alexander Campbell, and formed the Campbellite church. Andrew Clark, Lydia Huffman, Daniel Kiser and wife, Moses Stout, Elizabeth Crowell, Elizabeth Bowen, and Rachel Bradford were dismissed because they held to the old doctrines. This little band kept together, and formed the nucleus of the present First Baptist congregation.

May 15, 1817, the Rev. Philander Chase preached in Dayton, and the Parochial Association of St. Thomas was formed. The papers were signed by Blakewell Stephens, George Grove, Ally Grove, William M. Smith, Betsy Smith, John Collins, and Joseph H. Crane. The Association was not incorporated until 1835, before which time the name was changed to Christ Church. Their first building, on South Jefferson Street, was consecrated November 17, 1833, by Bishop McIlvane, on his first visit to this parish.

In 1828 nine persons met at the home of Father Bruen and organized a New Light society. They erected a building on Main Street, long known as the Union Meeting-house.

The congregation is now known as the Broadway Christian Church.

In 1833 the Rev. David Winters organized the German Reformed Church, with six members, Adam Artz and wife, Valentine Fryberger and wife, Mrs. David Winters, and Mrs. Valentine Winters. For many years the services were held alternately in German and English. Mr. Winters remained pastor of the church for twenty-seven years.

Almost from the time when the city was founded, United Brethren families were residing in Dayton and in the country adjacent. Bishop Newcomer preached in the town in 1810, and conducted a two days' meeting near by. The first congregation was not formed, however, till about 1835, when Bishop Joseph Hoffman moved to what is now Dayton View. It is not generally known that he built the house now occupied by Mr. J. O. Arnold, on Superior Avenue, and that he provided in his plan for two large rooms, with double doors between them, with a view to accommodating a large audience. He was a preacher of unusual power, and soon there was organized in his house a class of about forty-one members. He removed from Dayton about 1838, and the history of the congregation is not now known. However, in 1840 we have notice of a congregation in the city; it may have been the same or another congregation. Mrs. Mary Somers was a member of the first organization in 1835, and is still living in Dayton. She was born February 14, 1812, came here in 1832, and was baptized by Bishop Joseph Hoffman in the Miami River below Bridge Street about 1835. The first permanent organization, that of the First United Brethren Church, was made in 1847.

The United Brethren Publishing House was established in Circleville, Ohio, in 1834, and removed to Dayton in

1853, when its present location, then occupied by Strain's Hotel, was purchased for eleven thousand dollars.

In 1839, during a visit of the Rev. Reuben Weiser, the First English Lutheran Church was organized, and articles of agreement were signed, July 6, at a meeting in Frederick Gebhart's store.

The first Catholic priest in Dayton was Father E. T. Collins, who came here in 1832. In 1833 a congregation formed under Father Emanuel Thienpont, and Emanuel Church, a one-story brick building, on Franklin Street, was erected and dedicated in 1837. The parochial schools connected with this church were started in 1833.

The African Methodist Episcopal Church was organized in 1840, and a frame building erected on the northeast corner of Plum and McLain streets, dedicated by Bishop Paul Quinn. Occasional services were held as "ministers of the faith" visited the congregation, and Father Willis, a local preacher, did much good, but after the mob in 1841 the congregation disbanded. It was reorganized in 1868.

Of the many other church organizations in Dayton all are too young for a place in this little history of first beginnings. Dayton may well be called a city of churches.

The first school in Dayton was taught by Benjamin Van Cleve in the blockhouse during the winter of 1799–1800. The second was held in 1804, in a cabin on Main Street, by Cornelius Westfall, of Kentucky, and in 1805 by Chauncy Whiting, of Pennsylvania. In 1807 the Dayton Academy was incorporated by James Welsh, Daniel C. Cooper, William McClure, David Reid, Benjamin Van Cleve, George F. Tennery, John Folkerth, and James Hanna, Mr. Cooper donating two lots, numbers 139 and 140, to the trustees, at the corner of Third and St. Clair streets, on part of which a two-story brick house, with belfry, was built. Mr. Cooper, in addition to his other donations, gave the bell. The first teacher of the academy was William Smith. In 1815 he was succeeded by Gideon McMillen, a graduate of the University of Glasgow, who advertised that he would teach all poor children free of charge. In 1819-20 the trustees adopted the Lancasterian system of instruction and erected a long, one-story brick building just north of the Academy. It was heated by direct radiation, the floor being of brick, with flues running lengthwise under it. At one end of the building was an opening, like the arch in a brick kiln, in which the fire was made and kept up by pushing in long sticks of wood. The principle of the Lancasterian method was "mutual instruction," the pupil being placed on honor, and no examinations held. In 1822 Gideon McMillen was succeeded by Captain John McMullen, of Lexington, Virginia. The next principal was James H. Mitchell, a graduate of Yale College, who, after a fair trial of the Lancasterian method, discontinued it. In 1831 the trustees of the Academy, Aaron Baker, Dr. Job Haines, Obadiah B. Conover, James Steele, and John W. Van Cleve, sold the St. Clair Street property and bought lots 1 and 2 of the plat of Samuel Pierson on the southwest corner of Fourth and Wilkinson streets, where, in 1834, the school opened with E. E. Barney principal. In 1839 Mr. Barney resigned, and was succeeded by Collins Wight, and in 1844 he was succeeded by Milo G. Williams, of Cincinnati. The catalogue of the Academy for the year ending July, 1850, gives the list of instructors: Milo G. Willliams, Instructor in Mathematics, Natural Philosophy, Natural Science, etc.; R. Dutton, A.B., Instructor in the Classics, Chemistry, etc.; Rev. A. Hordorf, Instructor in the German Language; Louis De Corn, M.D., Instructor in the French Language; William C. Bartlett, Instructor in Constitutional Law; Edmund

Smith, M.D., Instructor in Anatomy and Physiology; Instructor in Drawing, Daniel P. Nead.

Following are some of the pupils whose names appear in this catalogue: James O. Arnold, John J. Achey, Winslow R. Bidleman, Henry Brown, Eugene Barney, Samuel W. Davies, Arthur Estabrook, George B. Edgar, William T. Herrman, Milo G. Newcom, Hy. Eugene Parrott, J. Merrick Phelps, Robert Patterson, Samuel B. Shoup, Gates P. Thruston, Dickinson P. Thruston, Ebenezer M. Thresher, Benjamin F. Wait, and others, many from a distance.

In 1833 David Pruden opened a manual-labor school in a large brick building at the corner of Jefferson and Warren streets, with Milo G. Williams, of Cincinnati, in charge of the academic department. The school was very popular, boys coming from Cincinnati and other places. It was not, however, a financial success, and Mr. Williams returned to Cincinnati, but was recalled to Dayton in 1844 as principal of the Academy. He was one of the founders and the first president of the Dayton Library Association.

In 1825 the first law authorizing a tax for schools was passed by the Legislature, and in 1838 the law authorizing a special tax for public-school buildings was passed. A meeting was at once called of the Dayton citizens, two school buildings decided upon, and the amount to be raised fixed at six thousand dollars. The schools were opened in the fall—one on Perry Street, with Collins Wight principal, and the other on East Second (the old "Eastern School"), with D. H. Elder principal. In 1842 four schools were opened,—two in rented rooms,—and as the Board was determined not to go into debt, they were only continued for one quarter, one month, and one week, using the last dollar of the fund. In 1841 a special act was passed by the Legislature providing for a German school, and in 1849 music was introduced in the schools, with James Turpin as teacher. In 1872 William H. Clark was elected superintendent of music, and when he resigned in December of the same year, Mr. Turpin was elected to fill that position, but died before his term of office expired.

In 1850 Henry L. Brown offered to the Board the following: "*Resolved*, That this Board do now establish the Central High School of Dayton, in which shall be taught the higher branches of an English education and the German and French languages, besides thoroughly reviewing the studies pursued in the district schools." The school opened April 15, 1850, in the Eastern District, with James Campbell principal, Miss Mary Dickson assistant, and James Turpin teacher of music. James Campbell, who came here in 1847 as principal of the Eastern School, was a graduate of Rensselaer Polytechnic Institute, a B.N.S. of the class of 1843. He was the first superintendent of schools in Dayton, his appointment being opposed by a progressive citizen as an unnecessary expense. When the High School was fairly established, the trustees discontinued the Academy, and offered the use of their building for the High School free of rent, and in the fall of 1850 it opened in the Academy building. In June, 1857, the Legislature having granted an enabling act, the trustees of the Academy deeded the property to the Board of Education to be used exclusively for school purposes for all time, and the Board at once erected the old Central High School building.

As early as 1805 the Rev. William Robertson, Dr. John Elliot, William Miller, Benjamin Van Cleve, and John Folkerth secured from the Legislature an act of incorporation for the Dayton Library Association, the first act of the kind passed in Ohio. It was sustained by voluntary

STEELE HIGH SCHOOL.

OLD EASTERN SCHOOL.
ONE OF THE TWO ORIGINAL BUILDINGS ERECTED.

From "Early Dayton," by permission of the U. B. Publishing House.

DAYTON PUBLIC LIBRARY AND COOPER PARK.

subscription, and a fine assortment of books was collected for that day; but during 1835, when times were hard and money scarce, the subscriptions failed, and the library was sold at auction from the clerk's office on September 12. The Dayton Lyceum was established in 1832, for "the diffusion of knowledge and the promotion of sociability." The Mechanics' Institute, for "moral, literary, and scientific improvement," with library and reading-rooms, was organized in 1833, Henry L. Brown secretary, and on July 1 General R. C. Schenck delivered a public address at the Court-house in behalf of the institute. The Adelphic Society of the Dayton Academy, in 1837, had a very fine library, the books, probably, all being selected by E. E. Barney. On December 10, 1846, a meeting was held and a committee appointed to draft a constitution for a library "worthy of the city," and on December 29 the constitution was adopted. A list was prepared by Judge Joseph H. Crane, John W. Van Cleve, Dr. John W. Hall, and Milo G. Williams, over a thousand books purchased, and the Dayton Library Association opened its library on the second floor of the building that was torn down when the Callahan Bank Building was erected. When J. D. Phillips was erecting the new Phillips Building, at the southeast corner of Main and Second streets, he finished a room on the second floor for the library and leased it to the Association at a reasonable rent.

By the school law of 1853 a tax was allowed for libraries in the schools. The money in Dayton amounted to one thousand four hundred dollars, with which one thousand two hundred and fifty books were purchased, and in the fall of 1855 the library was located on the second floor of the United Brethren Publishing House building, to be open only on Saturdays, with W. H. Butterfield, principal of the

Second District School, in charge. When the Central High School building was completed, the library was moved there. In 1860 the Library Association, on vote, presented its library, including many valuable books and the files of all the Dayton newspapers from 1808 to 1860, and also its furniture, to the Board of Education, and the Public School Library was removed to the rooms in the Phillips Building. Mrs. Hiley Davies was then appointed the first regular librarian. In 1867 the library was moved to the old City Hall, and when the new City Buildings were erected a room was fitted up for its use. In 1884, on the recommendation of the committee,—Dr. J. W. Conklin, A. Junikl, George Neder, and Elihu Thompson,—the Board of Education decided to erect a fireproof building for the library. The committee, to which were added Louis Reiter, C. L. Bauman, and A. A. Winters, obtained the consent of Council that the building should be placed in Cooper Park, decided on plans furnished by Peters & Burns, and in January, 1888, the library was moved to its present permanent quarters. According to the latest report of the librarian (Miss Dryden), there are now thirty-five thousand three hundred and twenty-five books, with a circulation the past year of one hundred and six thousand.

SHINPLASTER OF VINCENNES BANK OF INDIANA.

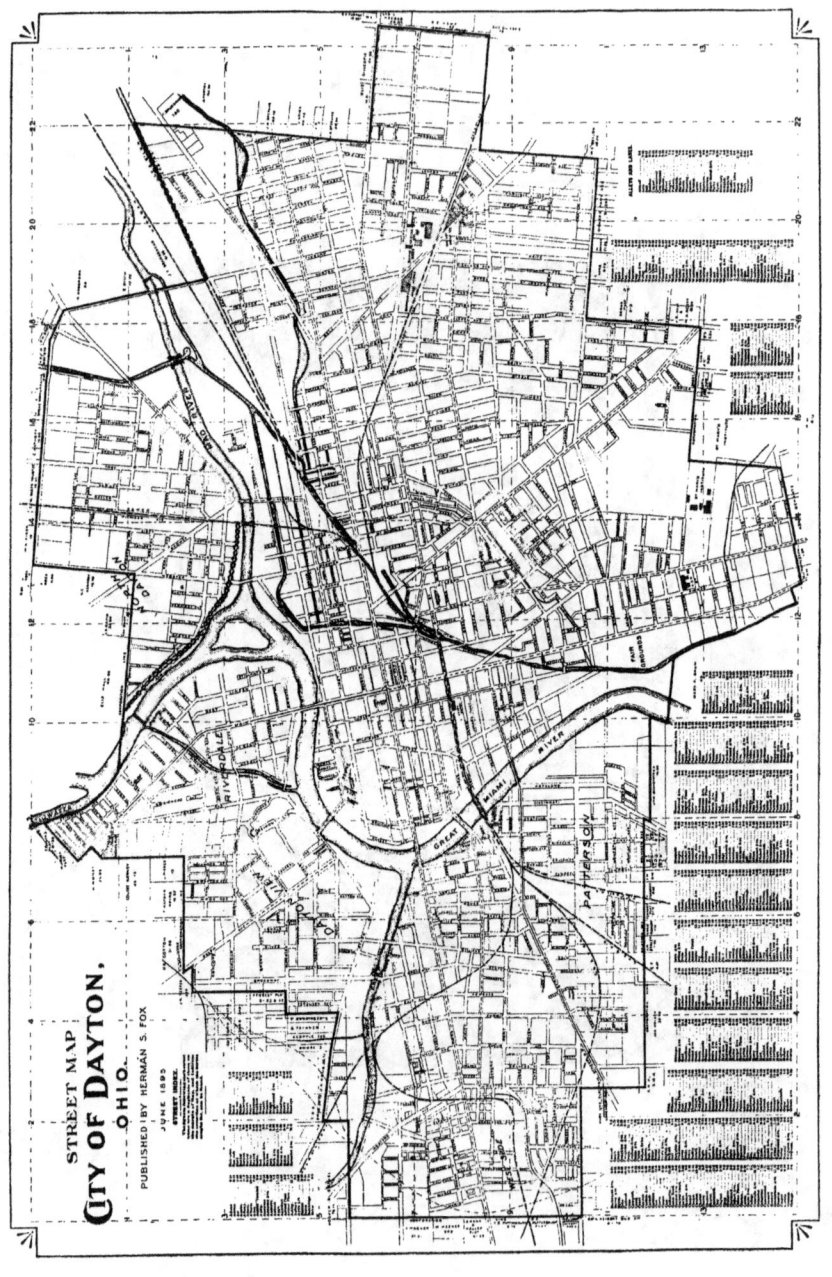

INDEX.

Accidental death, 28.
Achey, John H., 174, 228.
Achey, John J., 251.
Adams, George, 56.
Adams, President John, 59.
Adelphic Society, 253.
Administration, letters of, 85.
African Methodist church, 249.
Allen, Colonel William, 222.
Allen, Rev. Ethan, 116.
Altick, Daniel, 217.
Altick, William, 217, 228.
Anderson, Charles, 90, 211.
Anderson, Colonel Richard C., 187.
Anderson, John, 196.
Andrews, Captain Hugh, 86, 91.
Andrews, James, 32.
Archer, Benjamin, 84.
Archer, Samuel, 148.
Archibald, Captain, 199.
Arnett, Thomas, 51.
Arnold, Gorton, 182, 205.
Arnold, James Oliver, 69, 206, 248, 251.
Articles of agreement, 35, 38.
Artz, Adam, 248.
Asbury, Bishop, 246.
Ashby, Bladen, 78.
Ashton, Daniel, 203.
Assessors' fees, 49.
Atchison, Henry, 85.
Atkins, William, 133, 222.
Aughenbaugh, Peter, 190, 191, 236.

Babbitt, T. S., 213.
Bachelor's Alley, 31, 75.
Bachelors' Society, 120, 176.
Bacon, Henry, 203, 211, 218.
Bacon, Samuel, 111, 203, 208.
Baer, Peter, 195.
Baker, Aaron, 100, 177, 203, 246, 250.
Baker, David C., 32, 100.

Baker, John, 28.
Baker, John L., 28.
Banks—
 Dayton Manufacturing Company, 27, 172, 185.
 Dayton, 173, 208, 234.
 Dayton Branch, State, 174.
 Dayton National, 174.
 Harshman, Winters & Company, 209.
Baptist church, 18, 247.
Barnett, Joseph, 190, 222, 224, 236.
Barnett, William, 224.
Barney, Albert C., 226.
Barney, Edward E., 226.
Barney, Eliam E., 135, 225, 250, 253.
Barney, Eugene J., 225, 251.
Bartlett, William C., 250.
Bauman, C. L., 254.
Beal, Gideon, 217.
Bebee, Lovell, 204.
Beck, James, 140.
Beckel, Daniel, 70, 118, 229.
Beckel House, 233.
Bellaw, Peter, 140.
Belville, John L., 215.
Benham, Robert, 49.
Berkdoll, Mrs. E. E., 23.
Beulah Church, 242.
Bickham, Major W. D., 89, 201.
Bidleman, John, 219.
Bidleman, Winslow R., 251.
Bigger, James, 85.
Bigger, Joseph, 85, 86.
Bimm, Ezra, 42, 189.
Bimm, John, 189.
Blackburn, Rev. Gideon, 145.
Blockhouse, 31, 50, 57, 58, 243.
Blodget, Dr. William, 186.
Blue, Barney, 85.
Board of Trade, 213.

INDEX

Boats, canal, 122, 198, 199.
    flat, 22, 41, 54, 123, 128, 139, 144, 166, 168, 182.
    keel, 138.
    packet, 131.
    steam, 197.
Bomberger, George, 199.
Bomberger, Mrs. Sarah, 124, 245.
Bomberger, William, 124, 125, 147.
Bond, Joseph, 32.
Bonner, John, 133.
Boogher, Daniel G., 131.
Boogher, Gideon, 131, 231.
Boogher, Jesse, 132, 231.
Boogher, Samuel, 131.
Boundary lines, 16, 48, 106.
Bowman, Benjamin, 85.
Boyd, Miss Maria, 231.
Boyer, Frederick, 218.
Boyer, J. F., 218.
Brabham, Elisha, 70, 193.
Bradford, John, 64, 85.
Brady, James, 48.
Brenner, Jacob, 123.
Brewster, Elder William, 111.
Bridges, 45, 110, 181, 190, 191.
Broadwell, Ephraim, 184.
Broadwell, Silas, 184.
Brooks, James H., 228.
Brough, Governor, 91.
Brown, Enson, 205.
Brown, General, 51.
Brown, Henry, 88, 251.
Brown, Henry L., 86, 89, 90, 172, 252, 253.
Brown, Lewis Hamblin, 194.
Brown, Robert Patterson, 90.
Brown, Samuel N., 220.
Brown, Thomas, 195, 205, 219, 232.
Brown, William H., 180.
Browne, William, 79.
Bruen, David H., 87.
Bruen, Luther, 86, 232, 247.
Bruen, Luther Barnett, 87, 188.
Burnett, David L., 203.
Burnett, G. W., 36.
Burnett, Isaac G., 38, 143, 145, 146, 172, 202.
Burnett, Judge Jacob, 36.
Burnett, Rev. D. S., 131, 247.
Burns, John G., 169, 172.
Butler, Paul, 36, 51, 63, 138.
Butt, Henry, 129.
Butterfield, A. A., 206.
Butterfield, W. H., 253.

Cabins, 25, 27, 34, 65.
Cabintown, 149, 177, 179.
Calvary Cemetery, 165.
Campbell, Alexander, 247.
Campbell, James, 252.
Campbellite church, 247.
Camp-meeting, 242, 246.
Canal, Miami and Erie, 35, 116, 131, 188, 189, 198, 202, 237.
Car Works, 225, 237.
Carey, John, 84, 232.
Carpenter, Thomas G., 182, 183.
Cass, Colonel Lewis, 158.
Catholic Church, Emanuel, 249, 252.
Census, 58, 63, 78, 147, 200, 241.
Central High School, 252, 254.
Charter amended, 231.
Chase, Rev. Philander, 247.
Chase, Salmon P., 59.
Chenoweth, William, 23, 29.
Chillicothe, 56, 59, 96, 102, 110.
Cholera, 233.
Christian church, 202, 247.
Churches —
    African Methodist, 249.
    Baptist, 18, 247.
    Beulah, 242.
    Campbellite, 247.
    Catholic, Emanuel, 249, 252.
    Christian, 202, 247, 248.
    Episcopal, Christ, 247.
    German Reformed, 248.
    Lutheran, First, 249.
    Methodist Episcopal, Grace, 175, 231, 245, 246.
    New Lights, Broadway, 247.
    Presbyterian, First, 39, 81, 89, 124, 135, 143, 187, 194, 242, 243.
        Fourth, 245.
        Park, 245.
        Third Street, 245.
    United Brethren, First, 248.
Cincinnati, 18, 19, 20, 22, 30, 33, 41, 44, 64, 81, 117, 131, 132, 142, 147, 158, 192.
Claflin, L. F., 230.
Clark, Andrew, 247.
Clark, General George Rogers, 14, 16, 96.
Clark, T. R., 195.
Clark, William, 230.
Clark, William H., 252.
Clay, Henry, 135.

INDEX

Clayton, Rev. Mr., 84.
Clegg, Joseph, 210, 218, 229.
Clegg, Thomas, 210.
Clingman, John, 194.
Coleman, Henry, 41.
Collins, Father E. T., 249.
Collins, Rev. John, 246, 247.
Comly, John P., 201.
Comly, Richard N., 201.
Comly, William F., 201.
Compton, John, 137, 139, 165, 172.
Conklin, Dr. J. W., 254.
Conover, Adam Jewett, 224.
Conover, Harvey, 170, 174.
Conover, Obadiah B., 169, 203, 250.
Conover, Obadiah M., 171.
Conover, Peter Post, 224.
Conover, Samuel Dolley, 224.
Conover, Wilbur, 171, 221.
Constitutional convention, 59, 223.
Cooper, Daniel C., 20, 21, 25, 33, 35, 42, 43, 49, 51, 54, 86, 107, 117, 120, 137, 140, 189, 192, 204, 244, 249.
Cooper, David Zeigler, 36, 40, 110, 212, 234, 236, 240.
Cooper Hydraulic, 168, 227, 237.
Cooper Park, 39, 121, 149, 158, 234.
Cooper Seminary, 74, 136, 225.
Cooper's Mills, 28, 34, 35.
Coppock, Thomas, 86.
Corwin, Hon. Thomas, 159, 211, 221.
Corwin, Robert G., 88.
Cotterel, Lorenzo Dow, 169.
Cotterill, John, 27.
Cottingham, William, 246.
Cottom, Leven, 165.
Cottom, Thomas, 165, 246.
Court-house, 18, 26, 74, 80, 81, 82, 109, 145, 232.
Craighead, Dr. John Boyd, 221.
Craighead, John P., 222.
Craighead, Joseph Boyd, 222.
Craighead, Samuel, 171.
Craighead, William, 222.
Crane, Joseph G., 93.
Crane, Judge Joseph H., 73, 86, 92, 143, 146, 172, 211, 213, 221, 247, 253.
Croome, George L., 24.
Crowder, John, 192, 235.
Croy, Mrs. Elizabeth, 23.
Culbertson, Joseph, 23.
Curwen, quoted, 21, 63, 82, 147.
Cut money, 193.

DARST, ABRAHAM, 126, 195, 233.
Davies, Edward W., 70, 93, 110, 119, 211, 236.
Davies, Joseph Peirce, 212.
Davies, Mrs. Samuel Hiley, 254.
Davies, Samuel Hiley, 113.
Davies, Samuel W., 212, 251.
Davis, David, 66, 182, 183.
Davis, James, 169.
Davis, John, 23, 28, 54.
Davis, Owen, 28, 227.
Davis, Thomas, 23, 28, 85, 86, 227.
Davis, William C., 166, 218.
Dayton, site purchased, 16.
　laid out and named, 21.
　settlement, 22.
　made county-seat, 78.
　incorporated, 106.
　received its charter, 107.
　township, 48, 78, 106.
Dayton, General Jonathan, 20, 21.
Dayton Academy, 133, 134, 137, 249.
Dayton Gas Light and Coke Company, 179, 229.
Dayton Hydraulic Company, 70, 118.
Dayton *Journal*, 73, 89, 201.
Dayton *Journal and Advertiser*, 200.
Dayton Library Association, 251, 252, 253.
Dayton Lyceum, 253.
Dayton Philharmonic Society, 235.
Dayton *Watchman*, 190.
De Corn, Louis, 250.
De Graff, Andrew, 239.
Decatur, Commodore James, 224.
Deichler, Henry, 195.
Dennison, Mathias, 98.
Dickey, Robert R., 209, 229.
Dickey, William, 229.
Diehl, Henry, 164, 182, 195.
Dillon, J., 173.
Disbrow, Henry, 138.
Dodds, James, 206.
Dodds, John, 105.
Dodson, John, 202, 204.
Dolley, Samuel, 213, 224.
Donnell, Jonathan, 21.
Dorough, John, 23, 29.
Dover, John, 79.
Dow, Lorenzo, 246.
Dryden, Daniel H., 206.
Dryden, John W., 206.
Dunlap, Captain John, 17, 20, 21, 31.
Dunlevy, Hon. Francis, 84, 93.
Dustin, Judge C. W., 219.

258 INDEX

Dutton, R., 250.

EAKER, WILLIAM, 127, 172, 212, 232.
Earthquakes, 150.
Edgar, George B., 251.
Edgar, John F., 45, 47, 218, 236, 240.
Edgar, Robert, 20, 21, 26, 35, 40, 41, 51, 85, 189, 244.
Edgar, Robert Andrew, 45, 47, 128, 180, 222.
Edgar, Samuel D., 45, 47, 70, 118.
Edwards, Dr. Abraham, 144, 148.
Eells, B. F., 230.
Eells, Marcus, 206.
Eichelberger, L., 109.
Elder, D. H., 251.
Elections, 78, 79, 141, 148.
Electric Light Company, 239.
Elliot, Dr. John, 92, 143, 154, 252.
Elliott, James, 28, 99, 161.
Engle, David W., 207.
Engle, John, 207.
Ensey, John, 32, 162.
Ensley, Jozabed, 45.
Episcopal Church, Christ, 247.
Este, Dr. Charles, 144, 147, 150.
Esterbrook, Arthur, 251.
Esterbrook, Joel, 174.
Esterbrook, Warren, 174.
Evening Herald, 213.
Ewery graveyard, 242.
Ewing, John, 50, 71, 84, 172, 244.
Ewing, Thomas, 36.

FALLEN TIMBERS, battle of, 19.
Female Charitable and Bible Society, 89, 93, 118, 174.
Ferrell, Daniel, 23, 29.
Ferries, 62, 108, 160, 190.
Filson, John, 98.
Fire department, 195.
Fire-engines, 195, 196.
Fire-wardens, 115, 120, 127, 187, 195.
First bank, 27.
First birth, 22.
First book published, 202.
First brick house, 108.
First brickyard, 230.
First canal-boat, 198.
First carding-machine, 140.
First circus, 193.
First colored person, 37.
First colored Sunday school, 205.
First county convention, 141.

First court, 26, 81, 84.
First death, 28.
First drug-store, 144.
First election, 78.
First female resident, 32.
First gas-fitter, 181.
First iron moldboard plow, 43.
First justice of the peace, 37.
First locomotive, "Seneca," 240.
First market building, 177.
First meeting-house, 243.
First mill, 35.
First minister, 22.
First opera-house, 134.
First panic, 34.
First postmaster, 31, 142.
First recorded juries, 85.
First recorded wedding, 31.
First secret society, 141.
First show, 192.
First stage line, 191.
First State fair, 136.
First store, 26.
First stove store, 178.
First Sunday school, 124.
First Territorial legislature, 50.
First theater, 176.
First town clock, 246.
First undertaker, 115.
Fisher, Maddox, 172.
Flatboats, *see* Boats.
Floods, 107, 108, 175, 184, 202, 234.
Folkerth, John, 38, 133, 137, 141, 249, 252.
Folkerth, Russel, 133.
Foot-bridges, 25, 29.
Fords, 50, 108.
Forrer, Christian, 188.
Forrer, Howard, 188.
Forrer, Samuel, 187.
Fort Adams, 139.
Fort Erie, 51.
Fort Greenville, 57.
Fort Hamilton, 20, 24, 25, 88.
Fort Laramie, 89, 104.
Fort Meigs, 98.
Fort Recovery, 19.
Fort Washington, 56.
Fourth of July celebration, 141, 146, 156.
Foutz, Josiah, 112.
Francisco, Calvin, 233.
Franklin, Benjamin, 156.
Freeman, Trueman, and Hardin, 19.
Fry, Stephen, 235.

INDEX 259

Fryberger, George, 134.
Fryberger, Valentine, 134, 248.
Fullerton, Dr., 57.

GADDIS, THOMAS, 124.
Gahagan, William, 21, 23, 24, 33.
Game, 15, 25.
Gano, John Stites, 17, 77, 158.
Gas, 210.
Gebhart, Alexander, 227.
Gebhart, Frederick, 227, 249.
Gebhart, Herrman, 174.
Gebhart, John, 227.
Gebhart, Joseph R., 230.
Gebhart, Josiah, 227.
Gebhart, Mrs. Susan, 27.
Gebhart, Simon, 204.
Gebhart, Walter, 227.
George, Augustus, 45, 126, 203.
George, William, 124, 142, 147, 191.
George, William G., 126.
Gerard, John, 85.
German Reformed church, 248.
Gilbert, P. E., 232.
Gillespie, James, 85.
Gist, 15.
Goforth, William, 17, 78.
Gorman, Jonathan Harshman, 217.
Gosney, Fielding, 173.
Goss, Solomon, 23, 29.
Gould, Judge, 186.
Grassmire, Abraham, 23, 29.
Graveyard, 39, 45, 76, 102, 153, 244.
Green, John W., 218.
Greene, Charles Russell, 120, 172, 173.
Greenville, treaty of, 20, 33.
Greer, Admiral James A., 226.
Greer, Colonel James, 226.
Greer, Horace, 227.
Greer, John E., 27.
Gridiron, 196.
Griffin, David, 172.
Grimes, Alexander, 67, 70, 110, 118, 174, 176, 195, 212, 236.
Grimes, Colonel John, 109.
Grimes, James, 166.
Groves, George, 173, 247.
Gump, Andrew, 212.
Gunckel, Hon. Lewis B., 103, 105, 204.
Gunckel, O. I., 103, 105.
Gunckel, Philip, 100, 137, 172.
Gustin, Mrs. F. R., 40.

HAGENBAUGH, CHARLES, 236.
Haines, Dr. Job, 72, 187, 194, 195, 203, 250.
Hall, Dr. John W., 253.
Halsey, Ichabod B., 78.
Hamer, Dayton, 23.
Hamer, William, 22, 33, 51, 245.
Hanna, James, 137, 140, 176, 244, 249.
Hardin, Robert, 102.
Harker, S. T., 202.
Harker, William, 218.
Harmer, General, 29, 56.
Harries, John W., 24, 216.
Harrison, General William H., 14, 73, 114, 135, 145, 159, 223.
Harshman, Jonathan, 121, 122, 208, 236.
Hart, Ralph, 211.
Hatfield, James, 102.
Hatfield, Owen, 85.
Hatfield, William, 85.
Hawes, C. L., 230.
Hayden, C., 235.
Haynes, Judge Daniel A., 185.
Hays, A. T., 190.
Hays, John, 240, 241.
Heck, David, 184.
Henderson, James, 28, 161.
Henry, Governor Patrick, 97.
Herrman, Henry, 89, 213.
Herrman, William T., 251.
High School, Central, 252, 254.
Hoff, William, 228.
Hoffman, Bishop Joseph, 248.
Holden, Joel, 237.
Hole, Dr. John, 57.
Hole, Zechariah, 57, 58.
Hole's Creek, 56, 58.
Holt, Colonel Jerome, 20, 21, 30, 40, 41, 51, 58, 77, 141, 156, 159.
Holt, Judge George B., 185, 200, 211.
Honey Creek, 17, 29, 33, 63.
Hood, Andrew, 244.
Hoover, Daniel, 38, 137.
Hordorf, Rev. A., 250.
Horticultural Society, 73.
Houk, Adam, 67, 109.
House furniture, 52.
Houston, George S., 118, 119, 173, 176, 190, 191, 202.
Howard, John, 113.
Hudson, Shadrach, 85.
Huffman, Mrs. Lydia, 247.
Huffman, William, 167, 176, 247.
Huffman, William P., 167, 195.

260 INDEX

Hull, General, 158.
Hunt, Nathan S., 191.
Huntington, Samuel, 148.
Huston, John, 242.
Huston, Judge David, 242.

IDDINGS, BENJAMIN, 85.
Iddings, Daniel W., 222.
Idylwild, 45, 50, 69.
Improvements, 148, 198, 203, 234.
Indian agents, 89, 113, 144, 154.
Indian hunting-grounds, 15.
Indian supplies, 89.
Indian villages, 15, 97.
Indians, early experiences with, 19, 41, 42, 43, 94, 97.
Indians, treaties with the, 13.
Indians, wars with the, 14, 15, 18, 19, 56.
Infirmary, 67, 164.
Irwin, A. Barr, 89, 91, 208, 221.
Irwin, Andrew, 89, 208.

JACKSON, GENERAL, 190.
Jail, 26, 79, 80, 82.
James, Colonel John H., 93.
Jeff, Tom, 235.
Jefferson, President, 63, 96.
Jewett, Dr. Adams, 216.
Jewett, Dr. Henry, 203.
Jewett, Dr. Hibbard, 174, 216.
John, Joseph, 176.
Johnston, Colonel John, 31, 89, 144, 154.
Johnston, Stephen, 47.
Johnston, Stephen, 154.
Journal office, 196, 201.
Junikl, A., 254.

KEIFER, DANIEL, 170, 246.
Keifer, Philip, 232.
Kemp, George W., 72, 132.
Kemp, Lewis, 132.
Kemper, James, 242.
Kennedy, Gilbert, 70.
Kincaid, R. D., 170.
King, Augustin, 226.
King, Colonel Edward A., 226.
King, Rufus J., 226.
King, William, 59, 176, 191, 203, 222, 244.
Kingry, Joseph, 85.
Kiser, Benjamin, 163.
Kiser, Daniel, 112, 164, 247.
Kneisley, John, 236.

Knotts, Nathaniel, 85.
Kobler, Rev. John, 246.
Koons, George, 85.
Kuhns, Jacob, 169.

LA SALLE, 13.
Lancasterian system, 250.
Laymon, David, 228.
Leatherman, Henry, 70.
Lehman, David, 130.
Lehman, Peter, 130.
Libraries, 253, 254.
Licenses, 62, 108.
Light, Peter, 214.
Light, Samuel B., 214.
Lincoln, President, 201, 211.
Lindsley, David, 152, 172.
Lindsley, Ephraim, 152, 190.
Lindsley, L., 109.
Local officers, 77.
Location of the first settlers, 51, 129.
Locomotive engines, 231, 240.
Log cabin, 73, 201.
Logan, Colonel, 14, 97.
Logan, Shawnee chief, 14.
Long, Jacob, 85.
Loomis, Hezekiah, 224.
Loomis, James Decatur, 195, 224.
Losantiville, 30, 33.
Loury, Fielding, 40, 113.
Loury, General Fielding, 40, 112.
Lowe, Jacob D., 191.
Lowe, John G., 119, 212, 224.
Lowe, Peter P., 119, 129, 200, 203, 210.
Lowry, Archibald, 54.
Lowry, David, 21, 23, 54.
Lowry, Fletcher, 23.
Lowry, William C., 23.
Ludlow, Colonel Israel, 20, 21.
Lutheran Church, First, 249.
Lyon, Mr., 191.

MAD RIVER, 14, 15, 16, 17, 18, 19, 20, 21, 32, 34, 39, 42, 50, 51, 54, 70, 96, 97, 110, 141, 190, 212, 236, 237, 239.
Mad River & Lake Erie Railroad, 111, 209, 239.
Madison, President, 156.
Mails, 142, 143.
Marietta, 17, 36, 120, 157.
Market-house, 177, 189, 194.
Marot, Lewis, 201.
Marshall, Robert, 242.

INDEX 261

Mason, William, 85.
Mathison, Thomas, 231.
McCleary, Nat, 235.
McClelland, William, 78.
McClure, Mrs., 24, 33, 51.
McClure, William, 38, 137, 138, 142, 244, 249.
McConnaughey, David, 99.
McConnaughey, John C., 100.
McConnell, Alexander, 148, 163.
McConnell, Thomas Jefferson, 67, 163.
McCullum, Hugh, 38, 67, 81, 108, 174.
McGrew, John, 50.
McIlvaine, Bishop, 247.
McKabe, John, 84, 85, 244.
McMillen, Gideon, 250.
McMillen, William, 49.
McMullen, Captain John, 250.
McNamer, Richard, 242.
McReynolds, John, 129.
McReynolds, Joseph, 129, 181.
McReynolds, Robert, 181.
Mead, Benjamin Wicks, 213.
Mead, Daniel E., 218.
Mechanics' Institute, 253.
Medicines, list of, 144.
Meigs, Governor R. J., 40, 148, 157, 159.
Mercer, Edward, 22, 23.
Mercer, Jonathan, 21, 22, 23.
Methodist Episcopal Church, Grace, 175, 231, 245, 246.
Mexican War, 226.
Miami and Erie Canal, *see* Canal.
Miami land warrant, 17.
Miami Republican and Dayton Advertiser, 200.
Miami River, Great, 15, 16, 17, 48, 58, 59, 63, 69, 141, 240.
Miami River, Little, 15, 16, 17, 48, 63, 96.
Miami tribes, 16.
Miami Valley, 15, 16.
Mikesell, John, 85.
Miller, Daniel, 64, 65.
Miller, James, Sr., 85.
Miller, John, 55, 244.
Miller, Rev. Jacob, 85.
Miller, William, 252.
Miller's Mills and Ford, 65, 87.
Milligan, James, 242.
Mitchell, James H., 189, 250.
Montgomery, Brigadier-General, 57, 78.
Montgomery County, 39, 57, 58, 67, 74, 78, 102, 105, 125, 141.

Montgomery County Agricultural Society, 235.
Montgomery County Bible Society, 93.
Montgomery County Pioneer Association, 186.
Montgomery House, 188, 233.
Moral Society, 115, 120, 176.
Morrell, Calvin, 48.
Morris, Charles, 211.
Morris, James, 23, 29.
Morrison, David H., 183.
Morrison, Thomas, 182, 202, 205, 234.
Morrow, Jeremiah, 78.
Moyer, Michael, 85.
Munger, Edmund, 79, 85, 137.
Munger, General, 157, 158.
Munger, Warren, Sr., 163.
Murphy, Dr. William, 143.
Musgrove, Jacob, 192.

NAMES of the five families in 1802, 63.
National Hotel, 233.
National Road, 236.
Nead, Daniel P., 251.
Neder, George, 254.
Neff, John, 69.
New Lights, Broadway, 247.
Newcom, Colonel George, 23, 25, 42, 49, 51, 63, 78, 79, 84, 148, 173.
Newcom, George, Sr., 27, 43.
Newcom, Milo G., 28, 251.
Newcom, William, 23, 28.
Newcomer, Bishop, 248.
Newell, Augustus, 73.
Newspapers, 138, 145, 146, 189, 200, 201, 213.
Noop, John, 85.

ODLIN, PETER, 119, 129, 174, 211, 221, 224, 245.
Ohio admitted into the Union, 59.
Ohio Centinel, 145, 146, 148.
Ohio Insurance Company, 229.
Ohio Land Company, 15.
Ohio Republican, 146, 174, 189.
Ohio River, 16.
Ohio State Agricultural Association, 136.
Ohio Valley, 13.
Ohio Watchman, 189, 190, 200.
Ohmer, Augustus, 229.
Ohmer, Francis, 229.
Ohmer, George, 229.
Ohmer, Michael, 229.
Ohmer, Nicholas, 229.

INDEX

Ohmer, Peter, 229.
Oliver, James Bracy, 66, 205.
Opdyche, Henry, 246.
Original topography, 51.
Osborn, Cyrus, 48, 49.
Osborn, E. F., 240.
Overlease, Abraham, 195.
Owens, Matilda, 114.
Oyer, Valentine, 50.

PARKER, CALEB, 225.
Parks, Robert, 244.
Parrott, Hy. Eugene, 251.
Patterson, Colonel Robert, 14, 37, 86, 89, 94, 148, 191, 242, 251.
Patterson, Francis, 245.
Patterson, Jefferson, 14, 159.
Patterson, John, 176, 242, 243.
Patton, Matthew, 115, 139, 176, 195, 244.
Peace declared, 160.
Pease, Charles E., 204, 230.
Pease, Horace, 174, 229.
Pease, Perry, 229.
Pease, Walter, 230.
Pease, Webster, 230.
Peasley, A. M., 232.
Peirce, David Z., 116, 174.
Peirce, Jeremiah Hunt, 116, 188.
Peirce, Joseph, 116, 134, 142, 143, 172, 173, 191, 245.
Peirce, Joseph Crane, 116.
Penn, Madison, 235.
Perrine, James, 153, 173, 195, 202.
Perrine, John, 152.
Petticrew, James, 85.
Phelps, J. Merrick, 251.
Phillips, H. G., 40, 70, 90, 117, 165, 172, 173, 174, 191, 192, 223.
Phillips, J. D., 118, 119, 174, 253.
Phillips, T. A., 46, 174.
Phœnix Hotel, 233.
Piatt, John H., 192.
Pierson, Samuel, 250.
Piner, Joe, 235.
Pirogue, 23, 24, 30, 162, 204.
Plans of a town, 18.
Plats of the town, 38, 160.
Pleyel Society, 73.
Postmasters, 143, 226.
Potter, Maxwell, 114.
Presbyterian Church, First, 39, 81, 89, 124, 135, 143, 187, 194, 242, 243.
  Fourth, 245.

Park, 245.
  Third Street, 245.
Pritz, William, 224.
Pruden, David, 251.
Public School Library, 253, 254.

QUINN, BISHOP PAUL, 249.

RAILROADS, 239, 240.
Read, Andrew, 246.
Read, Thomas Buchanan, 190.
Rebellion, War of the, 113, 119, 221, 226.
Reeve, Judge, 185
Regans, Jephthah, 200, 203, 208, 217.
Reid, Colonel David, 111, 141, 157, 172, 191, 244, 249.
Reid's Inn, 111, 144, 147, 175, 187, 192, 193, 197.
Reider, George, 30.
Reiter, Louis, 254.
Rench, John, 121.
Rench, John, Jr., 122, 123.
Repertory, 138, 139, 145.
Retrospect, 241.
Revolutionary War, 13, 28, 30, 56, 57, 71, 92, 109, 143, 212.
Reynolds, Aaron, 96, 97.
Rhea, Captain J., 147.
Rieman, Joseph H., 211.
Ritchie, John, 244.
Robertson, Rev. William, 252.
Robinson, Henry, 176.
Robinson, Rev. William, 54, 85, 242.
Rogers, G. W., 174.
Roth, William, 115.
Rouzer, John, 164.
Rouzer, William H., 201.
Ruffin, William, 63.
Russel, James, 85.

SCHENCK, ADMIRAL JAMES F., 91, 220.
Schenck, Caspar, 221.
Schenck, General Robert C., 93, 136, 211, 221, 224, 253.
Schenck, John N. C., 172.
Schenck, Woodhull, 221.
School tax, 251.
Schools, 50, 137, 162, 249.
  Central High School, 252, 254.
  Dayton Academy, 249, 252.
  manual-labor, 251.
  parochial, 249.
  public, 251.

INDEX

Scott, Benjamin, 84, 85.
Scott, James, 85.
Seely, Morris, 231, 236.
Select Council, 107, 194, 231.
Shakers, 242, 243.
Shellabarger, John, 99.
Shoup, Joel Ohio, 168.
Shoup, Samuel, 168, 174.
Shoup, Samuel B., 251.
Shuey, Adam, 104.
Shuey, John Martin, 103.
Shuey, Martin, 104.
Shuey, Rev. William John, 105, 265.
Sidewalks, 148.
Simms, William Henry, 217.
Simonds, A. A., 239.
Simpson, Moses, 179.
Site of Dayton, 15.
Skinner, Robert J., 189.
Slaght, James, 245.
Slaves, 24.
Sloan, Wilson, 66.
Smith, C., 109.
Smith, Edmund, 251.
Smith, Edwin, 208.
Smith, Ezra, 204.
Smith, General S. B., 219.
Smith, George, 138.
Smith, George W., 127, 128, 217.
Smith, Hon. John, 113, 204.
Smith, Hon. T. J. S., 37, 218.
Smith, J. McLain, 219.
Smith, L. S., 211.
Smith, Moses, 118.
Smith, Preserved, 225.
Smith, Thomas, 246.
Smith, William M., 172, 203, 247, 250.
Snodgrass, Alexander, 85.
Somers, Mrs. Mary, 248.
Soule, Charles, 213.
Southard, John, 242.
Southerland, John, 89.
Spining, Charles, 72.
Spining, Judge Isaac, 71, 84, 86, 122, 147, 172.
Squier, David, 114, 141.
Squier, Timothy, 114, 192, 233.
Squier's Hotel, 199.
St. Clair, Governor Arthur, 20, 85, 86.
Staunton, Ben, 211.
Steele, Dr. John, 68, 144, 175, 176, 189, 203, 216, 245.
Steele, Judge James, 40, 134, 137, 148, 159, 173, 191, 195, 250.

Steele, Robert W., 75, 135, 174.
Steele, Samuel, 237.
Steele, William, 187.
Stephens, Amos, 230.
Stephens, Blakewell, 247.
Stewart, William, 242.
Stilwell-Bierce Company, 239.
Stites, Benjamin, 16, 17, 18.
Stoddard, Asa Patterson, 185.
Stoddard, E. Fowler, 185.
Stoddard, Henry, 68, 130, 184, 193.
Stoddard, John W., 185.
Stone, Charles A., 215.
Stone, David, 214, 215.
Stone, William B., 215.
Stoneberger, Peter, 191.
Stout, Atlas L., 179, 210.
Stout, David, 174, 178.
Stout, David Orion, 179.
Stout, Elias R., 179.
Stout, Moses, 178, 247.
Strain, John, 140, 147.
Strain, Robert, 179.
Strong, Hiram, 90, 171.
Sturr, Jacob, 230.
Stutsman, Daniel, 180.
Stutsman, David, 140.
Stutsman, John Grove, 180.
Stutsman, Jonathan, 181.
Suburbs, names of, 149.
Sullivan, Thomas, 246.
Sunderland, Peter, 84.
Swain, C. G., 174.
Swaynie, Alexander, 193, 233.
Swaynie, Robert, 30.
Symmes, Daniel, 84.
Symmes, John Cleves, 16, 17, 18, 20, 21, 34.

TATE, SAMUEL, SR., 168.
Tavern signs, 112.
Taverns, 26, 27, 42, 55, 79, 81, 84, 110, 190.
Taxes, 49, 58, 63, 79, 147, 149.
Taylor, General, 224.
Tecumseh, 14, 15.
Tennery, George F., 84, 137, 142, 249.
Tharp, Beniah, 230.
Thespian Society, 190, 196.
Thienpont, Father Emanuel, 249.
Thomas, Rev. Thomas E., 245.
Thomas, Richard S., 86.
Thomas, Walter E., 211.
Thompson, Christopher, 227.
Thompson, Elihu, 205, 254.

264 INDEX

Thompson, James F., 49, 80, 85, 205.
Thompson, John, 242.
Thompson, Ralph Langton, 28, 227.
Thompson, Samuel, 24, 30, 32, 50, 51, 204.
Thresher, Ebenezer, 225, 251.
Thruston, Dickinson P., 251.
Thruston, Gates P., 251.
Thruston, Robert A., 112, 119.
Tiffin, Governor Edward, 71.
Toasts, 146, 147, 199.
Todd, Captain Levi, 96.
Tull, Charles, 245.
Turnpikes, 236.
Turpin, James, 252.
Twightwees, 15.
Tyler, William, 166.

UMBAUGH, GEORGE, 129.
United Brethren Church, First, 248.
United Brethren Publishing House, 105, 180, 248, 253, 265.

VAN CLEVE, BENJAMIN, 20, 21, 24, 27, 29, 30, 31, 38, 50, 63, 84, 120, 127, 141, 142, 146, 173, 243, 245, 249, 252.
Van Cleve, John, 19, 29, 30.
Van Cleve, John W., 19, 32, 72, 112, 136, 175, 195, 200, 201, 202, 203, 227, 250, 253.
Van Cleve, William, 23, 30, 159.
Van Cleve Park, 26, 27.
Van Tuyl, H., 191.
Vansel, John, 85.
Venice, 18.

WAGNER, PHILIP, 64.
Wait, Benjamin F., 251.
Walls, Captain John, 95.
War of 1812, 14, 44, 51, 57, 98, 109, 112, 156.
War of the Rebellion, 90, 93, 169, 171.
Ware, J. T., 132.
Waring, Francis, 217.
Washington, George, 229.
Watervliet, 243.
Wayne, General, 19, 20, 25, 33, 50, 89.
Wead, Ebenezer, 55.
Weakley, Captain T. J., 213.
Weakley, Edward, 212.
Weakley, George Willis, 213.
Weakley, Herbert H., 213.
Weakley, Thomas, 212.

Weber, John, 232.
Weiser, Rev. Reuben, 249.
Welch, Sylvester, 188.
Wells, William, 144.
Welsh, John, 51.
Welsh, Rev. James, 63, 89, 143, 146, 190, 243, 249.
Westerman, William, 210.
Westfall, Cornelius, 249.
Westfall, George, 63.
Weston, Joseph, 218.
Weston, Washington, 217.
Wheeler, Joseph, 235.
Whiting, Chauncy, 249.
Wiggim, Andrew, 206.
Wiggim, Huey, 206.
Wiggim, John, 206.
Wiggim, Samuel, 206.
Wight, Collins, 171, 250, 251.
Wild-cat currency, 234.
Wiles, Mr., 190.
Wilkinson, General James, 20.
Williams, Harbert S., 65, 66.
Williams, James Lockhart, 65.
Williams, John H., 65, 148, 172, 185, 244.
Williams, Micajah T., 198.
Williams, Milo G., 250, 251, 253.
Willis, Father, 249.
Wilson, James, 148.
Wilson, Rev. Dr. J. L., 175.
Wilt, Jacob, 195.
Winters, A. A., 254.
Winters, John P., 207.
Winters, Jonathan H., 209.
Winters, Rev. David, 203, 207, 248.
Winters, Rev. Thomas, 194, 207.
Winters, Valentine, 191, 195, 207, 208, 236.
Wolf Creek, 65.
Wonderlich, Jacob, 191.
Wood, Dr. P., 144.
Woodland Cemetery, 74, 126, 135, 136, 188, 189.
Worley, Nathan, 92.
Worthington, John G., 119.
Wyatt, Hiram, 227.

YERGER, COLONEL, 94.
York, Jeremiah, 84.
Young, James R., 209.
Yount, George, 85.

BIBLIOGRAPHY.

BLACK, ALEXANDER. *Story of Ohio.* Boston. 1888.

BROWN, ASHLEY. History of Dayton in the *History of Montgomery County, Ohio.* Chicago. 1882.

CURWEN, MASKELL E. *A Sketch of the History of Dayton.* 1850.

EDGAR, JOHN F. *Pioneer Life in Dayton and Vicinity;* 1796-1840. 310 pp., 12mo. Illustrated. Dayton, Ohio: W. J. Shuey, United Brethren Publishing House. 1896.

HOWE, HENRY. *Historical Collections of Ohio.* 1847.
—— *The Same.* Revised and enlarged. 2 vols. Columbus. 1889.

KING, RUFUS. *History of Ohio.* Boston. 1888.

Newspapers from 1808 to 1896, on file in Dayton Public Library.

Records of the Dayton Academy. 1808-1847. MS.

STEELE, ROBERT W. *Historical Sketch of the Dayton Schools.*
—— *Historical Sketch of the Woodland Cemetery Association.* 1875.

STEELE, ROBERT W., AND STEELE, MARY DAVIES. *Early Dayton; With Important Facts and Incidents from the Founding to the Hundredth Anniversary—* 1796-1896. 300 pp., 12mo. Illustrated. Dayton, Ohio: W. J. Shuey, United Brethren Publishing House. 1896.

STEELE, ROBERT W., WOOLDRIDGE, J., AND OTHERS. *History of Dayton, Ohio.* 728 pp., quarto. Dayton, Ohio: W. J. Shuey, United Brethren Publishing House. 1889.

VAN CLEVE, BENJAMIN. *Memoranda.* MS.

VAN CLEVE, JOHN W. *Brief History of the Settlement of the Town of Dayton.* Published in Journal of Historical and Philosophical Society of Ohio, page 73.

Note.— For a more complete bibliography see *Catalogue of the Dayton Public Library.*

THE RUBICON FACTORY,

Two miles below Dayton.

THE subscribers inform their friends and the public, that their Carding and Spinning machines are now in complete operation, having this season made considerable improvement in their Factory—they are prepared to Card and Spin wool in the best manner.

For Carding common wool 6 1-4 cts. per lb
" Spinning chain per doz. 18 3-4 cents,
" do filling per do 15 do.
" Carding, Spinning and Weaving Cloth to 500 Reed, } 31 1-4 do.
" do. all above 500 in proportion,
" do Casinett, do.
" do. Satinett, 37 1-2 cts.

Every attention shall be paid to work committed to them, that it shall be done in the best manner and to the satisfaction of those employing them.

Produce will be received, in part payment, at the market price.

R. PATTERSON,
H. HYATT.

May 12th, 1823. 73 tf

From the notched stick to the National Cash Register
The Progress of One Hundred Years

CHEAP SUMMER GOODS,

H. G. PHILLIPS

Is just receiving a large and general assortment, including

DRY GOODS,
HARDWARE,
BOOKS & STATIONARY,
BONNETS,
LOOKING GLASSES,
MILL & X CUT SAWS,
IRON & STEEL. &c. &c.
GROCERIES,
MEDICINES,
PAINTS & DYE STUFFS,
SHOES,
SADDLERY, AND
PLATED WARE,
CASTINGS,
COTTON, &c. &c.

The above were purchased on the best terms, and are offered WHOLE-SALE or RETAIL, at the most reduced prices for CASH, COUNTRY LINEN, BEES WAX, WHEAT, WHISKEY, &c.

Dayton, May 12th, 1823. 21 tf.

P. M. HARMAN & CO.,

Dealers in Carpets, Mattings, Linoleum, Rugs, Draperies, Wall Papers, and

Household Furnishings

Our stock will always be found large and complete in all departments. Prices within reach of all. We invite inspection.

Telephone 381.

P. M. HARMAN & CO.,
30 & 32 North Main Street.

Dayton, Feb. 17, 1829.

COACH MAKING.

THE subscriber very respectfully informs the citizens of Dayton and the surrounding country, that he still continues to carry on the COACH MAKING business in all its various branches on Main Cross street one door west of the jail. He will make Coaches, Barouches, Gigs, and Dearborns, of the newest fashion or according to order on reasonable terms; those who may favor with their custom may depend on having their work according to their order.

SAMUEL DOLLEY.

Dayton, July 4, 1828.

N. B. Stage contractors can be accommodated with Post Coaches made of the best materials and in the newest fashion.

If any person should want further information they can inquire of Timothy Squier, stage owner and contractor in Dayton.

1796

The Leidigh Carriage Co.

Invite you to read the "ad" on opposite page and then call on them for first-class Vehicles of every description. ❧ ❧❧They carry a very large stock at their repository, 1224 and 1226 East Third Street, ❧❧ ❧❧❧❧ Dayton, Ohio.

1896

M. OHMER'S
FASHIONABLE CABINET AND CHAIR
WARE ROOMS,
SMITH'S FOUR STORY BUILDING,
CORNER OF MAIN AND SECOND STREETS,
DAYTON, O.

M. O. keeps all kinds of Cabinet Furniture, at as low prices, and warranted as well made as at any Cabinet Wareroom in this city or Cincinnati.

The M. Ohmer's Sons Co.,

Corner Main and Fifth Streets,

Opposite Post Office.

Seven immense floors filled with the latest production of the ✣✣✣✣✣✣✣

Furniture Designer's Art.

The largest and best-lighted rooms in the State. Every description of Furniture, the commonest as well as the most elaborate and expensive. Compare our stock with any in Cincinnati. It is as large, and fresher and cheaper.

THE M. OHMER'S SONS CO.,

Corner Main and Fifth Streets.

SHOE MAKING.

I have opened a Shoe Shop, two doors south of H. G. Phillips's Store, in Main street, where I intend carrying on the

BOOT & SHOE Making Business,

in all its branches. Having employed good experienced hands and laid in a stock of Leather of the Best quality, I flatter myself that work will be done in the neatest manner and on terms best to accommodate the times.

J. BROADWELL.
Dayton, June 23d, 1823

Dayton's Centennial Year finds us with a stock of SHOES that for

FIT, STYLE, AND COMFORT

cannot be excelled. The prices are right, and our clerks are scientific fitters. We invite your inspection.

DIERS & TANNER,

CASH SHOE STORE,

DAVIES BUILDING,

104 SOUTH MAIN ST.,   DAYTON, OHIO.

SILAS M'DERMED,

Jacob Stutsman,
COPPER-SMITH.

RESPECFULLY informs the public that he has commenced the Copper-Smith Business, in all its various branches, in Market-street, between G. W. Smith's granary and the Presbyterian church, where every description of STILLS will be made and old ones repaired, together with TEA KETTLES, and a variety of other Copper Ware. He will attend to any orders in the line of his profession with punctuality.

Dayton, May 11th, 1824.   21 tf

Brooks & Son

1863-1896.

Plumbers

Steam and Gas Fitters.

Hot Water and Steam Apparatus.

Natural Gas Fitting.

42 North Jefferson Street, Dayton, Ohio.

Watch & Clock Making.
Silver Smith and Jewellery.

THOMAS DOVER returns his thanks to the public for the encouragement he has received, and informs them that he still continues the business and will pay the strictest attention to the Repairing all kind of Watches, Clocks and every kind of complicated Instruments, Surveyors' Compasses, Musical Boxes, Seals, &c. &c.

WARRANTED.

For the encouragement of the more general use of Silver Articles, I will sell 28 per cent lower than the common price. $1 per oz. with the addition of making; (and to those that are tired of their wooden clocks,) I will sell them some that requires winding but once in 8 days. First quality Brass Clocks for one third less than customary.

FOR SALE

1 First rate Jewelled Watch, low for cash or whiskey.—Gold, Silver and Steel Chains, Seals, Keys, Ear-Rings, Finger Rings, Breast-Pins, Clasps, Thimbles; gold and silver Eagles, Amulet Beads of superior quality, and will be sold almost for cost.—Old Gold and Silver taken in payment.—Cash given for old Silver

T. DOVER.

September 1st, 1823.   89 tf

A. Newsalt,

Watches, Diamonds, and Fine Jewelry.

Solid Silverware, Fine French and American Clocks.

Cor. Main and Fourth, Dayton, Ohio.

JAMES MILLER,
NANCY GUILE, *Adm*
June 19th 1823   79 6t

WRITING ACADEMY.

D. EASTON

HAS just commenced giving lessons in PENMANSHIP, at the Academy near the Lancasterian Seminary. He teaches the *Swift Angular Running Hand* without ruling, the *Round Running Hand*, the *Waving Hand*, the *Ornamental Italian Hand*, and various others both plain and ornamental. He also instructs in making *pens*.

Ladies attend at 4 o'clock P. M. Gentlemen at 8 in the evening; and at those hours the bell will be rung. Scholars furnish Stationary. Letter paper is preferred. A considerable number of Ladies and Gentlemen have already subscribed. If there are any others wishing to attend, they will do well to commence soon.

Specimens of scholars' improvement may be seen at the Academy. References to the Rev WM. GRAHAM, GENL SMITH, and COL. DAVID REID.

Dayton, July 22d, 1823.

Beck's Dayton Commercial College and Shorthand Institute

Is one of the Largest and Most Complete Young People's Business Training-Schools in Ohio.

Beck's Penmanship, Bookkeeping, and Short Methods, and Munson's Pitmanic Shorthand, as elaborated and taught by John Collins, who has been for over eighteen years a court reporter, and does the most rapid and technical reporting, are a guaranty of efficiency in all departments. No extra charge is made for assisting students to positions. Catalogue free. Address

JOHN K. BECK, Principal.

John Collins, Manager Shorthand Department.

TELEPHONE 1015.
KUHNS BUILDING.

.yton, Feb. 10, 1829. 11–tf.

HYMN BOOKS

DOBELLS' HYMNS, Watts' do. in Morocco binding, pocket book form, common do. Rippons do. Methodist do. Goddards do just received and for sale at the Journal Printing Office, by

J. REGANS.

March 24, 1829. 17–tf

PAPER.

JUST RECEIVED and for sale at the *Journal Printing Office*, a lot of Paper from J. LOWRY & CO'S. new Paper Mill, at Springfield, Clarke county, to-wit:

No. 1, Writing Paper,
No. 3, do. do.
Wrapping and Tea do.
Bonnet Boards.

Which will be kept constantly on hand, and will be sold at Mill prices for Cash or Rags.

J. REGANS.

Dayton, *April* 28th 1829.

FOR SALE

After Sixty Years

OF

BOOK,
STATIONERY,
AND
PUBLISHING
BUSINESS.

THE

United Brethren Publishing House

IS BETTER
PREPARED
THAN EVER
TO SUPPLY

BOOKS OF ALL CLASSES, STATIONERY, ENGRAVING AND EMBOSSING FOR HOME AND OFFICE, PRINTING AND BINDING IN BEST STYLES, ELECTROTYPING, AND BUSINESS SUPPLIES. . . . .

CORNER MAIN AND FOURTH STREETS.

December 26th 1822.   *Admr.* 7 4

Samuel B Dover,

GUN-SMITH,

One door East of Squire Folkerth's Office, will make and repair GUNS PISTOLS, &c. of every description, on the shortest notice. And to accommodate the pressure of the times, will receive, in part payment, approved produce.

N. B. Cash paid for old Copper, Brass and Pewter.

Nov. 26th. 1822.   49 tf

NOTICE

LEADING HOUSE IN THE TRADE.

Telephone 593.

JAMES DODDS

Guns, Ammunition, Fishing Tackle, Cutlery, Tools, and Bicycles.

A FULL LINE OF BICYCLE SUNDRIES.

STERLING
REMINGTON
HUNTER
MAJESTIC
APOLLO
} Bicycles.
Best Makes at Low Prices.

Our Hand-Loaded Nitro Shells, No. 12, $1.75 to $2.50 per 100.
Machine-Loaded Black Powder Shells, No. 12, $1.25 per 100.

JAMES DODDS,

11 South Main Street.   DAYTON, OHIO.

NOTICE.

THE Ladies of Dayton and its vicinity, are hereby informed that the subscriber has opened a shop next door to captain H. G. Phillips' store; where she will keep on hand, all kinds of bonnets in the milinary line, of the newest fashions. She hopes from her attention and knowledge of her business, to meet with a share of the public patronage.— A quantity of goose feathers wanted.— Military gentlemen, can be accommodated with plumes of any size or colour. Hat covers of all sizes and colours for sale.

ANN YAMAN.

Dayton, June 26, 1815. *39—3t

New & Cheap Goods.

Mrs. Slater,

Fine Millinery

In all its branches. Imported Pattern Hats and Bonnets. Imported Mourning Veils and Trimmings. Special attention given to fine mourning work. Old ladies' Lace Caps and Bonnets made to order.

Mrs. J. Q. Slater,

New Ohmer Building,

9 West Fifth Street, Dayton, Ohio.

...on, Oct 12.

Wholesale or Retail
GROCERY,

At the head of the State Basin, sign of the
YELLOW CASK.

Chests of Tea,
Bags superior Rio Coffee,
" Prime Havana do.
Barrels of Sugar,
lbs. of Loaf do.
Kegs White Lead,
Boxes 8 by 10 Glass,
Tubs Mackerel, &c. &c.

Together with an assortment of articles commonly kept in a Grocery—Foreign and Domestic Liquors, and
RECTIFIED WHISKEY,
All of which is offered at Cincinnati prices, by   CHARLES G. SWAIN.
Dayton, Oct. 20. 1829.

ON CONSIGNMENT—A few dozen Goodwin's SADLE TREES, at Manufacturers' prices.

CASH paid for Country Produce.
C. G. S.

Speculators

Telephone 271. **E. BIMM & SONS,**

Grocers

313 and 315
East First Street.

The Bimm Dayton Ice Co.,

The Best Ice for all purposes. Orders filled promptly for large or small quantities.

Telephone 271.

www.ingramcontent.com/pod-product-compliance
Lightning Source LLC
Chambersburg PA
CBHW071958220426
43662CB00009B/1178